THE FORGIVENESS TO COME

just ideas

transformative ideals of justice in ethical and political thought

series editors

Drucilla Cornell

Roger Berkowitz

THE FORGIVENESS TO COME

THE HOLOCAUST AND THE HYPER-ETHICAL

Peter Banki

FORDHAM UNIVERSITY PRESS
NEW YORK 2018

the modern language initiative

THIS BOOK IS MADE POSSIBLE BY A COLLABORATIVE GRANT FROM THE ANDREW W. MELLON FOUNDATION.

Fordham University Press also publishes its books in a variety of electronic formats. Some content that appears in print may not be available in electronic books.

Visit us online at www.fordhampress.com.

Library of Congress Cataloging-in-Publication Data
available at http://catalog.loc.gov.

Printed in the United States of America

20 19 18 5 4 3 2 1

First edition

Contents

readings of Simon Wiesenthal's *The Sunflower* (1969), Jean Améry's *At the Mind's Limits* (*Jenseits von Schuld und Sühne*) (1966), Vladimir Jankélévitch's *Forgiveness* (1967), and Robert Antelme's *The Human Race* (1947). In addition, I analyze the documentary film *Forgiving Doctor Mengele* (2006) on Eva Mozes Kor. Each of these works bears witness to "aporias," or unsolvable impasses, of forgiveness, justice, and responsibility in relation to the Holocaust. All of the texts chosen, and especially those written in the late 1960s, are at grips with the idea that the crimes committed by the Nazis are inexpiable. To this extent, they contend in different ways with the limits of a dominant understanding of forgiveness within the Abrahamic tradition.

While a great deal of secondary literature exists on the work of Jean Améry, Robert Antelme, and Simon Wiesenthal, in general this literature relies on an understanding of forgiveness grounded in the metaphysical presuppositions that Derrida's thought puts into question (i.e., the autonomous subject, the performative utterance, and the belief in an end or *telos* without remainder). Even when the value of forgiveness is declared to be dead (Jankélévitch) or superseded by the crimes of the Nazis (Améry), it is always the same metaphysical or "ontotheological" understanding of forgiveness that is presumed.

While I believe it is necessary and justified to assert that forgiveness of the Holocaust is impossible, today this response is, I argue, insufficient. In an epoch of "worldwidization" (*mondialisation*), it may not be possible simply to escape what could be termed *the violence of forgiveness*.[2] This violence consists in, among other things, the worldwide proliferation of scenes and rhetoric which almost invariably portray apology, reconciliation, and forgiveness as accomplishable acts. As a way to become more sensitive to this violence, one may consider a memorable statement by Primo Levi: "Forgiveness is not my word, it has been inflicted on me."[3] He was referring to being asked by audiences repeatedly whether or not he could forgive those who perpetrated what happened to him and others at Auschwitz. From where comes this strange insistence on asking a survivor of Auschwitz whether or not he or she can forgive? In relation to the political obligations which drove Levi and others to testify to what happened in the Nazi extermination camps, it is in no way necessary to speak of forgiveness. And yet, one may speculate that something deep, if not intrinsic to Western culture, dominated by Judeo-Christian traditions, drives this insistence. Even though Primo Levi had said that forgiveness is not his word and that it had been inflicted on him, he nonetheless did agree to answer. Echoing a thinking deeply rooted in the Abrahamic tradition, he said: "No, I have not forgiven any of the culprits, nor am I willing to forgive a single one of them, unless he has shown (with deeds, not words, and not too long afterwards) that he has become conscious of the crimes and the errors, and is determined to condemn them, to uproot them from his conscience and from that of others, because an enemy who sees the error of his ways ceases to be an enemy."[4]

One must ask what are the limits of an understanding of forgiveness that is conditioned on the perpetrators' consciousness of their crimes and their determination to condemn and expiate them. In such an understanding the perpetrator as such is not forgiven, nor is the crime itself, but only the perpetrator who has later agreed to reform themselves; the one who in Levi's terms "ceases to be an enemy". One could go so far as to ask if in this understanding *there is really any forgiveness at all.* In the name of a more marginal strand of thinking within the Abrahamic tradition, one that emphasizes unconditional forgiveness, Jacques Derrida argues that a forgiveness worthy of the name *must not require* that the perpetrator be in conscious agreement with their victim about the nature of their crimes and that they reform themselves in conformity with this agreement. Rather, it should be extended to the perpetrator as such, that is, as unreformed and unrepentant, as they were at the moment when they committed their crimes. Such forgiveness would imply therefore that the perpetrator could commit the same crime again and again, even against the same victims without ever making a promise to reform themselves: "You kill me, I forgive you, you kill me again, I forgive you", and so on ad infinitum.

At first sight it may be difficult, even impossible, to understand the necessity of such a thought, which would seem to be in greatest proximity to the very worst, to the idea that through forgiveness the Holocaust could be permitted to happen again and again, as it were, in a sort of Nietzschean eternal return. And indeed, when I first heard Derrida speak of "pure forgiveness," it was this very implication, which he did not seek to hide, that I found to be most impermissible and even angering, for it challenged one of my most deeply held political beliefs. And yet, if such a thought has any justification, it lies perhaps in the insufficiency of a certain "worldwidized" language and scenography of apology and forgiveness in the context of what are called crimes against humanity. The unconditional forgiveness of which Derrida speaks is not the accomplishable act of a subject who could ever say with good conscience "I forgive" or "I can forgive." If in an epoch of "worldwidization" it is not possible simply to escape the violence of forgiveness, then it is necessary to rethink what forgiveness is, the conditions under which it supposedly takes place, and especially its relation to justice. The implementation in international law of a concept of "crimes against humanity" calls for—even necessitates—the thought of a forgiveness, which does not imply closure of the infinite wounds of the past. Such forgiveness would be distinguished from personal and political reconciliation. What are the conditions under which this forgiveness may be thought or dreamed? How can it be dreamed without renouncing political vigilance? Must this political vigilance itself today be rethought?

To forgive is not my verb. It has been inflicted on me.

—Primo Levi, *The Voice of Memory*

When talking about this book [*weiter leben* in German or *Still Alive* in English] to German audiences, I was invariably confronted with the anxious question whether I could "forgive." It was not clear whether I was to forgive the perpetrators or all Germans . . . [H]ow can I "forgive" the murder of my teenage brother when I have had my life, and he didn't get to have his? And perhaps the adult I am now cannot forgive even in the name of the child I was then. This was not a free decision, I would explain: it was simply not in my power to grant the kind of absolution that is implied in the plea or demand for forgiveness.

—Ruth Kluger, "Forgiving and Remembering"

Whether you are an agnostic or a believer, I do not know, but your problem belongs to the realm of guilt and atonement and . . . therefore is a *theological* one, and as such, it does not exist for me as an atheist who is indifferent to and rejecting any metaphysics of morality . . . Because I can only see the problem of forgiveness in political terms, I must abstain from approving or condemning your behavior . . . Politically, I do not want to hear anything of forgiveness! . . . What you and I experience must *not happen again*, never, nowhere. Therefore I refuse any reconciliation with criminals.

—Jean Améry, in response to Simon Wiesenthal's *The Sunflower*

We are asking forgiveness by reading. Somewhere I wrote that as soon as I write, I am asking for forgiveness, without of course knowing what will happen. But forgiveness is implied in the very first speech act. I cannot perform what I would like to perform. That is why things happen.

—Jacques Derrida, in response to Robert Gibbs

Die Welt ist fort. Ich muss dich tragen.

—Paul Celan

Introduction

To Forgive the Unforgivable

In a scene composed by Ingeborg Bachmann for her unfinished novel *Franza* (1965–66), the protagonist, Franza, visits a "doctor" who had taken part in medical experiments at Dachau and in the Nazi euthanasia program at Hartheim. He now lives as a free man in Cairo, Egypt. After having confronted him, by telling him that she has read all the documents and knows who he is, she is surprised by the words she then says to him:

> Forgive me [*Verzeihen Sie*], she said. The two of them stood there; he no longer pressed at her and she also didn't move.
>
> She suddenly realized that she had said to him: Forgive me [*Verzeihen Sie*].[1]

Franza's strange and thought-provoking request for forgiveness is split across an interval of time. In the first moment, when she speaks, she is not aware of what she says to the man. Only a moment later does it occur to her. What was at first perhaps said only as an empty phrase, a *Floskel* in

German, suddenly appears more meaningful and disturbing. The man to whom she has just said, "Forgive me," is from the SS. He is an unpunished and unrepentant murderer.

Rather than the guilty asking the innocent for forgiveness, the reverse has apparently taken place. Franza, who has not committed any crimes, comes to see this man, the SS-Assault Leader Dr. Kurt Körner, presumably for the purpose of confronting him. Then, after having done so, she unexpectedly asks him for forgiveness. However, because the text marks that Franza is not aware of what she says when she says, "*Verzeihen Sie*," what she means or intends by this phrase is not decidable. The text holds in suspension the differences between "*Verzeihen Sie*" as a mechanical formula (which one might translate into English as "Excuse me") and "*Verzeihen Sie*" as a request for forgiveness addressed to the SS man as such.

If indeed Franza does request forgiveness of the SS man, then what would it be for? For having confronted him? For then not knowing what to say? For not being able to account for why she is there?[2] Or, more radically, for being as such, as if being alive in front of an SS man were itself a sin? Or, on the other hand, might "*Verzeihen Sie*" be a request for forgiveness made for the SS man, on his behalf, for the crimes for which he has neither asked forgiveness nor apparently shown any remorse? In her reading of this scene, the cultural theorist and literary critic Sigrid Weigel refers to Franza's "*Verzeihen Sie*" as a "*verkehrtes Verzeihen*," an inverted or perverted forgiveness; a forgiveness that is amiss or back to front.[3] While one may judge Franza's request to be perverted, even insane (later she returns to ask the SS man to kill her, to inject her with the same poison he used on his victims),[4] it also invites us to consider that it is most often the innocent, and not the perpetrators, who experience guilt. The irony of Franza's "*Verzeihen Sie*" calls attention to the abnormality, even perversity, of a situation that is accepted or tolerated as normal.[5]

In an oft-cited phrase from the same year (1966), the writer and survivor of Auschwitz Jean Améry testifies powerfully in his own name to the same ironic reversal of feelings of guilt and innocence:

> I am burdened with collective guilt, I say: not they. The world, which forgives and forgets, has sentenced me, not those who murdered or allowed the murder to occur . . . Everything will be submerged [*untergehen*] in a general "Century of Barbarism." *We*, the victims,

> will appear as the truly incorrigible [*Unbelehrbaren*], irreconciliable ones [*Unversöhnlichen*], as the antihistorical reactionaries in the exact sense of the word, and in the end it will seem like a technical mishap [*Betriebspanne*] that some of us still survived.[6]

There is a difference between the strange, not entirely translatable "*Verzeihen Sie*" uttered by Franza and the "forgiveness" which belongs to the motor of world history, to the logic of historically inevitable reconciliation, relativization, and normalization that Jean Améry, as a victim, and in the name of the victims, deems it necessary to refuse. It is necessary to refuse such "forgiveness" because it is founded on amnesia. The "forgive me" of Bachmann's Franza is, on the other hand, scarcely readable, like the "Forgive me, everybody" of Franz Kafka's hunger artist. It is a testimonial trace of multiple breakdowns and silences, which each in turn bears witness to the impossibility of what has taken place, and to the incapacity of institutions and languages adequately to account for it.

> Franza, in this still air, in this room, thought about forgiveness and records (*Protokolle*) and eradication (*Ausmerzung*). What did all that have to do with a man who stood there and knew so little what to say (*so wenig reden wusste*), as she did herself.[7]

A TRANSVALUATION OF THE IMPOSSIBLE

This book is concerned with the *aporias* of forgiveness, considered in relation to the legacy of the crimes against humanity perpetrated by the Nazis and their collaborators during World War II. Aporia, from the Greek *aporos*, signifies an impasse, a nonway: a passage that is either forbidden or impossible to traverse. Following Jacques Derrida's reading and employment of the term, "aporia" is not understood as a negative paralysis but as the endurance of an experience that is necessary for any responsible decision.[8] In relation to the crimes of the Nazis and their collaborators, survivors such as Simon Wiesenthal, Primo Levi, and Ruth Klüger have either refused forgiveness or argued for the radical impossibility of forgiveness beyond any subjective volition. They have justified this position on both moral and political grounds. Not only do they claim that they are not authorized to forgive in the name of those who have been murdered, but it is also feared that forgiveness (understood as reconciliation with the perpetrators) opens a space in which the crimes are more likely to happen again.[9] In a poem entitled "*Shoah* (or Dis-grace)," the philosopher Sarah Kofman goes even further. Echoing the position expressed by Jean Améry in the passage quoted above from *At the Mind's Limits* (*Jenseits von Schuld und Sühne*), she suggests that the Hegelian logic of history is nothing other than the logic of the Final Solution itself. By negating the crime in sovereign forgiveness or mercy (*Gnade*)—in Hegel's formulation, "to make un-happen what has happened" (*das Geschehene ungeschehen zu machen*)—the crime of the Final Solution is not negated but paradoxically accomplished inasmuch as its purpose was "to make the Jews' existence null, to make them un-happened."[10]

To support her reading, Kofman quotes at the top of her poem from a section of Hegel's *Elements of the Philosophy of Right* on the monarch's right to grant mercy (*Begnadigungsrecht*):

> The sovereignty of the monarch is the source of the right to pardon criminals, for only the sovereign is entitled to actualize the power of the spirit to undo what has been done [*das Geschehene ungeschehen zu Machen*] and to nullify crime by forgiving and forgetting [*im Vergeben und Vergessen das Verbrechen zu vernichten*].[11]

It is striking that Hegel uses the same verb to designate the sovereign action of pardoning as do the Nazis to describe that of the Final Solution: *vernichten*, *Vernichtung*, nullification, extermination. Moreover, in this description of legal amnesty, the right to pardon criminals that derives from sovereign power, Hegel links forgiveness (*Vergebung*) to forgetting (*Vergessen*). Forgiveness, as he points out elsewhere, should not imply forgetting but memory of the crime—a memory, however, from which the bad conscience has disappeared.[12] In this short passage Hegel brings together in effect the network of linkages that it will be the concern of this book to question and examine, that is, forgiveness, memory, forgetting, sovereignty, amnesty, and extermination. In her poem, after quoting the passage from Hegel, Sarah Kofman writes:

> Because the "final solution," the *Vernichtung*,
> is the diabolical will
> Wanting what happened not to have happened
> *Das Geschehene ungeschehen zu machen*
> It is wanting to turn the Jewish people to nothing . . . to make them un-happened.[13]

One of the central theses of this book is that, while it is necessary, it is not sufficient to insist simply on the impossibility to forgive the Holocaust.[14] Or, more precisely, the impossibility of forgiveness must be thought in another way. Affirming, as I believe one must, the impossibility of forgiving the Holocaust need not be the end of the discussion. The impossible may be transvaluated as the only "possibility" of forgiveness, that is, as an opening toward a reinvention of the value of forgiveness based on another reading of the Abrahamic tradition. What is henceforth called "forgiveness" may no longer resemble what until now has been identified under this name. What follows is a reading of Jacques Derrida's recent work on forgiveness, which will form the background against which the readings of Simon Wiesenthal's *The Sunflower* (1969), Jean Améry's *Beyond Guilt and Atonement* (*Jenseits von Schuld und Sühne*) (1966), Ingeborg Bachmann's *Franza* (1965–66), and Vladimir Jankélévitch's *Forgiveness* (1967) may be situated. With the exception of Derrida's recent work, all of the texts just mentioned were written in the late 1960s. Beyond a shared preoccupation with questions of guilt, responsibility, and forgiveness, these texts are also contemporary with the international public debate that arose following the implementation of legislation to abolish statutory limitations for crimes against humanity. An international convention to this effect was adopted in November 1968. European states also passed legislation independently: France in 1964, Austria in 1966, the Federal Republic of Germany in 1979, for example.[15]

The authors mentioned above actively participated in this international public debate. They signed petitions (Bachmann, Améry), wrote polemical texts (Jankélévitch), and, in the case of Simon Wiesenthal, mobilized hundreds of public figures to speak out. In collaboration with the Simon Wiesenthal Center in Los Angeles, Wiesenthal's Documentation Centre in Vienna organized a massive postcard campaign directed to the address of the then chancellor of the Federal Republic of Germany, Helmut Schmidt. Its purpose was to inform the world about the number of Nazi perpetrators still at large and to put pressure on the Federal Republic of Germany to pass legislation to preserve the only means by which they may be brought to justice. On the back of the postcards was written in several languages: "Justice for crimes against humanity must have no limitations."[16]

One cannot underestimate the political implications of the legal recognition of this unconditional demand. Not only has it made possible the trials of hundreds of Nazi perpetrators and their collaborators since the 1960s (notably, that of Maurice Papon in 1997 and Klaus Barbie in 1983), but it has also provided the basis for the prosecution in foreign courts of the perpetrators of the genocides in Bosnia and Rwanda.[17] In response to the seriousness and horrific magnitude of the crimes perpetrated by the Nazis and their collaborators during World War II, legislators and parliamentarians have been compelled to recognize the concept of a crime whose prosecution is and must be without limitations. Since the late 1960s a crime against humanity has been defined in international law as a crime that remains universally and eternally open to prosecution, that is, regardless of the place of its commission or the time elapsed since its commission.

What is the significance of this unconditional demand for the value of forgiveness? Jacques Derrida will argue that even though the domains of justice and forgiveness are heterogeneous (it is possible to forgive a crime without renouncing the claim to prosecute it before the law, just as it is also possible to refuse forgiveness while suspending judgment or granting amnesty), the unconditional demand implied in the legal concept of a crime against humanity is "a sign towards" the idea of the unforgivable and forgiveness—of the unforgivable. This argument is difficult to read and at first glance quite tenuous. In what sense could forgiveness be bound to justice if the two orders are fundamentally heterogeneous to one another? Derrida writes:

> But the abolition of statutory limitations [*l'imprescriptible*], I come back to this, signals towards the transcendent order of the unconditional, of forgiveness and the unforgivable, towards a sort of ahistoricity, even eternity and the Final Judgment, goes beyond history and the finite time of the law: for ever, "eternally," everywhere and always, a crime against humanity will always be subject to judgment, and it will never be effaced from the juridical archive. It is therefore a certain *idea* of forgiveness and the unforgivable, of a certain beyond of the law (beyond all historical determination of the law) which inspired the legislators and members of parliament, when, for example, they instituted in France the abolition of statutory limitations [*l'imprescriptibilité*] of crimes against humanity or, in a more general fashion, when they transform international law and institute universal courts.[18]

Elsewhere, in the course of a roundtable conversation on forgiveness, he elaborates this argument as follows:

> The international community, international law, with the institution of a universal penal court, and so on, are indications that humanity is entering a phase where the inexpiable should be denounced and judged as such, the inexpiable as such. That is why I took so much interest in the French law about imprescriptibility. Of course, I insisted that this law has nothing to do with forgiveness. If something is imprescriptible [not subject to a statute of limitations—*pb*], that does not mean it is unforgivable. Nevertheless, there is in this law a sign towards the eternal right to judge crimes, which are held inexpiable, beyond history, beyond time, beyond any period of time. That means that the horizon of forgiving the unforgivable is determining the human community, at least potentially. That is what interests me.[19]

Derrida's references to the "sign," the "transcendental order of the unconditional," and even to an "idea" of forgiveness and the unforgivable unambiguously invoke Kant's essays on the philosophy of history, and in particular, the section of *The Conflict of the Faculties* entitled "An Old Question Raised Again: Is the Human Race [*menschliche Geschlecht*] Constantly Progressing?" (1798).[20] In this section Kant famously argued that the disinterested sympathy (bordering on enthusiasm) of the observers of the French Revolution—even when the very utterance of this sympathy was fraught with danger—constitutes a sign of history (*Geschichtszeichen*) that indicates the moral tendency of the human race as a whole. Invoking Kant, Derrida argues that the recognition in international law of the concept of a crime against humanity is also a sign of moral progress, one which in turn opens a new horizon for humanity, that of forgiveness of the unforgivable. (However, this recognition of a sign of moral progress will not prevent him from *also* critically examining the ontotheological heritage, in particular, the fraternalist universalism implied in the concept of a crime against humanity.)[21]

It is striking that the "later" Derrida should invoke and implicitly countersign the Kantian concept of the sign of history (*Geschichtszeichen*), given the deconstruction of the concept of the sign in Rousseau, Saussure, and Husserl, for example, in earlier texts such as *Of Grammatology*.[22] Can one presume that Derrida employs the term "sign" above in the three senses that Kant gives to it in *The Conflict of the Faculties*, that is, *signum rememorativum, demonstrativum, prognostikon*, a sign that at once recalls, shows, and anticipates?[23] I would suggest one can presume that he does, as long as one does not read in these three senses or temporalizations (past, present, future) of the *Geschichtszeichen* the finality of a signified meaning—one that would be either presently available or promised as a hermeneutical horizon. *What Derrida calls "forgiveness" or "the unforgivable" is not the plenitude of a signified meaning,* which is indeed why the relationship of these ideas to what is called "the Holocaust" cannot be taken to be simply self-evident.[24] Derrida will attempt to define, or rather reinvent, the meaning of the term "forgiveness" on the basis of its very absence of "meaning," by which he understands its absence of finality or even intelligibility:

> Pure and unconditional forgiveness, in order to have its own meaning, must have no "meaning" [*sens*], no finality, even no intelligibility. It is a madness of the impossible [*folie de l'impossible*].
>
> For the common or dominant axiom of the tradition, finally, to my eyes the most problematic, is that *forgiveness must have a meaning* [*le pardon doit avoir un sens*]. And this meaning should be determined on the ground of salvation, reconciliation, redemption, expiation, I would even say sacrifice.[25]

I will return to the motifs of meaning and intelligibility below. Here, however, I underline that what links the concept of crimes against humanity to the idea of the unforgivable is precisely this absence of finality or what is above referred to as the *inexpiable,* that is, the idea of a crime or wrongdoing which cannot be expiated through apology or remorse, the work of reconciliation or even time. *It is the idea of the inexpiable that accounts for the necessity to think the orders of justice and forgiveness together, despite their fundamental heterogeneity.* What Derrida, following Vladimir Jankélévitch, calls "the inexpiable" is a sphere foreign to mediation, reparation, salvation, normalization, reconciliation, mourning, healing, apology, or excuse.[26]

As noted above, survivors such as Simon Wiesenthal and Ruth Klüger have argued that the crimes committed by the Nazis and their collaborators are unforgivable in a sense beyond subjective volition. "Not forgiving" (an imprecise designation) is not simply a choice, the free decision of a finite, supposedly autonomous subject. There is something like a prohibition, a law, which forbids the abusive substitution of a living subject in the place of the dead, who alone presumably would have the right to forgive what has been done to them.[27] Even though this prohibition cannot be a *certain* basis for a judgment or decision (it can be questioned, as we shall see), it is not clear that by simply disregarding the prohibition, forgiveness would or could take place. If the crimes of the Nazis are unforgivable, then they remain so: indifferent to the work of time, inexpiable through apology and remorse. Like the demand to prosecute crimes against humanity, the idea of the unforgivable is without conditions or limitations.

And yet, the same unconditional demand, which subtends the idea of the unforgivable, also calls for a reinvention of the value of forgiveness—one which puts into question the philosophical presuppositions on the basis of which forgiveness is generally presumed to take place, that is, the autonomous subject (who is able to ask for or grant forgiveness), the performative utterance ("I forgive you"), and, above all, the belief in the possibility of an end or *telos* without remainder. Inasmuch as the event of forgiveness is conventionally understood to be the end of trauma, guilt, resentment, hostility, pain, suffering, etc., it is arguably the philosophical and religious ally of the Nazi project of the Final Solution (*Endlösung*), with which it shares a fundamental metaphysical presupposition. As the drive toward closure and normalization, forgiveness has been interpreted, particularly since World War II, to be the enemy of justice.[28] More often, however, it has been interpreted as a way of self-healing of the individual and a therapy of national and international reconciliation. This, for example, is the position famously held by the Anglican Archbishop Desmond Tutu, who chaired the Truth and Reconciliation Commission in South Africa (1995–98): "To forgive is not just to be altruistic; it is the best form of self-interest."[29]

While among survivors of the Holocaust this position is unusual, there is at least one woman who passionately subscribes to it. Eva Mozes Kor, a victim of Josef Mengele's experiments on twins at Auschwitz between 1944 and 1945, shockingly, but in a way that commands our interest, has offered to extend forgiveness not only to Mengele but to all Nazi perpetrators, regardless of whether they have expressed remorse for their actions or have been caught or punished. She argues that forgiveness is essentially a means of individual self-empowerment. Through forgiveness one can overcome the trauma, pain, and helplessness of being a victim. On the fiftieth anniversary of the liberation of Auschwitz on 23 January 1995, she made a public statement before television cameras calling for amnesty for all Nazi war criminals: "Fifty years after liberation, I, Eva Mozes Kor, in my name only hereby give amnesty to all Nazis who participated directly or indirectly in the murder of my family and millions of others, because it is time to forgive, but not to forget. It is time to heal our souls."[30]

FORGIVING DOCTOR MENGELE: EVA MOZES KOR

Eva Mozes Kor made her call for amnesty in the name of an ethics of forgiveness that is widely promoted today (particularly since the Truth and Reconciliation Commission in South Africa). This ethics is not without force, for it seems to imply the promise of a more affirmative relationship to the past than that of those who outright refuse forgiveness or argue for its radical impossibility. Although it is necessary, I believe, to identify the confusions and limitations of Mozes Kor's position, I probably also share in the longing for a more affirmative relation to the past. Mozes Kor's position undoubtedly has the merit of breaking with a powerful taboo—both among survivors of the Holocaust and within the Jewish community more generally. For this reason among others, her decision and the autobiographical narrative she tells around it are worthy of a close reading (even though it is as yet scarcely acknowledged in the field of Holocaust studies).[31]

Eva Mozes Kor affirms an understanding of forgiveness that is apparently unconditional, that is, not bound to the atonement of the perpetrators or the demands of justice. Moreover, it cannot be said to imply simply the forgetting of what has happened. She has twice built a museum memorializing the victims of the Holocaust in the town where she lives, Terre Haute, Indiana; the second time after the building had been burnt down by neo-Nazis in 2003. The museum, CANDLES, welcomes thousands of visitors each year.[32] And yet, on the other hand, her position confuses forgiveness with amnesty while limiting the value of forgiveness to a teleology of self-empowerment and self-healing:

> So I thought about it, and the feeling that I had the power to forgive that god of Auschwitz, me, the little nothing, the little guinea pig, made me feel very good inside. And so I thought if I forgive Doctor Mengele, I might as well forgive everybody . . . Just to be free from the Nazis: that did not remove the pain they have inflicted upon me. As a victim all of us feel extremely helpless, things are done to us, we have no power over it. I had no idea that I had the power to forgive a Nazi. No-one could give me that power and no-one could take it away.[33] (FDM)

Where does the power to forgive a Nazi perpetrator come from? If, as she says, no one could give her this power, then she must have given it to herself, as it were, by an act of self-authorization or phantasmatic auto-affection—as if simply *believing* that she has the power were enough for her actually to have it. This recalls what Hélène Cixous calls "dreamexistence": the paradoxical structure whereby a thought or dream *proves* the existence of a thing, exemplarily, the existence of God.[34] Mozes Kor accuses the survivors who contest her authority to forgive Nazi perpetrators of not being able to understand, and thus of refusing the possibility to heal themselves: "Most of my fellow survivors are so hurting that they do not have the ability to even understand what I am talking about—and so many of them will die without ever feeling free of that pain" (FDM). Behind the self-certainty of this judgment is the interpretative determination of forgiveness as an unambiguous end, in this case, of trauma. Unlike her fellow survivors, she *has* freed herself from it. And because she believes she can affirm this without uncertainty or ambiguity, she can look back, or even down on the others who will remain enchained to it for the rest of their lives.

Eva Mozes Kor believes not only that she has the power to forgive Nazi perpetrators but that she has actually done so. This constitutes, arguably, one of the most serious problems with her reasoning, for can one ever say with certainty that one has forgiven—or that forgiveness has taken place? Moreover, if, as she claims, she forgives primarily in order to heal herself, one can ask to what extent such a gesture merits the name "forgiveness," because it gives absolute priority to the well-being of the forgiving subject, regardless, as it were, of the ones who are forgiven, or what they are forgiven for. In a response to a college student who asked her what the term "forgiveness" means to her, she resumed her position in the following terms: "Forgiveness to me means that whatever was done to me is no longer causing me such pain that I cannot be the person I want to be" (FDM). Within a capitalist culture that places a high value on the self-sufficiency of the supposedly autonomous individual, the promise held out to heal (infinite) wounds is powerful—*particularly if it is articulated by a survivor of Auschwitz.* Moreover, what could be more self-evident than the wish not to suffer? Particularly if this wish is justified in the name of forgiveness, which within Judeo-Christian civilization has almost always been regarded as a positive and praiseworthy act—indeed even as a divine and sacred value? A notable exception to this dominant interpretation is Nietzsche's *On the Genealogy of*

Morals (1887). What Mozes Kor calls "forgiveness" might usefully be read in terms of what Nietzsche in a famous passage of this text identifies as the self-negation or supersession of justice (*Selbstaufhebung der Gerechtigkeit*):

> It is not unthinkable that a society might attain such a consciousness of power that it could allow itself the noblest luxury possible to it—letting those who harm it (*ihren Schädiger*) go unpunished . . . This self-overcoming of justice (*Selbstaufhebung der Gerechtigkeit*): one knows the beautiful name it has given itself—mercy (*Gnade*); it goes without saying that mercy remains the privilege of the most-powerful man, or better, his—beyond the law?[35]

As noted above, Eva Mozes Kor's thinking confuses forgiveness with a declaration of amnesty, which was publicly delivered and signed before television cameras at Auschwitz on the fiftieth anniversary of its liberation on January 23, 1995. That she was careful to make this declaration "in her name only" does not remove its public, political character. On the basis of the authority bestowed on her as a victim and survivor of Auschwitz, she would claim to suspend or annul international law, which, as I emphasized above, recognizes no statute of limitations for the prosecution of crimes against humanity. The authority to which she lays claim is *phantasmatic* (which does not make it any less powerful—on the contrary). A Nietzschean reading of this scene might suggest that what is at stake is not at all a benevolent recognition of the humanity of Mengele and the other perpetrators but rather a luxurious dismissal of them as no longer able to inflict significant harm. As Nietzsche paraphrases: "'What are my parasites to me?' it might say. 'May they live and prosper: I am strong enough for that!'"[36] The feeling of self-empowerment to which Mozes Kor testifies after having made her declaration of amnesty-forgiveness should, I would argue, be read as the restoration of a feeling of narcissistic self-sufficiency, which results from the dismissal of those who for the longest time have been most hated and feared. And yet, this feeling of self-empowerment is not without a certain cost. For is Nazism really no longer dangerous? Is it not itself naïve and dangerous to adopt a sovereign gesture of any sort with regard to *that*? As the philosopher Jean-Francois Lyotard once noted: "The destruction of Nazism also leaves a silence after it: one does not dare to think out Nazism because it has been beaten down like a mad dog, by a police action, and not in conformity with the rules accepted by its adversaries' genres of discourse (argumentation for liberalism, contradiction for Marxism). It has not been refuted."[37] Mozes Kor's recourse to the word "healing" works to restore meaning and intelligibility to a gesture that would otherwise seem unintelligible—even insane: "If anyone would have told me ten years ago today that I was going to forgive the Nazis, I would have told them, please go and find the best psychiatrist and have your head examined, because you are crazy" (FDM). By virtue of the reference to healing, the madness of forgiving Mengele becomes "understandable," permitting a normalization of relations (in the first instance with oneself). As part of the same movement, the unconditional, aneconomical idea of forgiveness is restricted to a logic of calculation and exchange: being free from the wounds of Auschwitz is the return for forgiving Mengele. (This correlation between intelligibility and economic return is extremely thought-provoking. According to this logic, intelligibility itself would be an economic return, as would psychological normality. Thus the insane, the irrational would be, as it were, by definition not economical, or economical in a different way—according to another logic.)

Against the strong tendency of forgiveness to function as a means of closure and normalization, Derrida insists that the only forgiveness worthy of the name is one that does not take place in the service of a pregiven finality, even one that is noble and defensible. If the crime is insane, beyond comprehension, then the forgiveness must also be. Forgiveness must not be the nostalgic return to a state of affairs that existed beforehand, but the invention of something new. (In this sense, Derrida's reinvention of the value of forgiveness may be read as a response to Nietzsche's interpretation of mercy [*Gnade*] as the luxurious exercise of power.)[38]

> I shall risk this proposition: each time forgiveness is at the service of a finality, be it noble and spiritual (atonement [*rachat*] or redemption, reconciliation, salvation), each time that it aims to re-establish a normality (social, national, political, psychological) by a work of mourning, by some therapy or ecology of memory, then the 'forgiveness' is not pure—nor is its concept. Forgiveness is not, it *should not be*, normal, normative, normalising. It *should* remain exceptional and extraordinary, up to the test of the impossible [*à l'épreuve de l'impossible*]: as if it interrupted the ordinary course of historical temporality.[39]

If, as Jankélévitch and others have argued, forgiveness of Nazi perpetrators and their crimes is not only impermissible but radically impossible, then

unable to cope when identified as belonging to a *victimizing* group—and no longer only to a *victimized* group—does not mean that she simply refuses to forgive. However, it signals a breakdown in the logic of self-negation and preservation (*Selbstaufhebung*), which at least since Hegel has been understood in terms of reconciliation with the other and forgiveness: forgiveness interpreted as a form of reconciliation.[44] And yet, the unforgivable insists, it returns and haunts, if not on the side of the "Nazis," then on the side of the "Palestinians," if not on the side of the "Germans," then the barbed wire and the screaming. At one point in the documentary the husband of Eva Mozes Kor, Michael Kor, himself a Holocaust survivor, testifies in his own name: "I have forgiven the Germans, but not the stockade, not the wires, the shouting and the yelling . . . [He breaks down]. I don't want to see them again" (FDM).

"THE MELANCHOLIA IS NECESSARY"

Beyond the courage to break a powerful taboo, the trajectory of Eva Mozes Kor bears witness to a desire or dream for another future in relationship to what has happened. And yet, a close reading of her trajectory also strongly suggests that while the unforgiveable can be suppressed or displaced, it cannot be simply overcome. Jacques Derrida's thinking unconditionally accepts the idea of the unforgivable. Unlike almost all other conceptualizations of forgiveness, his thinking is not based on the presumption that infinite wounds can be healed. Moreover, he goes so far as to argue for the necessity of a *certain* suffering without end. This is, one might say, one of the most inassimilable, indigestible aspects of Jacques Derrida's thought. But for this reason, it is in all probability also one of the most important. His argument is not against health and happiness as such; it is a consequence of an understanding of responsibility as necessarily and always excessive:

> I, of course, have preferences. I am one of the common people who prefer their cat to their neighbour's cat, and my family to others. But I do not have a good conscience about that. I know that if I transform this into a general rule, it would be the ruin of ethics. If I put as a principle that I will feed first of all my cat, my family, my nation, that would be the end of any ethical politics. So when I give preference to my cat, as I do, that will not prevent me from having some remorse for the cat

> dying or starving next door, or, to change the example, for all the people on the earth who are starving and dying today. So you cannot prevent me from having a bad conscience, and that is the main motivation of my ethics and my politics.[45]

The discomfort of "bad conscience" bears witness to the original surplus of responsibility. For this reason it is transvaluated as the positive, indeed inexhaustible, condition of any ethical politics. "Good conscience," on the other hand, is never to be trusted, because it suppresses, denies, or ignores the testimony of "bad conscience," which from an ethical point of view is always prior. Thus one can say that, while Derrida does not repudiate the values of happiness and health as such, in the rejection of "good conscience" a rejection of a dominant interpretation of these values is in all probability implied.[46]

On the subject of mourning, of carrying the other within oneself, Derrida goes even further. He argues for the necessity of *pathological* suffering to resist "the good conscience of amnesia":

> According to Freud, mourning consists in carrying the other in the self. There is no longer any world; it is the end of the world, for the other at his death. And so I welcome within me this end of the world. I must carry the other and his world, the world in me: introjection, interiorization of remembrance [*Erinnerung*], and idealization. Melancholia welcomes the failure and pathology of this mourning. But if I *must* (and this is ethics itself) carry the other in me in order to be faithful to him, in order to respect his singular alterity, a certain melancholia must still protest against normal mourning . . . The "norm" is nothing other than the good conscience of amnesia. It allows us to *forget* that to keep the other within the self, *as oneself*, is already to *forget* the other. Forgetting begins there. Melancholia is therefore *necessary*. [*Il faut donc la mélancholie*.] At this point the suffering of a certain pathology dictates the law.[47]

What Freud designates as the process of "normal" mourning (introjection, interiorization, idealization) does indeed remember the other who has disappeared. However, the memory is kept in a manner that assimilates the otherness of the other to the sameness of the self. The inassimilable character of the other—his or her singularity or alterity—has a chance of not being forgotten only when the process of "normal" mourning fails, that is, when there is "pathological" mourning or *melancholia.* In Freud's terms, melancholia is when the other's disappearance is unacceptable, when there is a revolt; when not only the world *but the ego itself becomes poor.*[48] From this point of view, the verb "*falloir*" in Derrida's dictum "*il faut donc la mélancolie*" can also be read in the sense of lack or default, as if, perverse as it may sound, there were not enough—never enough!—melancholia.

One can apply the same argument to forgiveness when it is interpreted as a therapy of mourning or, what amounts arguably to the same, a form of personal and/or political reconciliation. Even when such forgiveness preserves the memory of the crime and its victims, it does so at the price of forgetting the inassimilable otherness of both. The exigency not to pay this price is at the heart of Jean Améry's revolt, quoted at the beginning of this chapter: "The world, which forgives and forgets, has sentenced me, not those who murdered or allowed the murder to occur . . . Everything will be submerged in a general 'Century of Barbarism.'"[49] Améry resists the tendency toward historical relativisation by insisting on what he believes to be the unique characteristics of Nazism and the Holocaust.[50] He proposes an ethics of *ressentiment* as the only chance of resistance against the world's amnesia and "forgiveness" (forgiveness interpreted here as a form of amnesia).[51] The restitution of the victim as a "fellow man" in, for example, international law may also be read as a symptom of the same process of assimilation and amnesia of mourning.[52]

One might say that in Western culture there is a great pressure to forgive, because it is believed that without forgiveness it is not possible to mourn, or otherwise, to bring mourning to completion.[53] But what if forgiveness were not a therapy of mourning, a means of normalization? There may be another "possibility" of forgiveness—more fragile, less assured of meaning—like the trembling of the body in laughter or a hopeless prayer. The implementation in international law of a concept of "crimes against humanity" calls for—even necessitates—the thought of a forgiveness that does not imply closure of the infinite wounds of the past. Such an unlimited, unconditional thought of forgiveness would be reserved *exclusively* for the worst of the worst, for crimes or wrongs which cannot be expiated though apology and remorse, and for which there is no possible reconciliation or mediation. What are the conditions under which such a forgiveness may be thought or dreamed? How can it be dreamed without renouncing political vigilance? Must this political vigilance itself today be rethought? (It is in fact not enough to say that forgiveness is reserved for the worst of the worst. By the strange, ambiguous logic of the gift/*gift* [gift/poison]: *it is the worst of the worst that calls the unconditional thought of forgiveness into being.* It is only when one speaks of the unforgivable that one really can speak of forgiveness.)

With the exception of Vladimir Jankélévitch's *Forgiveness* (1967), Derrida did not publish readings of the literary works discussed in this book, that is, Simon Wiesenthal's *The Sunflower* (1969), Jean Améry's *At the Mind's Limits* (1966), Ingeborg Bachmann's *The Book of Franza* (1965–66), and Robert Antelme's *The Human Race* (1947). While he had certainly read Vladimir Jankélévitch's *Forgiveness*, he did not undertake an extended commentary of it, choosing to focus his attention on the polemical essay Jankélévitch wrote two years earlier, *Pardonner?* (1965). While a great deal of secondary literature exists in German and English on the work of Améry, Antelme, Bachmann, and Wiesenthal, in general this literature relies on an understanding of the value of forgiveness grounded in the metaphysical presuppositions mentioned above (i.e., the autonomous subject, the performative utterance, and the belief in an end or *telos* without remainder). Even when the value of forgiveness is declared to be dead (Jankélévitch) or superseded by the crimes of the Nazis (Améry), it is always the same metaphysical or ontotheological understanding of forgiveness that is presumed. Derrida's idea of im-possible, unconditional forgiveness of the unforgivable opens, I argue, the intellectual space for different and, I wager, better readings of these literary and philosophical texts, which each addresses according to diverse paths the questions of forgiveness, justice, and responsibility in relation to the crimes of the Holocaust.[54] Derrida's idea of forgiveness might be inscribed within what Kant in *The Conflict of the Faculties* called the history of the future,[55] which is also to say, a thinking of peace: another thinking of peace than that of political or personal reconciliation, or the simple cessation of hostilities.

1

The Survival of the Question

Simon Wiesenthal's The Sunflower

In 1969, Simon Wiesenthal, already internationally recognized for his work in the Documentation Center of the Association of Jewish Victims of the Nazi Regime in Vienna, published an autobiographical narrative based on an exceptional encounter between himself and a dying, repentant Nazi soldier. On his deathbed this soldier confessed to Wiesenthal that he had participated in the murder of hundreds of Jews (including children) and asked Wiesenthal—at the time himself a prisoner in a concentration camp in Poland—for his forgiveness. Responding at the time with silence, Wiesenthal confessed nonetheless to being haunted by the dying man's request, unable to put the matter to rest, both during the period he was interned in the camps as well as afterward. Convinced of the importance of what he had experienced, he sent the narrative, entitled *The Sunflower: A Story of Guilt and Forgiveness*, to a number of distinguished figures of public life, including theologians, writers, philosophers, politicians, and religious leaders. The published text includes their responses.[1]

One of the most powerful responses to the narrative came from another survivor, the writer and essayist Jean Améry, who claimed that questions of forgiveness in relation to the Holocaust are politically irrelevant and, moreover, have no personal interest to someone who does not share a religious viewpoint or faith. What alone matters, he said, is that what happened to him and others does not happen again.[2] Simon Wiesenthal, however, ended his testimony by saying almost the opposite: precisely because it can happen again, it is necessary that the question of forgiveness be reappraised:

> Should I, should anyone, have forgiven him? Would I, would anyone, have permission to forgive him? Today the world demands of us that we forgive those who through their stance continue to provoke us. The world demands that we close the account and draw the line, as if nothing essential happened.
>
> Many of us who fought in that terrible time, and who still sometimes in their thoughts feel imprisoned by that hell, become silent when faced with this demand for forgiveness.
>
> This question will survive all trials and will continue to remain relevant when the crimes of the Nazis belong the distant past.
>
> Therefore I address it to people, who I believe have something to say about it. It should serve as an appeal [*Aufruf*]. For the events that have given birth to this question can happen again.[3] (SB 107–8; SF 97)

Why would someone who had spent almost his entire working life gathering information to bring Nazi war criminals to trial insist so strongly on the question of forgiveness? What connection did he see between the survival of the *question* of forgiveness and the possibility of repetition of these crimes? In this chapter I will attempt to explore these questions on the basis of a new reading of Wiesenthal's narrative and the archive of responses to it in several languages.

MUST FORGIVENESS BE A SPEECH ACT?

Reading closely the quotation above from the end of *The Sunflower*, one can note that the narrator refers to two different, yet related requests for forgiveness. The first, which forms the climax of the foregoing narrative, was made by a dying SS man during the war, that is, at a moment when the crimes were continuing: "Should I, should anyone, have forgiven him?"

Forgiveness accuses before it forgives. By accusing, by stating the injury, it makes the wrong irredeemable [*irremissible*]. It carries the blow all the way to culpability. [*Il porte le coup jusqu'à la culpabilité.*] Thus, all becomes irreparable; giving and forgiving cease to be possible."[10] In this passage, Blanchot argues for the necessity for an interdiction on forgiveness understood as a statement. For this reason, it is important for the argument I am proposing in this chapter. In order for forgiveness to remain possible, one must not say "I forgive you" or even, with Jesus of Nazareth, "thy sins be forgiven thee" (Matthew 9:2; Mark 2:5), for in so doing one *cannot not* at the same time also accuse the one who is addressed, and thus confirm culpability and erase any traces of nonknowledge and undecidability that remain in the interval between the blow (*coup*) and this confirmation. Such traces, Blanchot seems to argue, are necessary for any forgiveness without injury to have a chance.

On the other hand, or as another dimension of the same aporia, simply refusing to forgive is perhaps also never fully justified, particularly if, as the philosopher Vladimir Jankélévitch has noted, it is always possible to take advantage of and profit from the position of being innocent.[11] Indeed, this may be a reason why the narrator, despite the monstrous injustice done to him and the inequality that remains between him and the dying SS man, still feels disquiet for having left the room in silence.[12]

The question remains for the reading of *The Sunflower*, and also more generally, if forgiveness may—and even must—be communicated otherwise than with the words "I forgive you." This is not to ask if the same semantic content may be expressed by different means but rather if forgiveness may take place without being accredited to the sovereign, or more rigorously, phantasmatic power of the subject. The question bears not only on the subject's power to forgive but also on the subject's power to acknowledge guilt and request forgiveness, which is generally considered within both Judaism and Christianity to be the necessary precondition. If "I forgive you" credits phantasmatic power to the subject, so too does the "I apologize" and the "please forgive me." Is an acknowledgment of guilt or request for forgiveness possible without being expressly said by a subject, without a subject *being able* to express it as such? Such questions ultimately lead one to ask if forgiveness can mean something else than *closing the account and drawing the line*, as the narrator (following an entire tradition of thinking about forgiveness) seems to presume in the long quotation from the end of *The Sunflower* with which this chapter began:

> Today the world demands of us that we forgive those who through their stance continue to provoke us. The world demands that we close the account and draw the line [*einen Schussstrich zeihen*], as if nothing essential happened. (SB 107; SF 97)

Even though Simon Wiesenthal does not ask the questions mentioned above (perhaps never even thought of them), they belong to the future opened up by his and others' resistance to demands to close the account and draw the line (*einen Schlussstrich ziehen*), and correspondingly, to the announcement made at the end of the testimony that the question of forgiveness will survive all trials and remain relevant when the crimes of the Nazis belong to the distant past.

THE SPECULATIVE ECONOMY OF CHRISTIAN CONFESSION

I will return again to this announcement below, but before doing so I would like to suggest that the questions formulated above open the possibility of another reading of *The Sunflower*, one that to my knowledge has not been undertaken before. One can begin, or continue, this reading by drawing attention to the narrator's conviction that the SS man has expressed genuine remorse. Whether or not such remorse is sufficient to justify forgiveness is one of the central questions posed by the text. One can point out, however, that unlike the request for forgiveness, the SS man's expression of remorse is not directly *said* to the narrator as such:

> In his confession there was true repentance [*Reue*], even though he did not admit it in so many words. Nor was it necessary, for the way he spoke and the fact that he spoke to *me* was a proof of his repentance. (SB 61; SF 53)
>
> "So this Lemberg fellow showed signs of repentance, genuine sincere repentance for his misdeeds—that at least is how you described it."
> "Yes", I answered: "I am still convinced of that." (SB 91; SF 82)

The SS man does not apologize to the narrator, yet he confesses to him in detail the atrocious murders in which he took part. In the course of the confession his body trembles and convulses. His phrases are often broken up (*abgehacken*). The narrator notes that there was nothing in the SS man's confession that did not conform to a sequence of events of which the narrator was already aware.[13] While the narrator does not believe he is the correct addressee for this confession, he does take into account that the SS man could have called for a priest, which not only would be in accordance with the principles of the Catholic religion of his childhood but also easier and more assured. With a priest the dying SS man would be much more likely to receive "absolution" in the form of the response he desperately wanted. The ethical element, however, consists, I would argue, in the renunciation of such a calculation on forgiveness. The SS man's decision affirms, without regard to the instructions of the Catholic Church, that repentance, the acknowledgment of guilt, has force and meaning only if addressed to a "Jew," that is, to one who is a victim of the genocidal violence in which the SS man has taken part.

And yet, precisely because the addressee is a victim, a man who could—and in all probability will—die tomorrow of the same genocidal violence, the force or meaning of the SS man's repentance is at best difficult to situate, at worst derisory. Pressuring a prisoner destined to death, *eine Leiche auf Urlaub*, to listen to the confession of a dying perpetrator is also an act of violence. Several times during the interview the SS man must stop the prisoner from trying to leave the room by grabbing his arm and pleading with him. After, the narrator will testify that the interview had laid a heavy burden on him.[14]

> Here was a dying man—a murderer who did not want to be a murderer but who had been made into a murderer by a murderous ideology [*unbarmherzigen Ideologie*]. He was confessing his crime to a man who perhaps tomorrow must die at the hands of these same murderers. (SB 61; SF 53)
>
> In the last hours of my life you are with me. I do not know who you are, I only know that you are a Jew and that is enough. (SB 61; SF 54)

However, what makes the violence of the interview particularly intense is not the SS man's confession, shocking as it is, or even less, the genuine remorse that the narrator believes he is able to read in it. What makes the violence particularly intense is the request for forgiveness itself. This violence is obscured by the debate as to whether or not the narrator was morally justified at the time to respond with silence. Counterintuitive as it may seem, the SS man's request for forgiveness is culpable and even inexcusable under the circumstances.

> I think that he is now coming to what he wants from me. I cannot imagine that he ordered me here only to have a listener. [Ich kann mir nicht vorstellen, daß er nur nach mir verlangt hat, um einen Zuhörer zu haben.] (SB 60; SF 52)
>
> He sat up and put his hands together as if to pray. "I want to die in peace, and so I need . . ." (SB 61; SF 54)
>
> "I know that what I have told you is terrible. In the long nights while I have been waiting for death, time and time again I have longed to talk about it to a Jew and beg forgiveness from him. Only I didn't know if there were any Jews left . . .
>
> I know that what I am asking is almost too much for you, but without your answer I cannot die in peace." (SB 62; SF 54)

The request for forgiveness at the conclusion of the confession is a speculative teleological reappropriation. It recuperates the noncalculating, aneconomical character of the remorse, *which does not express itself as such*, back into the sphere of calculation on the future and self-interest. The SS man asks for forgiveness because he wants to have his conscience appeased, so that he may die in peace. The expression of remorse, absurd as it may seem under the circumstances, could still in the dying moments of his life have led to some political statement or action, which would unambiguously affirm his noncommitment to the SS and the Nazi project of the Final Solution. But the ontotheology of Christianization, the speculative economy of Christian confession stands in the way of such a possibility.[15]

The SS man has no moral grounds on which to ask for forgiveness, not only because his crimes are unforgivable but because, as a member of the SS in Nazi occupied Poland, he also continues to benefit from his crimes *even in death*. It is from this supplementary injustice that Wiesenthal's testimony draws its title, *The Sunflower*, which refers to the sunflowers that marked the graves of the dead Nazi soldiers that the narrator saw on the path from the Janowska concentration camp to the Lemberg college (*Hochschule*) where the meeting with the SS man took place.

> The flower heads seemed to absorb the sun's rays like mirrors and draw them down into the darkness of the ground as my gaze wandered down

> from the sunflower to the grave. It seemed to penetrate the earth and suddenly I saw before me a periscope. Colorful butterflies fluttered from flower to flower. Were they carrying messages from grave to grave? Were they whispering something to each flower to pass on to the soldier below? Yes, that is just what they were doing; the dead were receiving light and messages [*Botschaften*].
>
> Suddenly I envied the dead soldiers. Each had a sunflower to connect them with the living world. For me there would be no sunflower. I would be buried in a mass grave, where corpses would be piled on top of me. No sunflower would ever bring light into my darkness, and no butterflies would dance above my dreadful tomb. (SB 19; SF 14)

As mentioned above, Wiesenthal's text was first published in French translation in 1969, where the German title *Die Sonnenblume* was rendered *Les fleurs de soleil.*[16] Why should an autobiographical testimony written in German, dealing with questions of guilt and forgiveness for crimes committed in the name of "the German people," have been published first in another language? The French title, *Les fleurs de soleil*, refers to more than one sunflower. In this way it unambiguously invokes the sunflowers described by the narrator in the passage quoted above. The German title, however, while also invoking this passage, preserves a relationship to singularity, which is an essential aspect of Wiesenthal's approach to justice and guilt.[17] *Die Sonnenblume* refers most likely to the sunflower that *this* SS man will have on his grave. Facing death with a burning and unappeased conscience, the SS man knows in advance that there will be at least a sunflower, and this is consoling, as is the thought that there will be a living mother who will mourn for him, and a room of his own in which to die. When making his deathbed confession to the narrator, the SS man does not take into account that his addressee, just like his victims, will have been deprived of all these things. Had he done so, it would have been impossible for him to request forgiveness—at least in the same way.

> "Everywhere military cemeteries sprang up. I heard they were well tended and on every grave were growing flowers. I like flowers" . . .
>
> Therefore he knows that we will get a sunflower when he is buried. The murderer will own something even when he is dead. And I? (SB 58; SF 51)

That the SS man does not sufficiently take into consideration the historico-political abyss, the incommensurabilities between his own position and that of the narrator, is not by chance. The recognition of such incommensurabilities is incompatible with the speculative teleological structure of his confession, which, in order to function, presupposes that there is a common measure, a basis on which to exchange offers and requests of forgiveness. In order for there to be reconciliation, both parties, the one who confesses and the one to whom the confession is addressed, must *at some level* be able to identify with one another as the same, as fellow human beings. In the section of *The Phenomenology of Spirit* addressing the dialectic of evil and its forgiveness, Hegel describes confession and forgiveness as a movement of reciprocal recognition of two opposing self-consciousnesses. This reciprocal recognition is grounded in an act of putting oneself on the same level (*sich gleich machend*), recognizing the other against which one is opposed as in essence the same, which is to say, one-sided, finite, "wicked" (*böse*):

> By putting itself on the level with the doer [*dem Handelnden*] on whom it passes judgment, it is recognized by the latter as the same as himself. This latter does not merely find himself apprehended by the other as something alien and disparate from it, but rather finds that other, according to its own nature and disposition, identical with himself. Perceiving this identity and giving voice to it, he confesses this to the other, and equally expects that the other, having in fact put himself on the same level, will also respond in words in which he will give utterance to this identity with him, and expects that this mutual recognition will now exist in fact. His confession [*Geständnis*] is not an abasement, a humiliation, a throwing-away of himself in relation to the other, for this utterance [*Aussprechen*] is not a one-sided affair, which would establish his disparity with the other: on the contrary, he gives himself utterance solely on account of having seen his identity with the other.[18]

Within the Hegelian logic, it is essential that the confession of wickedness be said to the other, posited as a speculative proposition: "I am so" ("*Ich bin's*"). Only by being expressed in language does the innerness of self-consciousness step forth into concrete existence as a universal self: "*Das Dasein des Geistes als unmittelbaren Selbsts.*"[19] Likewise, the forgiveness offered by the other self-consciousness also must be expressed as a spoken, speculative proposition. It is the expectation that the other reciprocate, by recognizing its own one-sidedness and identification with the one who has confessed. The refusal to reciprocate is the hard heart (*das harte Herz*), who, in clinging to the divisive thought, in rejecting any continuity with the other, is therefore henceforth in the wrong. Hegel reads muteness (*Stummheit*) on the part of the one who should forgive as the most extreme form of the rebellion of the Spirit that is self-certain (*die höchste Empörung des seiner selbst gewissen Geistes*). The renunciation of this self-certainty is a necessary movement in exchange for which inner conviction is translated, or rather, sublated (*aufgehoben*) into objective knowledge that is mediated by the recognition of the other. Identification understood as equalization (*Ausgleichung*) is the very possibility of this economic transaction: equalization not at the level of wickedness or sin, but of the human beings, the self-conscious subjects who are not reducible to their sins.[20] The renunciation of self-certainty in the reconciling "yes" belongs to the teleological progression of history, understood as the dialectical unfolding of the absolute. The act is taken back into the Spirit. It is internalized, mourned, healed. The memory of the deed remains, but as a moment of the whole, it is no longer the life of the Spirit, which manifests itself as absolute in the word of reconciliation (*das Wort der Versöhnung*):

> The true, i.e., the *self-conscious* and *existent*, equalization of the two sides is necessitated by and already contained in the foregoing. The breaking of the hard-heart, and the raising of it to universality, is the same movement which was expressed in the consciousness that made confession of itself. The wounds of the Spirit heal, and leave no scars behind. The deed is not imperishable; it is taken back by Spirit into itself, and the aspect of individuality present in it, whether as intention or as existent negativity and limitation, straightway vanishes. The *self* that carries out the action, the form of its act, is only a *moment* of the whole, and so likewise is the knowledge, that by its judgment determines and establishes the distinction between the individual and universal aspects of the action.[21]

It should be underlined that I do not consider Hegel to be simply wrong to identify the fault of one-sidedness or self-certainty, nor is he in my view mistaken to think both the offer and request for forgiveness on the basis of an elementary need for recognition. The decisive point, however, is that the dialectic logic, whose force is reconfirmed in *The Sunflower*, is hopelessly insufficient. In particular, it insufficiently accounts for silence, which it interprets as one-sided self-certainty: the hard heart that does not break. In the early theological essay "The Spirit of Christianity and Its Fate," Hegel identifies this one-sided refusal with the spirit of the Jews, which *hates*:

> In the spirit of the Jews there stood between impulse and action, desire and deed, between life and trespass [*Verbrechen*], trespass and pardon, an impassable gulf, an alien court of judgment. When, then, they were referred to love as a bond in man between sin and reconciliation [*Versöhnung*], their loveless nature must have been outraged [*empört*], and, when their hatred took the form of a judgment, the thought of such a bond to their minds must have been the thought of a lunatic. For they had entrusted all harmony among men, all love, spirit, and life, in an alien object.[22]

According to his biographer, Hella Pick, Simon Wiesenthal considered *The Sunflower* to be his most important book, not only because of the questions it raises but also because "it sets out to demolish what he sees as a 'widespread perception of the Jew as a hater. I set out to show that if Jews do not forgive, it is because they are not empowered to do so.'"[23]

The extreme injustices described by Wiesenthal's testimony, and the consequences they have on the victims, bear witness to the limits of the presupposition of a common humanity as the speculative basis for both requests and offers of forgiveness. Despite the fact that the narrator believes in the genuineness of SS man's remorse and even admits at two points in the narrative to feeling compassion (*Mitleid*) for him (which is a form of empathic identification with the other), this under the circumstances is hopelessly insufficient.[24] The insufficiency lies not only, as the narrator points out, in the request that he, abusively, substitute himself for the SS man's victims and forgive in their name but also—and more importantly in my view—in the motivation behind such a request to "win paradise economically."[25] The SS man wants to have his conscience appeased and yet still keep a sunflower on his grave. In confessing his crimes to the narrator, *nothing at bottom is really risked.* Had he chosen or been persuaded to take some political action in favor of his victims, or in their memory (however feeble, however seemingly meaningless under the circumstances), he would have had to, at the very least, renounce the consolation of a sunflower.

The Ethical and the Hyper-Ethical

In her biography of Simon Wiesenthal, Hella Pick notes that Wiesenthal was encouraged to write the book by his French agent and publisher, Charles Ronsac (né Charles Rosensweig). The book was first published by Opera Mundi, where Ronsac worked as an editor. (It was later chosen as "Book of the Year" in France.) That the book was first published in translation undermines the habitual assumption that one can identify the language of the original without difficulties: "While Wiesenthal wrote the original by himself in German, some stylistic improvements were made by the French translators, which were afterwards incorporated into the German edition."[26] As at least one commentator of the French edition has pointed out, the French title does not employ the habitual translation of "*die Sonnenblume*," which would be "*le tournesol*."[27] *Les fleurs de soleil* is a poetic locution invented by the French translators, in all probability because it resonates with Charles Baudelaire's *Les fleurs du mal*. Like Wiesenthal's testimony, Baudelaire's collection of poems both describes and resists the speculative economy of Christian confession. In particular, the introductory poem, *To the Reader* (*Au lecteur*), articulates the mechanism by which the cultivation of remorse functions not to purify, but on the contrary to feed sin. Within this spiritual and sublime economy, evil becomes a flower, a poetic flower:

> La sottise, l'erreur, le péché, la lésine,
> Occupent nos esprits et travaillent nos corps,
> Et nous alimentons nos aimables remords,
> Comme les mendiants nourrissent leur vermine.
>
> Nos péchés sont têtus, nos repentirs sont lâches;
> Nous nous faisons payer grassement nos aveux,
> Et nous rentrons gaiement dans le chemin bourbeux,
> Croyant par de vils pleurs laver toutes nos taches.

> Foolishness, error, sin, niggardliness,
> Occupy our minds and work on our bodies,
> And we feed our mild remorse,
> As beggars nourish their vermin.
>
> Our sins are insistent; our repentances are limp;
> We pay ourselves richly for our admissions,
> And we gaily go once more on the filthy path
> Believing that by cheap tears we shall wash away all our sins.[28]

It seems incontestable that the sunflowers of Wiesenthal's narrative, which marked the graves of the dead Nazi soldiers, are flowers of evil: emblems of a perverted world, where the injustice of mass murder is openly rewarded. More than that, however, in the way that Wiesenthal poetically imagines them they also embody an almost childlike wish for reassurance. By virtue of the sunflowers, the dead soldiers retain a connection to the world, to butterflies and sunlight. The narrator, who imagines himself as already dead, cannot help but long for this connection. For him, *die Welt ist fort*: "Suddenly I envied the dead soldiers. Each had a sunflower to connect him with the living world, and butterflies to visit his grave. For me there would be no sunflower" (SB 19; SF 22). The narrator imagines the sunflowers as a kind of telecommunication channel between the living world and the dead. The light and information (*Botschaften*) they send into the earth do not resurrect the dead but keep them nonetheless in touch with the living. By virtue of the sunflowers, the dead do not disappear completely from the world's activity and awareness. Thus they are assured a kind of mortal survival, a "life" after death, which is not incompatible with a secularist or even atheist position: "Christians believe in the resurrection, but for a Jew, the grave is his last and also his perpetual home. That is why Wiesenthal always stresses that, for a Jew, the significance of his sunflower image is so important."[29] Even while the narrator seems to renounce any belief in the life of a human being after death, his longing for a sunflower remains arguably religious in its inspiration. Against his complaint that without a sunflower he will be cut off from the living, one might say that even in a mass grave there is still some underground microbial life that comes into contact with the dead. But that is not the point. What matters to the narrator is the relation to light and communication with the living world: "Gaily colored butterflies fluttered from flower to flower. Were they carrying messages from grave to grave? Were they whispering something to each flower to pass on to the soldier below? Yes, this was just what they were doing; the dead were receiving light and messages [*Botschaften*]" (SB 19; SF 22). Now all of this will have gone over to the other side. The narrator has a relation to light and the living world, only inasmuch as they remain for him infinitely out of reach, allied to an evil that is unforgivable. The ambiguity of the sunflowers is that as much as they express a childlike wish for reassurance, for a kind of mortal survival, they also testify to the possibility—even the ineluctability—of absolute disappearance. As the simulacrum of an aesthetic image or religious symbol, the sunflowers cannot not bear witness to what Jacques Derrida has called, also in memory of the victims of the Holocaust, *la cendre*: ash or cinder:

> The cinder, however, is an absolute non-memory, so to speak. Thus, it communicates with that which in the gift, for example, does not seek to be recognized or kept, does not even seek to economize itself. Well, to say that there are cinders there [*il y a là cendre*], is to say that in every trace, every writing, and consequently, in every experience (for me all experience is, in a certain way, an experience of the trace and writing), in all experience there is this incineration, this incineration which is experience itself. Of course, there are great, spectacular experiences of incineration—and I allude to them in the text—I'm thinking of the crematoria, of all the destructions by fire, but before even these great memorable experiences of incineration, there is incineration as experience, as the elementary form of experience.[30]

Derrida's argument on first appearance may appear quite scandalous. What happened to millions of victims of the Holocaust, that is, the murder in gas chambers and incineration in crematoria ovens is not an absolutely exceptional event of history but something that in a certain way is happening all the time: it is an elementary structure of experience itself as absolute non-memory, aneconomical loss, disappearance without return. While such an argument (and in particular, the use of the term "*la cendre*") may be interpreted as offensive or disrespectful to the victims of the Holocaust, it need not necessarily. Moreover, it need not imply a simple denial of the uniqueness of the Holocaust as may appear at first glance, but a more complex and discreet gesture.[31] Here I underline only that the speculative economy of forgiveness presupposes the cinder as the structural possibility of nonreturn or aneconomical loss. Rather than foreclose this possibility, it may be transvaluated, rethought not so much as the ethical but as the *hyper-ethical* condition of forgiveness. Rather than as a mechanism of repair and normalization, offers and requests of forgiveness should be pure gifts. They should not be grounded in the hope or expectation of a return on investment, in a speculation on the future—even in the first instance in the desire to seek recognition from the other. At the limit they should not even be spoken as such, because once expressed in language, as a word of apology or reconciliation, they already enter into the circuit of exchange.[32]

If, following Vladimir Jankélévitch, I underline the notion of a hyper- or hyperbolical ethics, it is because it is not certain that forgiveness is morally defensible.[33] Wiesenthal's decision to narrate the drama of the meeting with the SS man has perhaps no other purpose than to make this point as strongly as possible to those for whom the ethical character of forgiveness is an unquestioned given. As noted above, according to Hella Pick, Wiesenthal wrote *The Sunflower* because he wanted to counter the widespread perception of the Jew as a hater. Wiesenthal foresaw, one might say, an old/new anti-Semitism that arises perversely out of the very testimony of the Holocaust itself, a sort of self-fulfilling circular logic that takes the refusal or inability of the Jews to forgive what happened to them as an unforgivable fault. To resist this logic is no simple matter. On the one hand, the narrator of *The Sunflower* defends himself against this logic by arguing that he does not have the right to forgive in the name of others. On the other hand, however, he is not completely satisfied with this self-justification. Even though he believes he is able to account in moral terms for his decision to remain silent, he remains troubled by it. Moreover, being troubled by what happened is also something about which he does not have good conscience:

> Was I right after all to tell them what happened? I should think of the five men in the "pipe" ["*Schlauch*"] who had been shot that day. Was this SS man more to me than they were? . . . I feared that Arthur, the cynic, might say: "Just look at him, he can't forget a dying SS man while countless Jews are tortured and killed every hour." Then he would add something that would deeply affect me: "You have let yourself be infected by the Nazis. You are beginning to think that the Germans are in some way superior, and that's why you are worrying about your dying SS man." (SB 69–70; SF 62)

One might very tentatively inscribe Wiesenthal's narrative within a long and painful history of Jewish fascination with—even love for—the gentile, "Christian" other. The narrator is quite aware that he has no right to think obsessively about this man who is guilty, when so many who are not guilty in this manner have gone to their deaths unremembered and unmourned. But he cannot dispel his disquiet. It is stronger than he is. It follows him even into the death block at Mauthausen. The disquiet takes him "beyond" the realm of the "ethical," if by "ethical" one presupposes the ability to account for one's thoughts and actions and give reasons for them:

> Was this true? Did my unrest [*Unruhe*] come from my subconscious [*Unterbewußtsein*]? What drove me again and again to think about the

> encounter in the hospital? Why had I never been able to put it behind me? Why was this meeting [*Begegnung*] not finished and done with [*nicht abgeschlossen*]? The last question seemed to be the most important. (SB 90; SF 81)

One can say that this disquiet is the realm of the hyper-ethical, inasmuch as it bears witness to a surplus of responsibility that does not allow itself to be satisfied with pregiven rules, codes, norms, axioms—be they "Jewish" or "Christian." The narrator asks himself if his disquiet comes from his *Unterbewußtsein,* his sub- or unconscious. Shortly after the meeting, another one of the narrator's friends, Josek, seeks to reassure him by saying that he would have acted in the same way toward the SS man. And yet, unlike the narrator, he claims that he would have done so with full awareness and intention (*ganz bewußt und mit voller Absicht*). In Josek's estimation, the narrator had acted more unconsciously (*mehr unbewußt*):

> "I can see you are not entirely pleased with yourself. But I assure you that I would have done the same as you did. The only difference perhaps is that I would have refused forgiveness with full awareness and intention [*ganz bewußt und mit voller Absicht*]. You acted more unconsciously. And now you do not know if it was right or wrong. But believe me: it was right." (SB 73; SF 65)

Here one might say that the narrator receives from his friend the "I forgive you" that he had denied to the SS man. But this does not remove his disquiet. Recognition from another self-consciousness (who is "the same," a fellow prisoner) may perhaps provide temporary relief, but it does not make the symptoms disappear.

In the willingness to take seriously the possibility of unconscious motivations, as well as in the attention he gives to dreams, hallucinations, and jokes, Wiesenthal's *The Sunflower* is quite unusual among the testimonial literature of the Holocaust. Wiesenthal has an uncommon sensitivity for what escapes the sovereignty of the living present.[34] Such sensitivity is not unrelated to the demand for justice, above all, when this demand is felt to be unconditional. While the narrator of *The Sunflower* affirms that he did not believe that he would survive the war, he says that he never doubted that the Nazis would be called to account for their crimes. Even if the text reports that the prisoners cannot but laugh at the hope that God will save them, there is yet one thought in which the narrator says he never lost faith. Against the supreme principle the right of the strongest, Simon Wiesenthal helps us to read the thesis that justice, if there is any, is undeconstructible:[35] "I had still not lost the faith [*Glaube*] that the world would repay them for their crimes—despite their pompous victories, their measureless jubilation at battles they have won, and their boundless arrogance. The day will yet come when the Nazis will have to hang their heads, as the Jews do now (SB 41; SF 35). One of the questions that surprisingly has not been explored in any of the secondary literature about *The Sunflower* that I have encountered is whether there is a relationship between the central event recounted in the narrative and the work that Wiesenthal was to undertake after the war. Even the glaring irony has to my knowledge not been commented on, that is, that the narrator, the "Jew," chosen apparently at random to listen to the SS man's confession and to grant him forgiveness should be the one who will become the world's most famous "Nazi hunter." One can go further and ask if this traumatic encounter is not what gave Simon Wiesenthal his singular vocation? While I believe one must ask this question, it is impossible, of course, to know with certainty (even if Wiesenthal had himself affirmed this provenance of his work). What one can say, however, is that the narrator's disquiet (*Unruhe*) strongly suggests that he does not feel completely innocent of what happened.[36] Even if his refusal of the SS man's dying wish is just (and I believe it is), I would suggest that the narrator cannot foreclose the possibility—even the inevitability—that *he gains something from this refusal*, that he benefits from the opportunity that has been given to him, when, all of a sudden, between victim and perpetrator the tables have been turned. The narrator is, as it were, guilty automatically, by virtue of a logic that makes it impossible for him not to profit from being ethical and just:

> He sat up and put his hands together as if to pray.
>
> "I want to die in peace, so I need . . ."
>
> I sensed that something couldn't get past his lips. But I wasn't there to encourage him, to help him. I remained silent. [*Aber ich bin nicht dazu da, ihn zu ermutigen. Ich bleibe stumm.*] (SB 61; SF 54)

When the narrator avows, "But I wasn't there to encourage him," there is a moment of hardness, of noncompassion: a refusal to be generous. At that moment, the narrator cannot be called simply a victim or even only an eyewitness. In exchange for this moment of hardness, noncompassion, the narrator transcends his position as a Nazi victim to become one who in silence passes judgment on a murderer. His action no doubt is different from one who escapes, or who takes up arms, but it is potent nonetheless. Perhaps even—one might speculate—a life-affirming predatory instinct has been awoken in the course of this traumatic meeting with the dying SS man, one that will sustain Wiesenthal in the infinitely patient and frustrating research to which he will consecrate his energies after the war. And thanks to which a great many Nazi perpetrators, mass murderers, could not sleep.[37]

I believe, more than Wiesenthal said, this encounter with the SS man was for him a question of life and death. For had he done what the dying SS man had asked him to do, he would have at that moment compromised the sacred exigency within him to remain alive, not for his own sake, but for the sake of the victims to whom he wanted to give justice, and in all probability especially for his mother, Rosa Wiesenthal, whose murder several weeks before the encounter with the SS man is mentioned briefly in the narrative.[38] One can read *The Sunflower* as a request for forgiveness for being just.

IMPROBABLE LAUGHTER

In the *Phenomenology of Spirit* Hegel makes the bold assertion that "the 'yes' of reconciliation (*das versöhnende Ja*) is the manifestation of God in the midst of those who know themselves in the form of pure knowledge."[39] By contrast *The Sunflower* opens with an episode that testifies not so much to the discovery that God is absent, but to such a "discovery" being laughable. It becomes the object of a joke. One of the narrator's friends, Arthur, returns to the camp with news from an old lady in the ghetto:

> "What could the old lady have said? Does she perhaps know when we will get out of here? Or when they are going to slaughter us?"
>
> "Nobody knows the answers to those questions. But she said something else, something that we should perhaps think about in times like these. She thought that God was on leave [*daß Gott auf Urlaub sei*]." Arthur paused for a moment in order to let the words sink in. "What do you think of that, Simon?" he asked. "God is on leave."
>
> "Let me sleep," I replied. "Tell me more when He gets back." ["*Erzähl weiter, wenn Er wieder zurück ist.*"]

> For the first time since we had been living in the stable I heard my friends laughing, or had I merely dreamt it? (SB 11–12; SF 15)

How to read this improbable laughter? For the narrator's friend, Arthur, the news of God's absence comes as a revelation pregnant with meaning. For the narrator it is not news. It is something everyone has known for a long time: "So that should be news? [*Und das soll etwas Neues sein?*] That we live in a world that God has abandoned?" (SB 12; SF 16). What makes the friends laugh (if indeed they do laugh) is in all probability the insouciance with which the narrator responds to the thought of God's abandonment, his treating it as if it is nothing particularly important. What is more important at this moment is just sleep: "'Let me sleep,' I replied. 'Tell me more when He gets back.'"

But such a reading is not enough to account for the improbability of what happened. As an event, the laughter is more than the "joke" that supposedly caused it. It is quite possible that the narrator, who was half-asleep, did not even intend what he said to be funny. The laughter comes as a surprise: a rupture with the living present. The text suggests that it may have been a *dream of laughter*, leaving the ontological and epistemological status of what happened indeterminate and fragile: "For the first time since we had been living in the stable I heard my friends laughing, or had I merely dreamt it?" Now it is not just the friends' laughter that is held in epistemological and ontological suspension but almost everything that is recounted in the narrative. The text is littered with hesitations, question marks as to the reality of that to which the narrator bears witness. The narrator can scarcely believe the events to which he testifies. During this period, his entire existence appears to him illogical, unreal, dreamlike, even ghostly (*gespenstliches*) and uncanny (*unheimlich*). Such thoughts are particularly strong in relation to the meeting with the dying SS man.[40] To faithfully testify to what happened is also to testify to his disbelief, to the incredible, dreamlike character of what happened—and to the fact that what is called "reason" and "logic" could not be trusted.

It is certainly possible to interpret Wiesenthal's concentration camp humor as pleasure found in God's abandonment and rebellion against life's suffering. The expression *Gott auf Urlaub* is already a little bit humorous, as if God were just a human being on holiday. The narrator, who delivered the joke at the expense of what the old woman in the ghetto had said, is also careful to give reason to her: "What the old woman said in no way shocked me, she had simply stated what I had long felt to be true" (SB 13; SF 9). The humorous pleasure, rebellion, and even triumph is directed not against the suffering imposed on the prisoners by the Nazis but against that imposed by Judeo-Christian (i.e. monotheistic) culture itself, from where comes the hope of a miraculous intervention, the faith "in a world order in which God has a definite place" (SB 13; SF 9), and above all, in the dignity and sacredness of the life of a human being, because they have been made in the image of God (*imago Dei*). Under these circumstances, such hope and faith are laughable. It is alone what is laughable. Indeed the joke could not have provoked such improbable laughter among the fellow prisoners had they not, in addition to the monstrous suffering caused by the Nazis, also been carrying the weight of the metaphysics of Judeo-Christian (monotheistic) culture and the Abrahamic tradition. In a sovereign, life-affirming way, this weight is laughingly thrown off because it ceases to be useful—perhaps. The joke and the laughter it provokes offer a momentary triumph over metaphysics, which is humorously dismissed. In a more psychoanalytic vein, on the other hand, one might also suggest that the laughter is a release of unconscious aggression against God, who, having made the Jews His chosen people, has, by virtue of a perverse anti-Semitic reversal, caused them to be the chosen victims of extermination. In *Moses and the Monotheistic Religion* (1939), Freud memorably argues that among the deeper, more unconscious motives for the intensity and lasting strength of anti-Semitism is the surprising belief on the part of those who are not Jewish in the Jewish people's divine election: "What I am going to say will at first appear incredible. I venture to assert that the jealousy [*Eifersucht*] which the Jews evoked in the other peoples by maintaining that they were the first-born, favourite [*bevorzugte*] child of God the Father has not yet been overcome by those others, just as if the latter had given credence to the assumption."[41] Whether or not one interprets the laughter as deriving from atheism or theism, whether it was dreamed of or actually happened, it leaves undoubtedly a memorable trace. Everything remains the same, but by virtue of the laughter, it is "ever so slightly different." Perhaps. While it is certainly possible to read the laughter as a means of reconciliation and accommodation with "life" under such circumstances, I think such a reading would be superficial. What would be less superficial would be to suggest that the prisoners experienced in laughing a shared recognition of the impossibility of their current situation and that of any miraculous salvation or redemption by God. And in this shared recognition, they may have felt also some unspoken compassion for one another. And through this compassion perhaps even some forgiveness toward themselves and one another for having found themselves there, eyewitnesses and victims of such incomprehensible injustice.[42]

THE SURVIVAL OF THE QUESTION

> There is no testimony that does not at least structurally imply in itself the possibility of fiction, simulacra, dissimulation, lie, and perjury—that is to say—the possibility of literature . . . If this possibility that it seems to prohibit were effectively excluded, if testimony thereby became proof, information, certainty, or archive, it would lose its function as testimony. In order to remain testimony, it must therefore allow itself to be haunted.[43]

Whether the friends' laughter—like almost everything recounted in the narrative—was dreamed of or actually happened signals one of the most difficult dimensions not only of Wiesenthal's testimony but of the legacy of the Holocaust in general. It is, one might say, the point where testimony as a genre of autobiography intersects with the deconstruction of Western metaphysics and literature. On the one hand, as Wiesenthal and others do not fail to point out, this dreamlike, unbelievable character of the Nazi crimes works powerfully in the interest of the perpetrators and their objectives: "That was the Nazis' strength: they committed crimes that no-one before them could imagine" (SB 94). The destruction and/or contestation of evidence and testimony belong to the structure of the extermination itself, which targeted not only human beings but also the traces, the archive of what happened.[44]

On the other hand, however, precisely because it is always possible to contest or deny the evidence, one is compelled to recognize that a testimony, no matter how authoritative or compelling, cannot be considered to be a proof that what happened actually took place. No testimony can establish beyond all doubt the truth of that to which it bears witness. Because testimony is an appeal to belief, to faith, it may always be considered that the witnesses lie. In this sense, the question marks, the disbelief, the uncanny and haunted feelings to which the narrator of *The Sunflower* so frequently bears witness exemplify not only the effects of trauma but also a structural possibility of all testimony.

This haunting is not only at the level of the truth of what is told but also of its presumed meaning and importance. It is not certain that what the narrator has experienced is worthy of consideration in the public domain. In this sense, Jean Améry's response to the narrative, which I cited at the beginning of this chapter, is a necessary one, even if it is insufficient: "What difference does it make? [Was kommt's denn schon auf diesen einen an!]. . . . *Politically, it does not make any difference* [*Es gilt das politisch gleichviel*]" (SB 219; SF 107). The dimension of non-sense, and even pointlessness in speaking about what happened, is marked at least at one point in the narrative itself, where the narrator cries out in response to an hallucination about the SS man, while he is in the death block at Mauthausen at the end of the war. A Jewish prisoner, who is a doctor, comes to his assistance and offers to give him water: "I knew that he could not understand the few words I had spoken, and I was much too weak to tell him the whole story. What would have been the sense of it anyway? Not one of us was going to escape from this death block [*Todesblock*]. So I said nothing [*Ich schwieg deshalb*]" (SB 88; SF 88).

That the narrator will later recount the story of what happened with the SS man to Bolek, the Polish apprentice priest, does not negate the reasons he gives here for not speaking about happened. Like the laughter of the friends, the request for forgiveness is not reducible to an economy of meaning, any more than the crimes themselves. When at the conclusion of the story the narrator addresses his readers and takes the risk of speaking in the name of the survivors of the Holocaust, he inscribes the essential character of what happened within an "as if" of fiction: "Today the world demands of us that we forgive those who through their stance continue to provoke us. The world demands that we close the account and draw the line [*einen Schlußstrich ziehen*], as if nothing essential happened" (SB 107). It may be contested that what happened is essential. However, if it is essential, then this means that it is neither possible nor permissible simply to *close the account or draw the line* [*einen Schlußstrich ziehen*]. The very demand to do so, to close, end, "forgive" what happened is, one can argue, complicit with the crimes themselves, with the metaphysical drive implied in the name that the perpetrators gave to them. Now, according to Wiesenthal, this demand to forgive does not come from particular individuals or groups but from the world as such. How to read this reference to the "world" (which I recall was also decisive in relation to the sunflowers)? Here it is a placeholder for the perpetrators themselves, who with very few exceptions were unapologetic and without remorse. In the absence of a request for forgiveness on their part, the "world," as it were, asks forgiveness on their behalf: it says in sum that nothing essential has taken place. But who or what is the "world"?

One might be tempted to suggest that what Wiesenthal means by the "world" is the Christian world. But "Christianity" is not monolithic or univocal. It would be imprecise and unjust to equate Christianity *as such* with the drive to closure and normalization. And yet, a Christian inheritance speaks out in a powerful way whenever the world is understood in terms of the fraternity of men as neighbors, that is, whenever an essential unity and sameness of humanity is affirmed as an unquestioned presupposition. The "world" works in the service of closure and normalization by restituting the illusion of a fundamental human sameness and relatedness, forgetting the inassimilable otherness of the crime, its perpetrators and its victims:

> The world is neither the universe nor the cosmos. Even when Saint Paul spoke of the *cosmos* to designate the Christian world, he attributed a new meaning to the word *cosmos*, signifying the order of creatures, the fraternity of men as neighbours, etc. . . . One must recall this memory, which is both theological and philosophical, when one employs the word "worldwidization" [*mondialisation*]. The word "globalization" loses the reference to this memory.[45]

Despite his polemic with Wiesenthal, Jean Améry also makes a similar reference to the agency of the world. Whereas for Wiesenthal it is the world who demands forgiveness, for Améry it is the world that forgives and forgets. However, one can say that these two claims are but mirror reflections of one another. They diagnose the same geopolitical force (or logic) from opposing sides:

> The world, which forgives and forgets, has sentenced me, not those who murdered or allowed the murder to occur . . . Everything will be submerged [*untergehen*] in a general "Century of Barbarism." *We*, the victims, will appear as the truly incorrigible [*Unbelehrbaren*], irreconciliable ones [*Unversöhnlichen*], as the antihistorical reactionaries in the

> exact sense of the word, and in the end it will seem like a technical mishap [*Betriebspanne*] that some of us still survived.[46]

In a quasi-Hegelian fashion, Jean Améry identifies the agency of the world with history itself, with forgiveness and forgetting as the monstrosity of the natural time sense, which works without subject or intention, which happens automatically like a machine. He unambiguously interprets this machinery as complicit with the Nazi project of extermination. And yet, whereas Améry seeks to resist the machinery of the world's forgiveness by proposing an ethics of *ressentiment,* Wiesenthal has another strategy. In a prophetic manner, he announces *the survival of the question,* which he gambles will not be resolved by future generations. As quoted above: "This question will survive all trials and will continue to remain relevant when the crimes of the Nazis belong the distant past. Therefore I address it to people, who I believe have something to say about it. It should serve as an appeal [*Aufruf*]. For the events that have given birth to this question can happen again" (SB 107–8).

Not as the agency of the world or of history, but as a painful and disturbing question, an open wound, "forgiveness" will—Simon Wiesenthal affirms—survive not only the war but also the trials and testimonies of the war's aftermath. Wiesenthal's announcement of the survival of the question can be read as a "performative," a promise, even though it is not articulated in the first person.[47] It does not simply describe what will happen in the future; it makes the future that it announces. From the moment the survival of the question is predicted, the imminent closure and forgetting of the past will have been postponed. Henceforth, the *question* of forgiveness will stand in the way of the world's demand to close the account and draw the line "as if nothing essential had happened." The event of forgiveness will have been projected into a messianic "to come" beyond any foreseeable future. By announcing the survival of the question, Wiesenthal would be affirming that there is more promise in open wounds than in the healing of breaches, that prophetic utterance (rather than *ressentiment*) best resists the irresistible movement of closure and normalization.

In what one might identify as a classical philosophical gesture, Wiesenthal interprets the demand for forgiveness of the Nazis and their crimes *as a question*, which is to say, as an identifiable *topos* that can be situated and discussed as such. Such an interpretation may, however, be insufficient to account for the aporias to which both Wiesenthal and Améry bear witness. If, as they suggest, it is the *world* that asks for and grants forgiveness, then the "question" of forgiveness is not simply localizable. If the world is the agent, then there is no place that is simply beyond its influence. Even if the demand for forgiveness is impossible to answer, the nonresponse is still a response. Hence the insufficiency of an anti-Hegelian revolt, which may always be reinterpreted as self-certainty, the hard heart that reacts against the inexorable logic of history. In holding to the necessity of an ethics of *ressentiment*, Jean Améry also testifies bitterly to its powerlessness and insufficiency:

> I must encapsulate my resentments. I can still believe in their moral value and their historical validity. Still, but how much longer? The very fact that I must ask myself such a question demonstrates the immensity and monstrosity of the natural time-sense [*das Ungeheure und Ungeheuerliche des natürlichen Zeitgefühls*]. Perhaps already tomorrow it will lead me to self-condemnation . . . Our resentments—emotional source of every genuine morality, which was always a morality for the losers—have little or no chance at all to make the evil work of the overwhelmers bitter for them.[48]

Wiesenthal's prophetic announcement of the survival of the question is in all likelihood more powerful and life affirming than the ethics of *ressentiment* that Jean Améry nobly defends in despair. It is also, I would argue, more promising than the "I forgive" of Eva Mozes Kor in which an ethics of self-healing is affirmed at the expense of the unconditional demand for justice.[49] However, it should be underlined that *all three responses are ethical.* Each one answers to a profound necessity, even though they are fundamentally incompatible with one another. And yet, while all three are ethical, one is compelled to say that alone the response of Simon Wiesenthal deserves the name "hyper-ethical" because it is able to put itself into question, because it affirms itself in giving unconditional hospitality, or rather "hostipitality," to the other.[50] One can, as suggested above, read *The Sunflower* as a request for forgiveness for being just:

> Forgive me this my virtue;
> For in the fatness of these pursy times
> Virtue itself of vice must pardon beg.[51]

How to think the responsibilities of memory, justice, and education in an epoch when the trials are over and the eyewitnesses are dead? By announcing the survival of the question and calling the world to respond to it, Wiesenthal puts the very question of forgiveness to work in the service of the memory of the victims for future generations. One can read *The Sunflower* as the invention of a powerful resistance machine to the world's demand for closure and normalization.

It is a structural element of *The Sunflower* that there are many voices, differing and incompatible opinions, both within the narrative proper as well as beyond it. What is the purpose of such a debate? Why does Wiesenthal call for it and promote it, even among those who he could safely presume would have great difficulty agreeing with the decisions made by his narrator? In all probability, it is because he believes that such an open debate, *without restriction on dissent,* will best serve the memory of the victims of the Holocaust and the education of future generations. The ongoing debate, the ever-renewed critical examination (*Auseinandersetzung*) of the past, is alone what will keep the memory *alive.*[52] (This is the beginning of an answer to the questions I asked in the introduction, concerning why a Nazi hunter would insist so strongly on the importance of the question of forgiveness.)

While the first editions of *The Sunflower* included commentaries on the part of individuals to whom Wiesenthal had personally written and asked. Later editions, however, include responses from others, such that with each new edition there is effectively a new text, containing a mixture of old and new commentaries, either written specifically for one of the eight languages into which the text has been translated or otherwise recopied from other editions. What is created across the various publications of *The Sunflower* is thus also a testimony of time: each new edition is a palimpsest, containing responses that testify also to new historical events, changes in the perception of the Holocaust, as well as cultural and linguistic specificity. In responding to the narrative, many readers also testify in their own name to ethical dilemmas and injustices that they themselves have "experienced" (political dissidents, religious leaders, writers, activists, survivors from other atrocities, even a famous member of the Nazi elite).[53]

BEFORE ALL QUESTIONING

One can yet ask if, despite its prophetic character, Wiesenthal's affirmation of the survival of the question is still too much of a solution. To what extent do the aporias to which Wiesenthal bears witness exceed the question and the authority of the questioning attitude? What are the limits of the presupposition that "forgiveness" can be posed as a question and discussed as such? Must not forgiveness (be it as an offer or request) remain unavowed, indeed unavowable in language, if it is to resist recuperation into an economy of exchange; if it is to remain heterogeneous to any determination of the order of knowledge, of the self-presentation of an appropriable meaning?

In his reading of *The Sunflower*, Ulrich Baer has drawn attention to an *unstated* demand to listen as the unthought precondition for all discussions of atonement, guilt, and forgiveness in relation to the crimes perpetrated by the Nazis.[54] Can one think of listening as *already* a kind of forgiveness, even if this listening is violently imposed, as is very dramatically the case in *The Sunflower*? As several commentators have pointed out, at no point in the interview does the SS man ask the narrator for his name: "I don't know who you are, I only know that you are a Jew and that is enough" (SB 61; SF 54). For his part the narrator during the interview does not only refuse to respond to the SS man's request for forgiveness, but not give reasons for his refusal or otherwise say anything to the dying SS man of what is going through his mind. At the conclusion of the confession there is a radical interruption of communication between the two men.

> There was an uncanny [*unheimlich*] silence in the room.
>
> I looked through the window . . .
>
> I stood up and looked in his direction, at his folded hands. Between them there seemed to rest a sunflower. I had made up my mind and without a word I left the room. (SB 62; SF 55)

The silence between the two men in the room is an infinite silence, frozen, as it were, in time. After the narrator leaves the room, there will have been no way to rectify or change it. In this sense, one could say that the narrator's refusal is like a murder. What is the relationship between the silence between the two men in the dying room (*Sterbezimmer*) and the burning need to bear witness and solicit responses from others? Could it be that the narrator feels responsible for the SS man's death, as if he had lent a hand in it by refusing to assent to his last wish? Even further, might the narrator also feel responsible for the mass murders themselves, as if he, unwilling inheritor of the SS man's confession, were also responsible for the SS man's responsibility?[55]

It is certainly possible to read *The Sunflower* as a request for forgiveness for being unable to forgive, if "forgiveness" means closure, drawing the line, renouncing the demand for justice. However, it is also possible to read *The Sunflower* as an inventive, poetic gesture of forgiveness granted to the SS man, to whom the narrator feels bound by virtue of his remorse (despite its hopeless insufficiency). In Hebrew, the name "Simon," "Shimon" (שִׁמְעוֹן) means the one who has heard (Genesis 29:33). Because the narrator has heard the SS man, this is enough for Bolek, the apprentice priest, to believe that the SS man has been forgiven, that he has died in peace: "He died in peace because you listened to his confession. It was a proper confession [*richtige Beichte*]—even without a priest . . . Through his confession—though it was not a formal confession—his conscience was liberated and he died in peace because you listened to him" (SB 91; SF 82). This listening is not simply a choice, the decision of a sovereign subject. Listening is no more a choice than the compulsion to speak, to testify to what has happened. Simon Wiesenthal has listened so well that he can (or so he would ask us to believe) recall the smallest details of a meeting that had taken place twenty-five years prior to the first publication of *The Sunflower*. He will have planted a sunflower for this repentant Nazi in the form of a testimony, to remember him and connect him with the living—even to remember a part of his name (Karl). Perhaps this is forgiveness, if forgiveness means a new beginning without a definitive end or closure of the past. One can say that listening is the "yes," or more precisely, the "yes, perhaps" of forgiveness.[56]

2

Reading Forgiveness in a Marrano Idiom

(Jacques Derrida)

I have never found a concept that was grasped in a word. Should that be surprising? Has there ever been a concept that was really nameable? I mean nameable with a single name or a single word? The concept always demands sentences, discourses, work, and process: in a word, text . . . I sometimes feel I have never done anything, ever, other than to try to be coherent in this regard.

Jacques Derrida, *Paper Machine*

Many recent studies have focused on the contemporary proliferation around the world of requests and offers of apology, reconciliation, and forgiveness. Eliza Barkan, notably, has spoken of an "age of apology," referring to the impressive number of heads of state, leaders of the ecclesiastical hierarchies, and even multinational companies, who over the last twenty-five years have been asked to—and in some cases have made—public confessions, offers of apology, and requests for forgiveness.[1] It is to the detriment of many of these studies that they have not been informed by a careful reading of the work of the philosopher Jacques Derrida, who during the last ten years of his life elaborated a novel concept of forgiveness that took as its departure point a reading of this phenomenon quite different from that of anyone else.[2]

Derrida spoke of a contemporary "worldwidization of forgiveness" (*mondialisation du pardon*), whose historical novelty he traced back to the institution of the juridical concept of "crimes against humanity." His analysis focused on the global proliferation of *scenes* of apology, reconciliation, and forgiveness (transmitted via television and the Internet). Unlike Barkan and others, Derrida did not presume that, simply because there is this proliferation of scenes, that apology, reconciliation, and forgiveness is something that is actually happening in the world. Indeed, he argued almost the opposite: "The very dimensions of forgiveness tend to be effaced in the course of this worldwidization, and with it all measure and conceptual limitation."[3]

THE WORLDWIDIZATION OF FORGIVENESS AS A SYMPTOM OF THE DECONSTRUCTION OF CHRISTIANITY

Derrida's formulation "worldwidization of forgiveness" can and, I would suggest, must be read at least in three different ways. In the first instance, it draws attention to the fact that a certain language and scenography of apology, reconciliation, and forgiveness (which has its roots in an *Abrahamic*[4] religious heritage) have today become a universal idiom, imposing itself on radically different cultures, including those which do not have European or "biblical" origins. The stakes implied in such an internationalization are at once legal, political, economic, and diplomatic:

> I am thinking of those scenes where a Japanese Prime Minister "asked forgiveness" of the Koreans and the Chinese for past violence. He presented "heartfelt apologies" in his own name . . . Recently there have been real negotiations, this time official and serious between the Japanese and the South Korean governments on this subject. There will be reparations and a political reorientation. These negotiations, as is almost always the case, aimed at producing a reconciliation (national or international) favourable to a normalisation.[5]

When Derrida speaks of "a reconciliation favourable to a normalisation," this suggests that the formulation "worldwidization of forgiveness" should also be heard in a second, ironic sense, giving voice to the suspicion or, rather, the observation that the language and scenography of apology, reconciliation, and forgiveness function today as an ethico-political currency that can be bought and sold in a globalized marketplace. For such an economy to function effectively, it is useful, perhaps even necessary, that a single idiom be universally accepted, one that may be applied and translated into different contexts, in relation to crimes committed under absolutely heterogeneous conditions and for absolutely heterogeneous motives. And yet, with the universal adoption of a single idiom, one can foresee the possibility—even the inevitability—of further injustices.[6]

There is a third way of reading the expression "worldwidization of forgiveness" that is probably the most important of all, but it is also the most enigmatic and difficult to approach. Implied in the adoption of an Abrahamic language and scenography as a universal idiom is a worldwide process of Christianization and/or Latinization. What Derrida calls the "worldwidization of forgiveness" is coextensive with a globalization of Christianity itself, or more precisely, an understanding of globalization (*mondialisation*) as worldwide Christianization.[7] However, unlike the missionary efforts of the past, this universal or tendentially universal "convulsion-conversion-confession" does not conform to the implementation of a program or dogma. It resembles rather a *dissemination*, which, in order to be operative, no longer needs the Christian church or even, at the limit, the belief in God.[8] The globalization/worldwidization of Christianity corresponds, for Derrida (as it also does for Jean-Luc Nancy), to the deconstruction and self-deconstruction of Christianity.

> The "worldwidization" of forgiveness resembles an immense scene of confession in progress, thus a virtually Christian convulsion-conversion-confession, a process of Christianisation which has no more need of the Christian church . . . I propose to nickname "worldwide-latinization" (*mondialatinisation*) to take into account the effect of Roman Christianity which today overdetermines all language of law, politics and even the interpretation of what is called "the return of the religious." No alleged disenchantment, no secularisation comes to interrupt it. On the contrary.[9]

In chapter 3, I will return to the question of the Judeo-Christian underpinnings of the juridical concept of crimes against humanity, which Derrida contends is the main accusation as well as being the horizon of this worldwide proliferation of self-accusation, repenting, and asking for forgiveness. In this chapter, I will restrict myself to elaborating two fundamental—and radical—consequences of the thesis of globalization as worldwide Christianization.

Firstly, with regard to worldwide Christianization, whether or not one shares a religious viewpoint or confession is of no importance. Christianization takes place and is operative without it. In fact, for both Derrida and Nancy, it is precisely where Christianity appears today to be irrelevant and no longer recognizable that Christianization is most effective and powerful, for example, in the secular institution of international law. In the epoch of globalization there is no simple outside of Christianity.[10]

Second, what Christianity is or will be remains, however, open—yet to be decided. If worldwide Christianization corresponds to the (self)-deconstruction of Christianity, then this implies that what Christianity will become is unpredictable. It cannot, in a secular fashion, be reduced to a personal confession or a worldview (*Weltanschauung*).[11] Jean-Luc Nancy goes so far as to argue that atheism is realized Christianity:

> Christian assurance can take place only at the cost of a category completely opposed to that of religious beliefs: the category of "faith," which is faithfulness to an absence and a certainty of this faithfulness in the absence of all assurance. In this sense, the atheist who firmly refuses all consoling or redemptive assurance is paradoxically or strangely closer to faith than the "believer." But that means also that the atheism that henceforth determines the Western structure, which is inherent in its mode of knowing and existing, is itself realized Christianity [*christianisme réalisé*].[12]

Derrida suggests that Christianity is the most plastic, the most open religion, the one best prepared for unpredictable transformations, for the event, for what is coming: "If the deconstruction of Christianity develops we won't be able to recognize the roots of Christianity any more, and yet nonetheless, we will still be able to say that this is Christianity . . . [S]omething is happening to Christianity, an unpredictable earthquake, and that's not necessarily negative."[13] In his book *Beyond Guilt and Atonement* (*Jenseits von Schuld und Sühne*) translated into English as *At the Mind's Limits* (1966), the writer and survivor of Auschwitz Jean Améry argued that when crimes reach an order of magnitude that warrant the designation "crimes against humanity," questions of remorse and forgiveness cease to have any essential interest or pertinence. What alone matters is to analyze the causes, prosecute those responsible, and prevent the crimes from happening again. Inasmuch as forgiveness (with divine grace) belongs to the domain of theology, it has no place—or at best a secondary place—in a serious discussion about the Holocaust or other crimes against humanity in the modern secular world. Améry's quasi-Nietzschean position, implied in the title of his autobiographical reflections, *Beyond Guilt and Atonement*, is also expressed in his response to Simon Wiesenthal's narrative *The Sunflower* (1969), which testifies to the dilemma of a dying SS man's request for forgiveness, addressed to Wiesenthal while he was a prisoner in a concentration camp in Poland in 1943. In response to the question of whether or not Wiesenthal in the name of the murdered victims should have forgiven this man, Améry wrote:

> Whether you are an agnostic or a believer, I do not know, but your problem belongs to the realm of guilt and atonement and . . . therefore is a *theological* one, and as such, it does not exist for me as an atheist who is indifferent to and rejecting any metaphysics of morality . . . Because I can only see the problem of forgiveness in political terms, I must abstain from approving or condemning your behaviour . . . Politically, I do not want to hear anything of forgiveness! . . . What you and I experience must *not happen again*, never, nowhere. Therefore I refuse any reconciliation with criminals.[14]

Améry's exemplary response to Wiesenthal testifies to the limit or "disaster" of a Judeo-Christian value of forgiveness in a world without God, that is, in a world where the crimes of the Nazis take place beyond any horizon of promised redemption, security, or intelligibility. In such a world, not only is forgiveness no longer a divine or positive value, it is not even meaningful. While marking this limit, Améry also insists, however, on the *political* necessity to refuse forgiveness understood as any form of reconciliation with the perpetrators. Améry's two-part response has the virtue of drawing attention to what is unthought in the generally held presupposition that offers and requests of reconciliation and forgiveness are inherently ethical and/or meaningful.[15] However, as a strategy of resistance to the contemporary "globalization of forgiveness," Améry's response is, I argue, limited by the fact that it unreflectively relies on the distinction between the "theological" and the "political."

The "globalization of forgiveness" not only undermines such a distinction but also, more importantly, the premises on which it is based, that is, the opposition between reason and "religion" (or between thought or science and "religion"). If Christianity is in deconstruction, then it is not identical to itself. It is not stabilized and grounded in an identifiable origin or essence. As a symptom of the deconstruction of Christianity, the "worldwidization of forgiveness" undermines any distinction between the theological and the political, as well as the opposition between reason and "religion" (or thought or science and "religion"). Against a certain powerful tradition of the Enlightenment that extends from Voltaire to Heidegger (including Marx, Freud, and Nietzsche), Derrida and Nancy argue that it is not possible today to speak from a position that is purely and simply disenchanted from what is called religion, and in particular, from an experience of faith. This audacious claim does not, despite appearances, mean the abandonment of all critical and deconstructive vigilance with regard to the metaphysical heritage of Christianity (and/or monotheism in general) but rather, I would argue, suggests a deeper, more responsible way of addressing it.[16] Interpreting religion simply as ideology (Marx), illusion (Freud), error (Nietzsche), or, more radically, as having no place in thought as such (Heidegger: "Das Glauben hat im Denken keinen Platz")[17] does not permit one to account for the ways in which religion (in particular, Christianity) transforms itself in tandem with the development of secularization, reason, and techno-science, and forms ever new alliances with it. (Consider, for example, liberation theology, existential theology, Christian Science, even Christian Zionism.)[18] Moreover—and this is perhaps the most important point—antireligious vigilance in the filiation of a certain tradition of the Enlightenment, by virtue of its position of presumed disenchantment and outsider status, is at best limited in its chances of affecting how the great traditions of religious thought today are read and, consequently, the acts and decisions these traditions are presumed to authorize. Parting with the relative security of this outsider position (however powerful and necessary the insights that have come from it) may today be a political imperative.

> Now if the type of deconstruction that I try to do remains let's say Abrahamic—Jewish, Christian, Islamic—that would imply that it is part of this tradition, and also that it affects this tradition in an unpredictable way.[19]
>
> This year the seminar consists in analyzing in what way the Christian schemas are prevailing in the world. Beyond the Christian cultures,

> even in Japan and India, and so on. In the culture in which Christianity is present, and sometimes dominant, I try to understand what's going on. My language is marked by a number of Christian seals. It is sealed. Christian means also Jewish. There is a certain relation to Judaism and Islam, what I call Abrahamic traditions. My discourse is sealed by this complex Abrahamic tradition. My friend, Jean-Luc Nancy, is preparing a book entitled *The Deconstruction of Christianity*, and I know for having read some pages of the short text he has published on this subject that he also thinks that in fact we cannot escape what we call Christianity. It is in the name of Christianity that we get rid of Christianity. The death of God, for example—the death of God is a Christian theme. Nothing is more Christian than that. So perhaps what's going on today in the world under the name of what I call "mondialatinization," worldwide latinization, worldwide Christianization if you will, is a sort of self-deconstruction of Christianity.[20]

The above quotations further help to read what Derrida and Nancy understand by the thesis of the inescapability of Christianity, and how this is related to deconstruction and self-deconstruction. Just as Derrida had argued in the late 1960s that the end of metaphysics is a metaphysical category, in the late 1990s he insists that nothing is more Christian than the death of God. Like the metaphysics of presence, or rather, *as* the metaphysics of presence, Christianity is "inescapable" in the sense that simply refuting it, or claiming to overcome it, does not prevent it from returning in new ways. Therefore getting rid of what is called Christianity, if this remains the goal, must be approached otherwise. It is impossible to leap out, as it were, with both feet. And yet, on the other hand, if nothing is more Christian than the death of God, then this also means that the "Word" (what in the Bible is called the "Word" or *Logos*) can function and remain legible in God's absence, that is, without necessarily referring to a deciding or decidable instance, an origin or final addressee, that would guarantee and fix (its) meaning, (its) truth, indeed (its) very existence. Christianity is inescapable, not because it is "the only true religion," but inasmuch as it deconstructs itself into universally or almost universally employed schemas, which mark and seal the language(s) we speak. Consider emblematically the word "religion" itself, whose provenance is the Latin *religio*, which may remain untranslatable.[21]

One can say that the motif of the deconstruction of Christianity (and/or the Abrahamic monotheistic tradition) is both the same and also something quite different from that of the deconstruction of the "Greek" phonocentric philosophical tradition, from Plato to Husserl, Rousseau to Austin, and beyond. One could analyze the relation between the two as a relation of insistence.[22] Like the opposition between speech and writing, the oppositions between theism and atheism, and between the sacred and the secular, are so deeply entrenched in Western ("worldwide") thought and practice that they cannot be displaced in one go. Nor should such displacement be regarded simply as an accomplishable task.

RESISTING CHRISTIANITY FROM WITHIN: GIVING MEASURE AND CONCEPTUAL LIMITATION TO FORGIVENESS

> Ontotheology encrypts faith and destines it to the condition of a sort of Spanish Marrano who would have lost—in truth dispersed, multiplied—everything up to and including the memory of his unique secret. Emblem of a still life: an opened pomegranate, one Passover/Easter evening (*un soir de Pâques*), on a tray.[23]
>
> In my family and among the Algerian Jews, one scarcely ever said "circumcision," but "baptism," not Bar Mitzvah, but "communion."[24]

If it were necessary to distinguish between Nancy's and Derrida's readings of the deconstruction of Christianity, one would have to make reference to Derrida's avowed identification with the figure of the Marrano, which at one point he also suggests is a clandestine structure of identity in general.[25] The terms *Marrano,* and the slightly less pejorative *converso*, were applied in Spain and Portugal from the end of the fourteenth century to the descendants of baptized Jews, who in many cases continued to observe Jewish laws and customs in secret, in order to avoid further persecution. In Spanish *Marrano* means "pig," and it was employed by Christians as an expression of contempt and loathing, which later Jewry transvaluated to wear as a badge of honour—in this regard analogous perhaps to the labels "dyke" or "queer" today.

The interest of the Marrano tradition, which one would hesitate to locate simply within Judaism, is that it marks a clandestine resistance to Christianity from within Christianity. As noted above in the quotation from

"Circumfession," within Derrida's family and among the Algerian Jews, the language of the Christian sacraments was employed as a code, a *shibboleth.* The same language used to name the sacred rites of the dominant Christian (colonialist) culture was also used to designate other rites, testifying presumably to another faith.[26] Interpreting this (double) gesture would call for a long analysis, which I will not undertake here. I will simply suggest, as an introduction to what follows, that the word as well as the concept Derrida calls "forgiveness" may be usefully read with reference to this Marrano tradition. Unlike in other places where he invents new names to draw attention to the newness of his concepts (*differance, destinerrance, circumfession, grammatology, iterability,* etc.), his employment of the term "forgiveness" marks a more clandestine practice, comparable perhaps to the use Baruch (Benedictus) Spinoza made of the term "God" in his system.[27] Even though Derrida situates his concept within a Judeo-Christian or "Abrahamic" tradition of thought about forgiveness, what he calls forgiveness gives us to think something quite different than what has been previously understood by this term. For Derrida, forgiveness is not "closure," "reconciliation," "absolution," or even a therapy of mourning. Even though it is an event, nowhere does he determine forgiveness as the grandeur of a "new beginning" (as does Hannah Arendt, for example).[28] Forgiveness is neither an end nor a new beginning. Concretely, it may be closer to complicitous and denying laughter (*le rire dément*).[29] Or otherwise, it is an elementary condition of all forms of communication. Forgiveness is implied in listening, reading, speaking, and writing: "We are asking forgiveness by reading. Somewhere I wrote that as soon as I write, I am asking for forgiveness, without of course knowing what will happen. But forgiveness is implied in the very first speech act. I cannot perform what I would like to perform. That is why things happen."[30] To lend support to my reading, one can refer to at least one other place in Derrida's oeuvre where he refers to Marranism as a deconstructive practice. Toward the end of "Marx and Sons," Derrida offers to share the experience of the universal Marrano with Tony Negri, a Marxist autonomist who calls for "a post-deconstructive ontology." Rather than attack Negri for this apparently regressive metaphysical maneuver, Derrida suggests to him the possibility of using the word "ontology" to mean something other than what it means normally in the tradition of Western philosophy: "In philosophical company we could act as if we were still speaking the language of metaphysics or ontology, knowing full well, between us that this was not at all so."[31] Such a practice pretends to speak the language of theology and metaphysics, but in so doing speaks another language entirely. It hides an alterity and at the same time protects it, but also at the risk of losing it or rendering it unrecognizable.

Unlike Heidegger, who clearly also recognized worldwide latinization (*mondialatinization*), Derrida does not attempt to resist its domination by searching for another idiom that would be more proper. Through worldwidization, the Abrahamic heritage has become ineluctable. Derrida rethinks the value of forgiveness—and the name "forgiveness"—through a novel rereading of the Abrahamic heritage itself. Not simply by returning to a Hebrew thought of forgiveness, of which he is also aware, but, as we shall see, by rereading the Latin idiom of the gift in its alliance with forgiveness (the verbal link of "don" and "pardon").

Returning to the discussion above concerning the "globalisation of forgiveness," one can note that if an Abrahamic language and theatricalization of apology, reconciliation, and forgiveness have today become a universal idiom, it would *seem* that one concept or understanding of forgiveness has effectively triumphed, to become the universal concept that may be functionally applied and translated into different contexts, in relation to crimes that have been committed under absolutely heterogeneous conditions and for absolutely heterogeneous motives.

One can say that Derrida's position on this question is subtle. If there is today a universal concept of forgiveness employed internationally (in conjunction with a language and scenography of apology, reconciliation, and so on), it is a concept whose contours have yet to be rigorously defined, and moreover, whose foundations are obscure. The apparent transparency and translatability of a particular idiom *does not* despite appearances signify the existence of a rigorous and coherent concept—or understanding—of what is taking place when one speaks of forgiveness, apology, or reconciliation. One could even suggest the opposite, thinking, for example, of what Heidegger says about the use of the word "being" (*seiend*) at the very beginning of *Being and Time*, that is, that an apparent clarity and self-evidence conceals a deeper disquiet (*Unruhe*).[32]

It is Derrida's interest to take such disquiet as seriously as possible—disquiet about not only the concept of forgiveness but also the immense tasks—or abysses—to which the scenography or idioms of "forgiveness," "apology," and "reconciliation" today bear witness. The point of such an inquiry is not to remove ambiguity in order to delineate, for example, a clearer concept that will work better. *The apparent good functioning today of the idioms of "apology," "reconciliation," and "forgiveness" is, for Derrida, symptomatic*—as indeed is the fact that these three "concepts" often appear together.[33] If anything, the inquiry should have the consequence of *slowing down* the globalization or worldwidization of forgiveness, by making the quasi-universal employment of certain idioms and conventions more difficult, because less self-assured. Against the tendency in this worldwidization toward the effacement of all measure and conceptual limitation, Derrida indeed will attempt to formulate a rigorous concept of unconditional forgiveness. However, it will be a concept that is internally split—one that, if anything, will accentuate, rather than diminish, contradictions, abysses, and impasses.

To what end? While this question should be left open (because one does not know what the effects of such a concept will be), I will argue nonetheless that there is an answer that one cannot avoid choosing. The purpose of such a concept is to make place for the dream of an unheard-of kind of forgiveness, a forgiveness of the unforgivable, that is, a forgiveness for crimes or wrongdoing whose seriousness and gravity is such that they cannot be expiated (through apology and remorse). As forgiveness of the unforgivable, such forgiveness would be as *unjustifiable*, indefensible even, as the crimes or wrongdoing to which it responds. As such, it would necessarily be grounded in a secret, not in the sense that it conceals some hidden or ineffable truth but rather that it cannot be reduced to the principle of sufficient reason, the possibility of an adequate explanation in the public, political, juridical, or even ethical domains.[34] As such, it would also be a leap of faith, which would not amount to forgetting (forgiveness, Derrida insists, is not equivalent to forgetting) but rather to a living, active memory of both the wrong and the guilty person:[35]

> The impossibility of forgiveness offers itself to thought, in truth, as its sole possibility. Why is forgiveness impossible? Not merely for a thousand psychological reasons, but absolutely impossible? Simply because what there is to forgive must be, and must remain, unforgivable. If forgiveness is possible, if there is forgiveness, it must forgive the unforgivable—such is the logical aporia. But, in spite of appearances, this is not only a cold and formal contradiction or logical dead end.

> It is a tragedy of compassion and of inter-subjectivity as destiny of the hostage, hôte, and madness of substitution of which we speak of with Levinas and Massignon. If one had to forgive only what is forgivable, even excusable, *venial*, as one says, or insignificant, then one would not forgive. One would excuse, forgive, erase, one would not be granting forgiveness . . . The forgiveness of the forgivable does not forgive anything: it is not forgiveness. In order to forgive, one must forgive the unforgivable, but the unforgivable that remains [*demeuré*] unforgivable, the worst of the worst: the unforgivable that resists any alteration, any historical reconciliation that would change the conditions or the circumstances of the judgement. Whether remorse or repentance, the ulterior purification of the guilty has nothing to do with this. Besides, there is no question of forgiving a guilty one, a subject subject to transformation beyond the fault. Rather, it is a matter of forgiving the fault itself . . . if it remains thus impossible, forgiveness must therefore *do the impossible*; it must undergo the test [*épreuve*] and ordeal of its own impossibility in forgiving the unforgivable. It must therefore undergo the test and ordeal, merge [*se confondre*] with the very test and ordeal of this aporia or paradox: the possibility, if it is possible and if there is such, the possibility *of* the impossible. And the impossible of the possible.[36]

How to read the intransigence of this thought or "logic" that enjoins one to do what one cannot do, and will not accept anything less? How to "*faire l'impossible*": not only "to do impossible" but also "to make the impossible," as if the impossible itself were each time an invention? Furthermore, how to respond or live—read, write, think—in relation to the authority of this heteronymic injunction, whose power or irony seems to increase by virtue of its contradictory character?[37] Derrida deploys the same paradoxical "logic" in relation to other unconditional concepts such as invention, testimony, hospitality, the gift, democracy-to-come, and even reading ("the only possible invention would be the invention of the impossible . . . otherwise, it only makes explicit a program of possibilities with the economy of the same";[38] "the testimonial act is poetic or it is not a testimonial act: it must invent its language and form itself in an incommensurable performative";[39] "I cannot read what I can read. Only that which is illegible can be read").[40] While these unconditional concepts should not be seen as equivalent to forgiveness, they must by virtue of the paradoxical "logic" they share be in some way related to each other.[41]

If deconstruction is both a thinking of the impossible *and* the unconditional injunction to *do* and/or *make* the impossible, then it necessarily implies both a thought and an experience of forgiveness. Why? Because when faced with the impossible, *one cannot not ask for forgiveness.* The request for forgiveness is an inescapable corollary of the injunction to do and/or make the impossible: "If I have been multiplying the detours and the contortions since a moment ago, including the place where I humbly ask for forgiveness and commiseration, it is because I am, I am placed; I have placed myself, in an untenable position, faced with an impossible task. Forgiveness and pity: mercy."[42] One can notice that in the citation above the rhythm of articulation slows down and falters. This faltering step ("it is because I am, I am placed; I have placed myself, in an untenable position . . .") testifies that the "I" is at a limit of its capacities. Even if the demand to do the impossible enjoins a request for forgiveness, forgiveness itself remains out of reach . . .

Following the argument that Derrida elaborates elsewhere on the gift,[43] forgiveness—from the moment it appears as forgiveness—necessarily submits to an economy of exchange, and thus to the possibility of inmixing and contamination. Even the most generous, heartfelt, authentic, sublime act of contrition or forgiveness never appears without being haunted by the possibility of a return—in the form, for example, of a reward or profit (intentional or otherwise) within, for example, a horizon of reconciliation, expiation, or redemption.

This transcendental style of argument about the nature of forgiveness or its "condition of (im)possibility" might be read as an attempt to broach the question of whatever link there may be between the Judeo-Christian concept of forgiveness (and its metonymies of confession, contrition, reconciliation, etc.) and the possibility of genocide and crimes against humanity. If "pure" forgiveness is impossible, then the Judeo-Christian notion of sincere, genuine, heartfelt forgiveness is *necessarily insufficient*; it cannot be equated with forgiveness; it is in a sense the destruction of any chance of forgiveness because it pretends to make present what cannot be made present. The employment of this notion, at least in its habitual understanding, is henceforth—if not simply forbidden—displaced, reinterpreted in such a way that it can no longer be employed with a good conscience and without irony:

> If forgiveness happens, then this experience should not be the object of a sentence of the kind "S is p" . . . if I say that I know that I forgive, if I say, lightly, "I forgive you" this sentence in the present, with a verb in the present tense, is absolutely the destruction of forgiveness. That is because it implies that I am able to forgive, that I have the power to forgive, the sovereign power to forgive, which introduces me into the scene of the economy of exchange.[44]

It seems to me necessary to point out that Derrida's argument has two separate moments, which seem to go in two apparently contradictory directions. On the one hand, it affirms that pure forgiveness—forgiveness as such—is impossible; on the other hand, if such a thing were ever to be imagined, it must be other than what has always been thought of or understood as forgiveness. And it is in the name of—or for the sake of—this something else that we are henceforth called to think and to speak. In this context, he refers to the "im-possible" (which holds the possible and impossible in suspension) and elsewhere, after Angelus Silesius, to "the more than impossible" (*das Überunmöglichste*).[45]

What would be at stake here is, as I suggested above, the elaboration of a concept of forgiveness that is radically foreign to any kind of instrumentalization or exchange. Such a concept is, at one level, only a more rigorous development of the thought of unconditionality and generosity that was already implied in the Judeo-Christian notion of genuine, sincere, heartfelt forgiveness. The cost or advantage of this "more rigorous" concept is a certain "im-possibility," a forgiveness that cannot be made present as such—or appropriated by a subject in the present.

What would *also* be at stake here is the elaboration of a concept of forgiveness that preserves as rigorously as possible a place for the otherness of the other, an other who could not be reduced to an horizon of identification, knowledge, understanding, and so on. It is in this sense that Derrida's theorization of forgiveness should be related to the Levinasian tradition of ethics and responsibility as *prima philosophia*. It is also in this sense that I would suggest that one read Derrida's insistence that one must also think forgiveness without the request for forgiveness: "There is in forgiveness, in the very meaning of forgiveness a force, a desire, an impetus, a movement, an appeal (call it what you will) that demands that forgiveness be granted, if it can be, even to someone who does not ask for it, who does not repent or confess or improve or redeem himself, beyond, consequently, an entire identificatory, spiritual, whether sublime or not, economy, beyond all expiation even." And again: "This link between forgiveness granted and forgiveness asked for does not seem to me to be a given, even if here again it seems required by an entire religious and spiritual tradition of forgiveness. I wonder if a rupture of this reciprocity or this symmetry, if the very dissociation between forgiveness asked for and forgiveness granted, were not *de rigeur* for all forgiveness worthy of the name."[46] No doubt the traditional insistence on the request for forgiveness is justified on the basis that without it one is given over to the worst risk, the risk that a crime may be repeated over and over again, without any commitment on the part of the perpetrator(s) not to repeat it or to compensate for it—at the limit without even the recognition that a crime has been committed. The expression of apology and remorse would seem particularly indispensable in the fields of contemporary international politics, where newly created criminal tribunals rarely, if ever, have the means of prosecuting all those responsible. A sincere public statement of responsibility and contrition on the part of (at least some of) the perpetrators offers victims a kind of loose (in many cases *very* loose) compromise, where—in the absence or hopeless insufficiency of a criminal tribunal—the injustices that have been done to them are at least recognized as injustices, and there is, at least implicitly, the commitment to another, better future (by virtue of a transformed relation to the past).[47]

And yet, if there truly is such a thing as alterity of the other, an alterity that cannot be reduced to the possibility of identification, knowledge and so on, then it cannot be taken for granted that there would be in each case an elementary agreement as to whether there has been a crime and as to who is the victim and who is perpetrator of it. It is unreasonable to presume, on the basis of such a hypothesis, that the conditions necessary for an admission of responsibility could be in each case satisfied or satisfiable. For a sincere admission of responsibility, an offender must at the very least be *conscious* of their fault and have the ability to confess to it. In the case where an offender can neither be presumed to be conscious nor able to confess, expiation of the fault is impossible. Forgiveness is out of the question, because it could not even be asked for.

It is perhaps to the possibility of this kind of ethical impasse—an impasse where at the limit there is no agreement that there even is an impasse—that Derrida's unconditional thought of forgiveness responds. The necessity and urgency of such a thought of forgiveness appears, for example, when someone may be wrongly accused—and yet unable to *prove* their innocence. In such circumstances, an "offender" could not ask for forgiveness without perjury (either by confessing to something that they did not do, or do not believe that they did; or by pretending to agree that a given act was an offense when they at bottom do not consider it to be one). In such situations, the "offender" submits to a situation where forgiveness is the playing out of a ritual, an actor wearing a mask. And yet, one can ask if it is ever possible to ask for forgiveness, without wearing a mask, without some hypocrisy?

AN ETHICS OR POLITICS OF THE DREAM

I will not attempt here to criticize Derrida's thought of unconditional forgiveness but rather will attempt to account for the chance and/or necessity to which it responds in terms of what he elsewhere calls "an ethics or politics of the dream":

> Could there be an ethics or politics of the dream which yields neither to the imaginary nor to the utopian, and is therefore not an irresponsible or evasive resignation? . . . The possibility of the impossible can only be dreamed. Thought, a totally other thought of the relation between the possible and the impossible . . . has perhaps more affinity with this dream than it does with philosophy itself. It would be necessary, while waking up, to keep the vigil of this dream. I try in my own way to draw out some of the ethical, juridical and political consequences of this possibility of the impossible—whether it concerns time, the gift, hospitality, forgiveness, decision or the democracy to come.[48]
>
> "Politics of the dream" is not a politics of dreamers or for dreamers. The dream I am talking about is a dream of thought, not the present collective phantasm of security, patriotism or revenge. A war such as the one that is currently being prepared cannot alone be the answer. The dream would be to say: let us invent something else.[49]

The dream or, as I will read later, Jewish joke of unconditional forgiveness is related to a thinking of disarmament and peace: one which acknowledges what Heidegger identified as the epochal removal (*Beseitigung*) of the distinction between war and peace,[50] and which is not the equivalent of death, as Kant feared.[51] Derrida distinguishes the dream (of unconditional forgiveness, of innumerable genders,[52] even of God)[53] from the phantasm (of absolute knowledge,[54] of indivisible sovereignty,[55] of the intact kernel),[56] although at other times he also seems to run the two terms together.[57] The two terms are very close, since they are both at grips with desire for the impossible. What is perhaps most important, however, is that for Derrida the dream is not separate from the "real," that is, from what happens. For this reason, it should not be understood as utopian in the sense of a fictional place or ideal:

> The deconstruction of logocentrism and linguisticism and economism . . . as well as the affirmation of the impossible, have always come forward *in the name of the real*, of the irreducible reality of the real—not the real as the attribute of the *thing (res)* . . . but the real as a coming or event of the other . . . [T]he real is this non negative im-possible, this im-possible coming or invention of the event, the thinking of which is not an onto-phenomenology . . . In this sense, nothing is more "realist" than deconstruction. It is what or who happens [*ce qui arrive*].[58]

In the course of elaborating her own theory of forgiveness, Julia Kristeva criticizes Derrida's dream for being "a little utopian" and, moreover, for presupposing "the existence of extremely flexible and evolved individuals, which is unfortunately not the case."[59] Kristeva makes the exemplary mistake of presuming that for Derrida forgiving the unforgivable would be the heroic act of a sovereign subject, who *is able* to do the impossible. But this is not what Derrida means. If the individual is called to do the impossible, the important point is that he, she, or it is not able to do it—will never be able to do it—in the same way that the unforgivable (which is to be forgiven) *remains* unforgivable. It is not something that can be achieved by an extremely flexible and evolved individual. If, however, the impossible happens (and for Derrida it is *only* the impossible that happens in strong sense, that is, as an event which is absolutely singular, new, surprising, unforeseeable, incalculable, etc.), then it is not the individual who makes this happen, but the other: "The only thing I can forgive is the unforgivable. If I can do that, if I have the sovereignty to do that, then I don't do this. If I do what I can, then I don't do anything. I must do what I cannot do, more or something else than what I can do. *Therefore it is not me who does this, but the other in me.* It is the other who forgives in this unconditional sense."[60] For this reason, as mentioned in a quotation several pages above, doing and making the impossible are not separate from undergoing the test and ordeal of this paradox (which is also, and perhaps firstly, a paradox of reading). Thus one can say that without doing the impossible one is *perhaps* also doing it; or rather, that one does the impossible by not doing it as such, that is, by creating a place or the conditions for it. Like unconditional hospitality, the dream of unconditional forgiveness makes the impossible. It calls the impossible into being as an absolute pole, from which the task then becomes to find the best "juridical" conditions to bring it about: "For that, you have to change laws, habits, fantasies—a whole 'culture.'"[61]

Derrida's thought enjoins "us" to ask what these conditions would be. They would undoubtedly look different from the scenography and idioms of apology, reconciliation, and forgiveness that currently dominate the world stage. In this book I have argued that to bring about unconditional forgiveness, one must first differentiate it from any form of political or personal reconciliation. Rather than as a mechanism of repair and normalization, offers and requests for forgiveness should be thought of and practiced as a pure gifts. They should not be grounded in the hope or expectation of a return on investment, in a speculation on the future—even in the first instance in the desire to seek recognition from the other. At the limit they should not even be spoken as such, because once expressed in language, as a word of apology or reconciliation, then they already enter into the circuit of exchange. Offers and requests of forgiveness should be approached as inventive, poetic tasks, always in relation to singular individuals and not directed by an end or finality. I can imagine that in certain situations just listening to the other or reading is already a profound event of forgiveness. Perhaps the very word "forgiveness" should not be used—it should be kept secret for fear that it would ruin any chance for forgiveness in a Derridean sense.

3

Crimes against Humanity or the Phantasm of "We, Men"

The necessity of displacing humanism, of questioning it or leaving it aside, this is the great and profound need of our times—provided that one knows how to see it as something other than a "super humanism" or a re-theologization.

—Jean-Luc Nancy, "On Derrida"

Le nazisme ne peut plus, ne doit plus se formuler simplement dans le langage d'une philosophie qui, pour des raisons essentielles, *n'y a jamais suffi* et que Heidegger nous a aussi appris à questionner: un certain état de l'éloquence sur le propre de l'homme . . .

Nazism can no longer, must no longer, I believe, be formulated simply in the language of a philosophy that, for essential reasons, *has never been sufficient for this* and that Heidegger has also taught us to question: a certain state of eloquence on what is proper to man (*sur le propre de l'homme*) . . .

—Jacques Derrida, "Comment Donner Raison?"

In the introduction, I analyzed in what sense the invention of a concept of "crimes against humanity" in international law may be interpreted as a sign of moral progress, a sign of history (*Geschichtszeichen*) in the Kantian sense. By virtue of this concept, the international community recognizes—at least in principle—a crime whose seriousness is such that it remains universally and eternally open to prosecution. In this chapter, I shall analyze in what senses the concept of "crimes against humanity" remains, despite this moral advance, bound to a humanist metaphysics whose limits today more than ever need to be acknowledged.[1] This chapter will include a reading of the legal statutes themselves, as well as Robert Antelme's *The Human Race* (*L'espèce humaine* [1948]): an autobiographical testimony of survival in the Nazi concentration camps where the humanist metaphysics underlying the concept of crimes against humanity is reaffirmed in an extremely memorable way.

THE SELF-EVIDENCE OF THE LOGIC THAT NOTHING IS WORSE THAN A CRIME AGAINST HUMANITY

Now, as mentioned in the chapter 2, Derrida traces the historical novelty of the "worldwidization of forgiveness" back to the international institution of the juridical concept of "crimes against humanity." Unlike the concept of "war crimes" or "crimes against peace" (violations of *Jus ad bellum*), "crimes against humanity" is a concept of international law that in principle overrides the sovereignty of the nation-state.[2] Since the precedent set by the Nuremberg trials in 1945 and 1946, a head of state—or members of a government or other officials of an organization exerting political power—can in principle be forced to appear before either a state or international tribunal on "crimes against humanity." In the case of such crimes, a plea of "Head of State immunity" will not constitute a defense, nor will it mitigate punishment: "The very essence of the Charter is that individuals have international duties which transcend the national obligations of obedience imposed by the individual state . . . if the state in authorizing action moves outside its competence in international law."[3] Consequently, crimes against humanity have a universal jurisdiction: *any* court *anywhere* is empowered by international law to try and punish them, irrespective of their place of commission or the nationality of the offender or the victims.[4] To the extent that the concept implies the idea of a universal human community, it can be said to belong to a legacy of humanism and enlightened cosmopolitanism, which dates back at least to the eighteenth century. (However, one can also trace the idea back to the Stoics and early Christianity.)[5]

While recognizing that the juridical concept of "crimes against humanity" undeniably corresponds to a certain progress in terms of the universal protection of human rights, Derrida argues that this concept in the last resort can only be justified by recourse to the sacredness of the human being: "Nothing is worse, in this logic, than a crime against the humanity of man and against human rights."[6] The seriousness of the topic would encourage one to *stall* the reading here, to proceed (if this is the right word) very slowly and tentatively: Where does the self-evidence of the logic that nothing is worse than a crime against humanity come from? What is at stake today that "the most serious crimes" are interpreted as crimes against humanity?[7]

No doubt such questions afford more than one response. Derrida's argument has the merit of creating a space where they may appear as questions rather than as self-evident truths. While the concept of crimes against humanity overrides and puts into question a powerful "concept" with theological roots (that is, the sovereignty of the nation-state and the immunity of its leaders to prosecution), the concept remains, according to Derrida, theological in another, deeper sense, by virtue of its reference to the idea of a universal human community, the desecration of which is considered unpardonable. If the concept of crimes against humanity overrides or does not recognize the sovereignty of the nation-state and the immunity it presupposes, it does so in the name of an idea that would be even more immune, more sacred: that of the universal human community. In his detailed study of the origins and implementation of the modern legal concept of crimes against humanity, Geoffrey Robinson (QC) testifies to this paradox (without seeming to notice it) at the moment when he analyzes the Nuremberg judgments:

> These were crimes that the world could not suffer to take place anywhere, at any time, because they shamed everyone. They were not, for that crucial reason, crimes against Germans (which therefore only Germans should punish); they were crimes against humanity, because the very fact that a *fellow human* could conceive and commit them diminishes every member of the human race. For this precedent alone, with its potential to destroy sovereign immunity, the Nuremberg judgement was one large legal step forward for mankind. (emphasis mine)[8]

Robinson's reading suggests that the reference to the "fellow human" and the unity of the human race is inseparable from the concept of "crimes against humanity" and the logic that there is nothing worse. For Derrida, this reference is in turn derived from "the Abrahamic memory of the religions of the Book" and "a Jewish, but above all, Christian interpretation of the 'neighbour' [*prochain*] or the 'fellow man' [*semblable*]."[9] Elsewhere, he calls this "a humanist and fraternalist universalism, in keeping with Jesus' message, for example, in Matthew 23:8: 'Yes, you have one rabbi and you are all brothers' (*unus est enim magister verter, omnes autem vos frates estis, pantes de umeis adelphoi este*)."[10] Such universalism would determine or overdetermine the meaning of "humanity" in the expression "crimes against humanity." Moreover, it would speak out, in an unacknowledged fashion, in the traditions of secular humanism and enlightened cosmopolitanism upon which modern international law is based.

But what exactly is "Judeo-Christian" universalism? And what is the meaning of the term "humanity" in the expression "crimes against humanity"? From what I can gather, this is not absolutely clear. Perhaps, as was suggested above concerning forgiveness, the lack of clarity is essential for these "concepts" to function. If one considers Article 7(1) of the Rome Statute of the International Criminal Court (1998), no definition is given of the term "humanity," and moreover, there is nothing that *explicitly* links the name of the crime to its definition. These are taken to be self-evident. And yet, what one can notice in the first instance is that an attack against a human being as such is *not* a crime against humanity—even if the attack is murder. A crime against humanity must be directed against a "population," that is, more than one individual, *and* exclusively a "civilian population," that is, one that is not militarily organized and thus presumably does not have the means to protect itself. According to the formal definition given in the Rome Statute of the International Criminal Court (1998), acts that constitute a "crime against humanity" must be committed "as part of a widespread or systematic attack directed against a civilian population, with knowledge of the attack."[11]

Significantly, the list of acts provided in subparagraphs 7(1) (a) to (k) is not exhaustive. The last subparagraph (k) leaves space for the inclusion of "other inhumane acts of a similar character intentionally causing great suffering, or serious injury to body or to mental or physical health." One might say, then, that "crimes against humanity" is a spacious concept. Employing the language of a certain Enlightenment heritage, one could say that the concept leaves room for its own *perfectibility*, that is, the inclusion of acts that either have not yet been recognized as "crimes against humanity," have yet to be invented, or have not yet being given a name.[12] This virtual (potentially infinite) list is restricted only by reference to a similarity with those acts outlined in the preceding subparagraphs. These acts constitute, however, an extremely heterogeneous ensemble, including—it should be underlined—not only murder and "extermination,"[13] but also enslavement, deportation, imprisonment, torture, rape, sexual slavery, enforced prostitution, forced pregnancy, enforced sterilization "or any other form of sexual violence of comparable gravity," enforced disappearance of persons, "persecution against any identifiable group or collectivity on political, racial, national, ethnic, cultural, religious, gender or other grounds that are universally recognized as impermissible under international law," and the crime of apartheid.

How could such a heterogeneous and open-ended ensemble be unified under a single concept of "crimes against humanity"? A clue might be in the employment of the term "inhumane" in the expression "inhumane acts of a similar character." Crimes against humanity are inhumane acts. According to the *Oxford English Dictionary*, "inhumane" is "destitute of compassion for misery or suffering in men or animals" and also "uncivilised, uncultured, impolite." But obviously it is also closely connected to humanity, understood as "the quality or condition of being human."[14] To be human is presumably to have humanity, or at the very least be capable of it, and hence the enigma and outrage of inhumane acts committed by human beings against other human beings. Understood as a crime of international law (i.e., one that warrants international scrutiny), "crimes against humanity" implies, as suggested above, the appeal to a collective unity of humankind. Humanity is *one*, and it is to humanity as one to which injustice is done when there are "crimes against humanity." Crimes against humanity are *as such* crimes against everyone: an injustice to all. There is therefore necessarily (and problematically) a universalizing and self-referential moment in the idea of common demand on the part of the international community in the name of "humanity."

For if the international community since 1945 has felt compelled to legislate in the name of "crimes against humanity," it can only be because such crimes radically put into question what is or has been understood as "humanity"—in every sense of the word, one would be tempted to say, which means in English at least: (1) "the quality and condition of being human . . . man in the abstract" (The semantic slippage between man and human belongs inerasably [it would seem] to the political historical legal philosophical nexus in question.);[15] (2) "the human race, mankind, human beings collectively"; (3) "the character or quality of being humane; behavior or disposition towards others such as befits a human being, civility, courtesy, politeness, good behavior"; (4) "disposition to treat human beings and animals with consideration and compassion." Under this heading is included a definition from the seventeenth century that is also noteworthy for its identifiably Christian overtone: "The vertue of humanity, that is, of being ready to shew love to man, as he is man."[16]

There is a further sense of the word in English, not present for example in the German equivalent (*Menschlicheit*), referring directly back to the etymological root "*humanitas*" as used by Cicero for example, and from where comes the designation "The Humanities," that is, (5) "learning or literature concerned with human culture: a term including the various branches of polite scholarship, as grammar, rhetoric, poetry, and esp. the study of the ancient Latin and Greek classics."[17] In this additional sense, which I would suggest is related in an important way to all the others, a crime against humanity would be *a crime against education*—or rather a particular (Western) understanding of education. According to a great Western secular humanist tradition, to be human is to be able to be formed, civilized, educated—to accede to *humanitas* as the development of human virtue.[18]

In all probability Derrida would say here that if the ideal of *humanitas* belongs to—or rather is inseparable from—a tradition of secular humanism, it presupposes as such a religious understanding and interpretation: "I don't believe there is anything secular about our time. First of all the concept of secularity is a religious concept. So when you understand something as secular you are already understanding and interpreting it as religious."[19] But what does "religious" mean for Derrida? In a paper that mimics Kant's gesture in *Religion within the Limits of Reason Alone*, Derrida identifies two sources or strata of the religious that, even while they can be associated with one another, should never be confused or reduced to one another. These are, on the one hand, "the experience of belief . . . that is always beyond proof, demonstrative reason, intuition" and, on the other, "the experience of the unscathed [*l'indemne*], of sacredness or holiness."[20] In this very complex and fragmentary text, Derrida proposes (and often repeats) a list of metonymies which can be read as interpretations or translations of what is meant by the term "sacred," that is, safe and sound, animate, healing, immune, intact, and in particular *unscathed* (*l'indemne*), and even further, phallic and fetish. (These, it should be noted, are at least in part derived from the attempt to translate into French the German words "*heilig*" and "*Heilige*" as interpreted by Heidegger in relation notably to Hölderlin.)[21]

Now if it is the case today that the most serious crimes are interpreted as crimes *against humanity*, this can, on the one hand, only suggest that "humanity" is considered to be the highest value, to be something sacred or sacrosanct. Such a position is supported by the fact that since the Convention adopted by the United Nations in 1968, the prosecution and punishment of "crimes against humanity" is not subject to any statute of limitations. In other words, for such crimes there would be no prescribed period beyond which it would no longer be possible to institute criminal proceedings and execution of penalties. "Statutory limitations" as they may exist in the states which signed the Convention are not applicable.[22] And yet, on the other hand—or as simply the other side of the same argument—it would be precisely the sacredness of "humanity" that is radically put into question by such "acts," up to, and including even, the elementary agreement that they can be called "crimes." In this sense, the juridical concept of "crimes against humanity" would be at once a defense against—as well as a testimony of—the possibility that *nothing at all* remains sacred, least of all "the humanity of the human being or man." If one were to employ one of Derrida's idiomatic concepts, what are called "crimes against humanity" would be an immunitary and auto-immunitary reaction.[23]

There would be, it appears, a profound need (that one hesitates to call simply a "human" or "ethical" need) that something of humanity remain intact, untouched, immune, unscathed; something that resists, while remaining beyond the reach of the seemingly inextinguishable forces of killing, maiming, starving, raping, torturing, enslaving, persecuting, discriminating, and making human beings disappear en masse. Without knowing exactly what this sacred is, it is necessary (it would seem) that there be some sacred of humanity, something of humanity that remains intact, that the inhuman human—or the inhuman in general—*cannot destroy*, and whose rights are recognized by international law.

THE HUMAN RACE BY ROBERT ANTELME

This position finds perhaps its most memorable formulation in a book entitled *The Human Race* (*L'espèce humaine*) (1947) by Robert Antelme.[24] Robert Antelme was a political dissident against the German occupation of France during the Second World War. He was deported to Germany as a slave laborer, first to Buchenwald (near Weimar), then a camp called Gandersheim; he was later led on a death march and was finally liberated in Dachau. *The Human Race* is a profound and detailed testimony of what he experienced, while also providing an essential reflection on the nature of humanity in general. The thesis of Antelme's book is explicitly stated in the preface, that is, that there is an indivisible unity of the human species.[25] This affirmation, which indeed recalls the "Judeo-Christian" doctrine of the brotherhood of men, must be read in the first instance as a politico-philosophical response to the genocidal mythology of the Nazis. There is no superhuman race; there is no subhuman race: there is *one* human race. This, as the title of the work suggests, is a quasi-biological affirmation, on the basis of which the SS *must* fail:

> If, between the SS and us—that is to say at the moment when the difference between beings is at its greatest, when the subjection of some and the power of others have attained such limits as to seem frozen into some supernatural distinction—we can perceive no substantial difference with regard to death or nature, we are obliged to say that there is one human species.
>
> But there is no ambiguity, we remain men, we will finish only as men. The distance separating us from another species remains intact. It is not historical . . . It is because we are men as they are that the SS will be finally powerless against us . . . The executioner can kill a man, but he cannot change him into something else.[26]

Those who unambiguously "remain men," and with whom the narrator identifies ("we"), possess in all probability the most stripped-away humanity or manhood that one can imagine. The "remaining men" of which he speaks is, dare I say, not the possession of some heroic power that would have been preserved through years of starvation under the permanent pressure of imminent death. And yet, on the other hand, it cannot be reduced to something purely physical either, for Antelme also calls it the single and final demand (*seule et dernière revendication*), the underlying motivation of our struggle (*ressort de notre lutte*).[27] It is that which, Antelme believes, even under the most extreme conditions of privation and injustice cannot be taken away. It does not save Antelme from death but rather, one might say, speaks through his death, sustains and preserves him in his relation to death, that is, what he designates in the preface as "an ultimate feeling of belonging to the human species" (*sentiment ultime d'appartenance à l'espèce humaine*).

> We do not believe that the heroes that we know from history or literature, whether they have cried from love, solitude, the anguish of being or non-being, vengeance, whether they have stood up against injustice, humiliation, have ever been led to express an ultimate feeling of belonging to the species as their last and only demand [*seule et dernière revendication*] . . . This was, however, what was most immediately and constantly lived and felt, and moreover, it was exactly what they wanted.
>
> The motivation underlying our struggle will only have been a furious desire, itself almost always experienced in solitude, to remain men, down to the very end.[28]

In a very traditional fashion, Antelme uses the terms "human" and "man" interchangeably. As I hope will be become clearer below, he writes about the struggle against the Nazis solely on the basis of an experience between men, which is seen as exemplary of that of humanity itself. I have not attempted to correct or rectify Antelme's phallocentrism, that is, his self-referential employment of the term "man" (homme), because I believe it to be intrinsic to the logic of his argument. A (virtually Christian) fraternalist universalism underlies Antelme's testimony of an ultimate feeling of belonging to the human species as the truth of his experience in the camps. A structural characteristic of this fraternalist universalism is the reduction of the otherness of the other to the same. In this logic all the specificities of the experience among the diverse groups who were targeted by the Nazis (the disabled, the Jews, the Sinti and Roma, homosexuals, Poles, Slavs, Jehovah's Witnesses, communists, members of the resistance and other political enemies, and so on) are subsumed under the banner of a fundamental contestation of the humanity of man. The violence of reducing the otherness of the other to the same can also be read in the initial Nazi gesture of identifying and naming a particular group to be targeted, a group often comprised of individuals of different nationalities, languages, cultural and religious practices, political beliefs, and so on. In which case, one can well argue that there is a hidden complicity between the fraternalist logic, which would claim to be the ultimate resource of resistance against Nazism, and that of Nazism itself.

If, as Antelme believes, there is such a thing as the indivisible unity of humanity, then logically there must be something that determines this unity and marks its specificity. One can say that for Antelme, the single trait that identifies the human *as* human is that he is indestructible. This indestructibility would constitute his "essence." This does not mean that he cannot be killed or destroyed, but precisely if and when he is, he nonetheless *remains a man*. Even in death, he is not, as it were, castrated. His being who he is, his self-sameness, is not put into question and remains intact: "The executioner [*le bourreau*] can kill a man, but he cannot change him into something else."[29] As part of the same resource of resistance—or as another dimension of it—Antelme also insists on the *humanity* of the ones who perpetrate the most serious crimes against him. As Maurice Blanchot points out, for Antelme the SS are not the enemy because in the camps he is reduced to a point where it is no longer possible in any way to take the posture of a warrior, either physically or psychologically. ("Our objective became the most humble, only to survive.")[30] The SS are for Antelme not the enemy, but the cold: "*le froid, SS.*"[31]

Antelme's political philosophical resistance—or what remains of it—is directed against this cold, which is to say, against the refusal on the part of the SS (who can be read here as exemplary for the perpetrators of any crime against humanity) to identify themselves in any way with their victims, to act toward them as if they were fellow human beings. Antelme recounts how one German, *a civil prisoner rather than a member of the SS*, and who for this reason was put in charge of the deportees in the ammunition factory, came up to them one day and said in a calm, almost nice voice: "*Langsam!*" (Go slowly). Antelme interprets this speech act as a discreet and profound act of resistance that unambiguously communicated to the deportees present this man's noncommitment to a work whose purpose is to extenuate the workers' ability to live, while in the service of producing materials that will cause others to die for no reason. Later, this man, who is identified only by the name "*le Rhénan*" (the Rhinelander—he is named by his place of birth, his regional "ethnicity"), offers again in a discreet manner to shake the hands of some of the deportees: "This secret, solitary gesture was not a private action, as opposed to the immediately historical, public action of the SS. Every human relation from a German to one of us was the sign of an intentional revolt against the entire order of the SS. One could not do what the Rhinelander did—that is to say, to act in a human way towards one of us–without thereby classifying oneself historically."[32] In this seemingly masculine gesture of shaking hands (*agir en homme avec l'un de nous*:

undecidably both "acting as a human being" and "acting as a man with one of us"), as well as Antelme's insistence on the irreducible humanity of those who perpetrate the most serious crimes against him, the possibility of "forgiveness" (understood as reconciliation) is already, one may argue, preprogrammed. Marguerite Duras's memoir *La douleur*, which is a record of Antelme's return from Dachau to Paris, and his subsequent convalescence, recounts how Antelme (here referred to as Robert L.) made at one point a final testament to the two men who brought him back:

> As soon as they left Dachau behind, Robert L. spoke. He said he knew he wouldn't reach Paris alive. So he began to talk, so it should be told before he died. He didn't accuse any person, any race, any people. He accused man. Emerging from the horror, dying, delirious, Robert L. was still not able to accuse anyone but the governments that come and go in the history of nations. He wanted D. and Beauchamp to tell me after his death what he had said . . . He spoke of the German martyrdom, of the martyrdom common to all men.[33]

Whether or not such a testament actually constitutes forgiveness is a question that should be suspended—not knowing exactly what forgiveness is, or if indeed it is at all possible. But, nonetheless, one has to acknowledge Antelme's displacement of the concrete responsibility of the Third Reich, and the SS in particular, onto the generalization "man" (*l'homme*). Such displacement is symptomatic of what Derrida called the "worldwidization of forgiveness." If it is "man" that it is responsible, then the responsibility is effectively diffused by becoming everyone's and therefore also no one's in particular (if it is true that an act of responsibility commits an individual always in a singular and irreplaceable manner in relation to an other (or others), as for example, the Rheinlander's "*Langsam!*").

When reading what Antelme is supposed to have said at the decisive moment of leaving Dachau, one should note that the narrator (Marguerite Duras), who reports Antelme's words, was not present. While it is not certain that Antelme or the others would have confirmed to the letter what Duras recorded in her dairy and later published, the accusation against "man" is (by virtue of its self-referential character) consistent, I would suggest, with the thesis put forward in *The Human Race*. If the Nazis and their collaborators are in their essence human beings, then what they have done is in essence a *human* crime. The "inhumanness" of their crimes *is* human; it belongs to the history of humankind. It is therefore "humanity," the humanness of the human that is responsible—and must be accused.[34]

While Antelme's thesis of the indivisible unity of the human species *appears* to be based on biological or anthropological grounds, it is not clear that it actually is. In the preface, Antelme writes of "an *almost* biological demand of belonging to the human species" (emphasis mine).[35] The remaining men, of which he speaks, cannot simply be a scientifically testable and thus falsifiable truth; for if, as Antelme believes, a dead man "cannot be changed into something else," that he remains a man, this would remain true even when the human body is no longer *intact* or identifiable, at the limit no longer accessible to biological or anthropological examination.[36] While Antelme's thesis undoubtedly derives its force and authority from being the testimony of one who survived the worst (?), one must note that it is in profound continuity with the thinking of perhaps the most powerful modern European humanist tradition, that is, the one that goes from at least Kant up to Heidegger (including Husserl and Hegel).

A CONTINUITY BETWEEN THE "WE, MEN" OF THE NAZI CONCENTRATION CAMPS AND THE "WE, MEN" OF MODERN EUROPEAN PHILOSOPHY

This philosophical tradition regularly distinguishes the truth or essence of man or the human (*der Mensch*) from any anthropological or biological characterization. And yet, it does so in a manner that is fundamentally ambiguous. Following Derrida's readings in the famous 1968 paper "The Ends of Man" ("Les fins de l'homme"), one can say that while the rational being in Kant and Husserl, consciousness in Hegel, and *Dasein* in Heidegger are in each case not identical with man in any biological or anthropological sense, they are, at the same time, however, *nothing other* than man (or the human): they are "man" determined in the specificity of his essence or truth.[37] While this essence or truth of "man"—what Derrida calls untranslatably *la relève de l'homme*—is interpreted according to diverse paths, in each case there is recourse to a "we" or "we, men," which in the last instance refers only to itself. In the absence of an anthropological or biological basis upon which to ground the specificity of the human, "metaphysics" has recourse to a self-referential "we" on whose basis the essence or truth of "man" may present itself to itself.

What appears to be at stake in the departure from anthropology and biology, from the natural sciences in general, is nothing other than human finitude. It is on this basis that I believe one can speak of a continuity between Antelme's "we, men" of the Nazi concentration camps and the "we" or "we, men" of modern European philosophy from at least Kant up to Heidegger. Without wishing to reconstruct here the ensemble of Derrida's readings in "The Ends of Man," one can note briefly and very schematically that when Kant, in the *Groundwork of the Metaphysics of Morals* (1785), argues that man's essence as a rational being (*zoon logon ekon*) announces itself to itself as an end in itself, this end is effectively an infinite end, that is, one that corresponds to the thought of the unconditioned. As the thought of the unconditioned, the rational being as an end in itself is a thought that rises above experience, which is to say, above finitude.[38]

Similarly, the third part of Hegel's *Encyclopedia* situates *The Phenomenology of Spirit* (and, in particular, "consciousness," as its point of departure) as the "sublation" (*Aufhebung*) of the *Anthropology*, that is, the science of man as "soul" or natural spirit (*Seele* or *Naturgeist*). When consciousness is designated in the final paragraph of the *Anthropology* as "the infinite relation to itself," this marks the end of man in two different senses according to the double meaning of the Hegelian concept of *Aufhebung*. Consciousness is the end of man as the end of finite man, of a "soul" or "natural spirit" who is not yet *thought* and *subject* for itself; but at the same time it is also the accomplishment of man's essence as the unity of the finite and the infinite: the end or *telos* of man as self-overcoming.

For Heidegger, unlike Kant and Hegel, it would not be a question of a rational, thinking, or self-reflecting being or "subject" that in any way rises above finitude. For Heidegger, there is no essential determination of man (*der Mensch*) that is *not* reducible to finitude (*Endlichkeit*). However, what "finitude" means for Heidegger does not correspond to any anthropological or scientific determination, any more than to what "finitude" means for Hegel or Kant. Nonetheless, at the beginning of *Being and Time* Heidegger also has recourse to a self-referring "we," when it is a matter of assuring the existence of a vague, everyday understanding of the meaning of the word "is," when we ask the question "what *is* Being?" ("Was *ist* Sein?") The *fact* of this preliminary understanding as well as the possibility of questioning (which is at once presupposed and grounded by this preliminary understanding) will in turn become the grounds for choosing "the being that we the questioners are ourselves" (des Seienden, das wir, die Fragenden, je selbst sind) as the exemplary and privileged entity whose analysis will provide the point of departure for the elaboration of the question of the meaning of being. In paragraph 2 of the introduction to *Sein und Zeit,* Heidegger writes:

> Wir wissen nicht, was "Sein" besagt. Aber schon wenn wir fragen: "Was *ist 'Sein'?"* halten wir uns in einem Verständnis des "ist," ohne dass wir begrifflich fixieren könnten, was das "ist" bedeutet. Wir kennen nicht einmal den Horizont, aus dem her wir den Sinn fassen und fixieren sollten. *Dieses durchschnittliche und vage Seinverständnis ist ein Faktum.*
>
> We do not know what "Being" [*Sein*] means. But even if we ask, "What is 'Being'?"" ["Was *ist 'Sein'?"*], we keep within an understanding of the "is," though we are unable to fix conceptually what this "is" signifies. We do not even know the horizon in terms of which that meaning is to be grasped and fixed. *But this vague average understanding of Being is still a Fact* [Faktum].[39]

Reading this passage, Derrida comments:

> In the absence of every other determination or presupposition, the "we" *at least* is what is open to such an understanding; it is what is always already accessible, and the means by which such a *factum* can be recognized as such.

And further:

> It is this self-presence, this absolute proximity of the (questioning) being to itself, this familiarity with itself of the being [*cette familiarité à soi de l'étant*] ready to understanding Being, that intervenes in the determination of the *factum*, and which motivates the choice of the exemplary being, of the text, the good text for the hermeneutic of the meaning of Being . . . We who are close to ourselves, *we* interrogate *ourselves* about the meaning of Being.[40]

At the moment when fundamental ontology is established as an inquiry prior to and therefore independent of any preestablished scientific thesis or axiom, and even of any thematic presupposition inherited from the history of Western philosophy (inasmuch as this tradition *in its entirety*, Heidegger contends, is grounded on an insufficiently elucidated understanding of

Being [*Sein*]), there would be recourse to a more hidden, more fundamental philosophical presupposition, that is, self-proximity and self-presence, as it is marked in the self-evidence of the "we," which ultimately refers only to itself. This self-referring "we" would take up the slack—fill the gap, if you will—when the simple presence of presumed knowledge is rigorously eschewed or bracketed.

Derrida points out in "The Ends of Man" that Heidegger's critique of humanism in the "Letter on Humanism" (1946) is undertaken in order to revalorize and restitute the essence of man beyond humanism's metaphysical presuppositions. Correspondingly, the "Letter on Humanism" contains a reelaboration of the notion of *humanitas* and the Kantian concept of dignity (*Würde*).[41] In a manner consistent with this movement, Heidegger affirms in *Being and Time* that the human dead are ontologically distinct from any other lifeless material thing (*Ding*), inasmuch as they are for *Dasein* the object of funeral rites, mourning, and burial. And, moreover, the death of *Dasein* ("the being that we the questioners are ourselves") is also ontologically distinguished from that of animals.[42]

Therefore one can say that although Heidegger would most certainly have rejected Antelme's thesis of the indivisible unity of the human species (on the grounds that the scientific categories of "species" or "race" are inappropriate to describe the dignity of man's essence (*der Mensch*), Heidegger's thinking in this regard is at bottom not inconsistent with that of Antelme. One can suggest that Heidegger provides only a more philosophically informed and radical (more *immunized* from criticism, one might dare say) interpretation of the same virtually Christian fraternalist universalism that sustains Antelme's testimony.

At this point in the argument, one should recall that of course not all survivor testimonies of the Nazi concentration camps teach that fraternalist universalism provides a final recourse of political resistance. Primo Levi, a scientist, who was deported for a different reason to Antelme, entitled his first book about Auschwitz: *If This Is a Man* (*Se questo è un uomo*). Between the titles of these two testimonies, *L'espèce humaine* and *Se questo è un uomo*, one can read a discreet dispute or *Auseinandersetzung* about the truth of the experience of the camps: whereas Antelme claims that it led him to reaffirm the unity and indestructibility of the human species, Primo Levi is less certain. The "if" of the title *If This Is a Man* may be read as the beginning of a conditional or hypothetical proposition (If this is a man, then . . .), or as the mark of an existential hesitation (Is this a man?): perhaps this is something or someone else (a child, for example, or an automaton, or that for which there is not yet a name). On the basis of Primo Levi's "if," one may have to rethink whatever allows itself to be understood today as "crimes against humanity," particularly wherever "humanity" is thought (implicitly or explicitly) on the basis of the "we" or "we, men" of modern European philosophy.

Might one dream of the existence of an international tribunal for the prosecution of "crimes against the otherness of the other"? Must not Nazism itself be thought of as something more and other than a crime against humanity?[43]

4

A Hyper-Ethics of Irreconcilable Contradictions

Vladimir Jankélévitch

The love of men is the most sacred of all values, but the indifference to crimes against humanity, to attacks against the very essence, the humanness of the human [*l'hominité de l'homme*], is the most sacrilegious of all faults. And we have no way of choosing one of these two superlatives over the other, nor any way of honoring them together: the choice of one Absolute necessarily leaves the "other Absolute" outside; concurrency and conciliation of the *two Absolutes* is impossible; the sacrifice of one Absolute leads to scruples and remorse; the synthesis of the two Absolutes would be a miracle: for the Absolute is plural and irremediably torn.

—Vladimir Jankélévitch, *Le pardon*

Until recently the work of French philosopher and musician Vladimir Jankélévitch (1903–1985) has been scarcely acknowledged in the English-speaking world. Over the last few years, some of his texts have appeared in English translation, in part because of the growing recognition of the importance of his moral philosophy for figures such as Paul Ricoeur, Emmanuel Levinas, and Jacques Derrida.[1] It is little known, for example, that Emmanuel Levinas acknowledged Jankélévitch as a source of the notion of the "absolutely" or "wholly other" (*le tout autre*).[2] Born of Russian Jewish émigrés, a student of Henri Bergson, about whom he wrote one of the most influential studies in French, he was also a member of the French Resistance during World War II.[3]

After the war and the discovery of the Nazi extermination camps, Jankélévitch systematically removed from his work any reference to German art, philosophy, or music. This is despite having written his doctoral dissertation on the philosophy of Schelling, whose understanding of human freedom will continue to inform his thought well after the war despite the disappearance of the name.[4] Jankélévitch maintained this protest against German culture more or less consistently for the rest of his life.[5] And yet as early as 1948 he also spoke of the possibility of forgiveness ("perhaps one day forgiveness will be possible, which has no meaning today").[6] Twenty-three years later, however, he declared forgiveness to be impossible and immoral: "Forgiveness died in the death camps."[7] Despite appearances, these two statements are not wholly incompatible with one another; for in both 1948 and 1971 what made forgiveness meaningless for him was—at least in part—the absence of a will to expiate on the part of those who were guilty:

> For as long as the inexpiable is not expiated, as long as France is not redeemed, amnesty can only be amnesia and forgiveness only indulgence or scandalous excuse, degrading complicity or betrayal. Purity is like love: it is something one must want.[8]
>
> The Germans are an "*unrepentant*" people . . . Why would we pardon those who regret their errors so little and so rarely? . . . To be pardoned one must admit to being guilty, without conditions or alleging attenuating circumstances.[9]

As will be consistently the case for Jankélévitch, the thought of forgiveness is associated with love. In a book entitled *Forgiveness* (*Le pardon*) (1967), Jankélévitch argued for a hyperbolical ethics of forgiveness that arises out of the duty of love. Such an "ethics beyond ethics" (that is, beyond norms and laws) implies an obligation to forgive even the unforgivable.[10]

What is the relation between Jankélévitch's enduring protest against German culture (the one which presumably *made possible* or *did not make impossible* the crimes of the Nazis) and his no less enduring impulse to think the possibility and limits of forgiveness? As I shall attempt to argue, Jankélévitch is unable to maintain a coherent position with regard to forgiveness and the Holocaust. However, this should not be considered to be simply a fault, a lack of moral and/or intellectual probity. The hyper-ethical exigencies to which he responds necessarily, I will argue, lead him into irreconcilable contradictions. There is *perhaps* something of the order of forgiveness—of a deeper, more clandestine order of forgiveness—in the willingness to give hospitality to such contradictions, to accept and expose them, without attempting to reconcile them.

TENSIONS AND CONTRADICTIONS IN FORGIVENESS (1967)

In his meditation entitled *Forgiveness*[11] (1967), the philosopher Vladimir Jankélévitch argues that forgiveness arises ultimately from an irresistible fraternal sympathy. Inasmuch as the bad or guilty one (*le méchant*) is a man like I am, what he has done I would also have been able to do and perhaps will do in the future. Inasmuch as, like him, I am human, finite (which for Jankélévitch also means fallible, solitary, weak, miserable), his fault could also be mine—and therefore in a certain sense is shared by me. The ethical movement of forgiveness consists in the refusal of the pride which shrinks back from any resemblance, any fraternity with the guilty man. This fraternal sympathy is in turn based on the thesis of the essential or irreducible resemblance of one man to another, or in other words, the indivisible unity of humanity.

What is marked here by "or in other words" is the *slippery*, still contemporary substitution of "man" for human, and "brotherhood of man" for the common belonging and relatedness of the humanity. This substitution is based on the presupposition of an essential similitude, which extends to women and children but not to animals and machines. For Jankélévitch, this essential human similitude is the basis for an explicitly Christian-like understanding of forgiveness. Because no one is without sin, and because as a human I a priori resemble the one who sins, and because every sin—however extreme—is a human sin, I am absolutely obliged to forgive: absolutely, that is to say, without conditions. Not to forgive would be effectively to consider myself as being of another essence to the one in the wrong (*le fautif*), to place myself on a totally other plane, and decide that I am beyond the possibility of this sin or outside of it, a priori untouchable by the guilt of this man and his act: "The man who pardons abstains from repudiating his essential similitude with the one who is guilty; he does not profit from the advantageous position that his innocence confers on him, he does not keep for himself this privilege of being alone infallible, impeccable, irreproachable, and on this point he renounces every monopoly; he sacrifices therefore a very brief and precarious superiority which perhaps is due to chance."[12] Forgiveness then, on this reading, involves sacrifice.

Jankélévitch is not concerned with the question of who has the authority to forgive—except to say that the guilty cannot forgive themselves.[13] As I shall attempt to show, a lot depends on the presence of the other in the scene of forgiveness. The other here must be a human being. While Jankélévitch presents a philosophical account of forgiveness that draws from the teachings of the New Testament, his account makes no reference—and does not need to make any reference—to God. The argument is constructed in such a manner that it functions without presuming a belief in Divine grace or redemption. And yet, even while this may be so, one can ask if a reference to God is nonetheless silently presupposed in the sacred value attributed to the love of men. If the love of men is sacred, it is because man's nature is divine, because man is created in the image of God (*imago dei*).[14] It is because the love of men is sacred that the movement of infinite resemblance stops at animals and machines, but not at women and children, who *are recognized as human only on the basis of their resemblance to man.*

According to Jankélévitch, whoever is not guilty, be they the victim or someone else, may—indeed must—forgive out of "the duty of love" (*le devoir d'amour*), which is unconditional and without restrictions. "The love of men is the most sacred of all values."[15] But if forgiveness is a question of sacrifice, then whoever is not at fault has something, or seems to have something, of which the one at fault is deprived. This something is like a possession, on which the "innocent" have the capacity, according to Jankélévitch, to capitalize—even to monopolize. This raises the question of exchange value and politics in, or as, the scene of forgiveness. There is a tendency to hold onto and to profit from the advantageous position of being innocent. Forgiving is the renunciation of this human, all too human, tendency; it is the paradox of giving away something that one does not really have, or that one has only in regard to this particular instance, "a brief and precarious superiority which is perhaps due to chance."

To be more precise: forgiveness implies the giving away of moral superiority and innocence *because* these are qualities which are only apparent, *because*, in other words, they are fictions. Thus there is in Jankélévitch (even if this seems pre-Kantian) not only an epistemological/ontological decision behind the moral injunction but also an ethico-moral decision in favor, as it were, of being and truth: it is *better* to be on the side of what is, than what is not; and therefore one *should* sacrifice what is not for the sake of what is. The hierarchical relation between the guilty and innocent is a fiction because we (men or human beings) resemble one another a priori and because to sin is intrinsically human. The fiction of moral superiority is produced by the tendency to forget our similitude with the other when we are wronged, and, moreover, such forgetting is itself a wrong, one which presumably in turn requires forgiveness.

It is significant and somewhat surprising that Jankélévitch's affirmation of the fraternal resemblance of humanity does not necessarily imply, as one might expect, a simple effacement of the *alterity* or otherness of the other. Almost the contrary, for the one who forgives in renouncing innocence and moral superiority also renounces the question of why. Jankélévitch distinguishes between excuse (*l'excuse*), which explains, gives reasons, justifies, and forgiveness (*le pardon*), which, as an ultimate recourse, does not need excuses: "One must in certain regards forgive the unforgivable without understanding it."[16]

> You are an hour late: I understand and excuse you. You didn't *want* to arrive on time, you did it on purpose,—and I forgive you (or don't forgive you . . .) Here all your excuses will be put aside, for one doesn't interpret a bad intention, it brings with it no nuances; and there exists no way to "understand" it . . . There is in fact nothing to understand in the mystery of gratuitous wickedness (*méchanceté*), if not that the wicked one (*le méchant*) is wicked.[17]

This insistence on nonunderstanding in forgiveness is the reason why Jankélévitch says that the two positions, forgiver and forgiven, are not exchangeable. The relationship is in the first instance heteronymous. On the one hand, it implies a reversal of the power relation between, for example, a victim and a perpetrator (a perpetrator cannot forgive him or herself and a victim's forgiveness is by no means automatic). On the other hand, however, by forgiving, the victim respects the secret of the perpetrator's intentionality. There is, as it were, between the two, a nonsymmetrical "recognition" of the other's otherness. And yet, and this is the twist, in order for forgiveness to take place, the one who forgives must be able to identify themselves with the other, there must be mirroring, and consequently the threat of losing oneself and fiction. The one at fault—like the fault itself—is an *inassimilable* otherness, which one "assimilates" nonetheless through a very particular kind of identification, one that in a certain way preserves the otherness of both the fault and of the freedom of the one who commits it.

I could have done, and perhaps will do, what you have done, even though I understand neither you nor it and renounce the effort of trying.

There is no interest in trying to hide that this is a contradiction in Jankélévitch's elaboration, or at the very least a tension that might threaten to make his argument collapse. But if one were to remain here and pursue the implications: at one level, the tension is not so serious, because under normal circumstances the guilty person is forgiven only after having asked for forgiveness, and thus having recognized his or her fault as such. There is therefore a prior identification *on the part of the one who is guilty* with the one who forgives. Before being forgiven, the one at fault has *already* distanced himself from the fault by acknowledging a resemblance with the one who accuses him, such that if he were in the accuser's place he would also complain of a wrong done to him. While the moment of nonunderstanding, what Jankélévitch also calls "the empty intellection of the incomprehensible" (*vide intellection de l'incomprehensible*) does play a role in the identificatory structure, it is one that is a priori circumscribed and limited. In forgiving the other, I identify myself not so much with the incomprehensible fault, or with the person who has committed it, but above all *with the person who has reformed themselves,* who has affirmed that they are not reducible to what they have done, or to the one they were when they did it. Without the prior request for forgiveness, however, which limits and circumscribes the incomprehensible character of evil liberty (*liberté méchante*), there is indeed in the act of forgiving the other the risk of losing oneself in the unknown: what one might think as a kind of masochistic ecstasy.[18]

Jankélévitch speaks of forgiveness as a spontaneous movement that is also madness. He entitles one of the chapters "Le pardon fou." That forgiveness should necessarily imply the nonunderstanding of the subject, an "empty intellection of the incomprehensible," also raises the question of the automaton, of automatic forgiveness. The "empty intellection" implies the possibility that forgiveness can happen all by itself, without my present intention, or even awareness that it has taken place. Of course, when Jankélévitch speaks of forgiveness as a mad spontaneous movement, he certainly does not mean that it is something that simply happens automatically. Despite an uncanny and thought-provoking proximity between the two concepts, spontaneity is in fact the opposite of automaticity. Inasmuch as forgiveness is a spontaneous event, the carrying out of a predetermined program is apparently excluded:

> Effectively, this hearty forgiveness [*pardon cordial*] would be an event, a relation with the person and a total remission . . . forgiveness is something which happens, and in this respect it is at the same level as sin, which is to say, of the contingent clinamen, and of the "having been able to be otherwise." Intellectualizing excuse does not happen: it is neither an act nor a decision . . . freedom, which is at work in gracious remission, here does not have a chance to intervene.[19]

Jankélévitch here makes use of the notion of the *clinamen* to account for the event character of forgiveness. Derived from the ancient philosopher, Lucretius, the *clinamen* is a spontaneous, unpredictable, nonsituatable and infinitely slight deviation in the chain of causality which has the effect of making possible what was previously impossible, a radical departure, a total change. The *clinamen* is for Lucretius the physical principle behind the creation of the world.[20] While Jankélévitch employs Lucretius's notion, unlike Lucretius he associates it with an event that for him must have a human agency. Forgiveness, even while remaining spontaneous and unpredictable, bringing with it the eschatological hope (*espérance eschatologique*) of a new order and a definitive end of rancorous rambling (*le radotage de la continuation rancunière*), is at the same time the free and intentional decision of a human subject. Grounded in an "I" who must be innocent of this particular fault, forgiveness is also groundless; it is "arbitrary," an event that "always begins by itself." To put the paradox more strikingly, while being without an origin, forgiveness must have a specific origin, which is *human freedom*: this origin without origin, which eludes the principle of sufficient reason like the navel of a dream, and which brings to forgiveness the irreducible element of contingency, interpreted here in terms of the *clinamen*.[21] Inasmuch as forgiveness is essentially and absolutely a question of human freedom, Jankélévitch can say that it is at the same level as the fault or sin (*à la mesure du péché*), although it is not to be confused with sin—*except, as we shall see, in one exceptional instance.*

It makes no sense and, strictly speaking, is not possible within the frame of this elaboration to forgive an animal or a machine (although both may indeed be responsible for acts that on the part of a human being could be considered a fault or sin, such as killing). This is not only because the animal and the machine are not considered to have freedom but also because they supposedly lack the potential for remorse. This additional feature is critical for Jankélévitch. Following the Judeo-Christian tradition, he affirms that in order for the guilty to be forgiven, they must first repent and request forgiveness: "The repentance of the criminal, and especially his remorse, alone give meaning to forgiveness, in the same way that despair alone gives meaning to grace . . . Before it can be a question of forgiveness, it first would be necessary that the guilty, rather than contesting, recognize themselves as guilty, without defense pleas nor attenuating circumstances, and especially without accusing their own victims: it's the least one can ask!"[22] It is curious that Jankélévitch names the necessity for repentance and remorse, which is the sine qua non of forgiveness, only a few pages before the very end of the book. In the previous 150 pages of discussion of forgiveness there is, strikingly, no mention of it at all. The expression used, "alone gives meaning," suggests that the meaning of forgiveness is imperiled. It discloses that under certain conditions forgiveness, or what is called "forgiveness," may have no meaning.

At this point Jankélévitch discloses that he has a personal stake in the discussion. The quasi-phenomenological style of meditation on the general conditions of forgiveness is interrupted and transformed by an indirect, but unmistakable, reference to a specific crime perpetrated by one group on another, and about which the signatory speaks at once as a victim and on behalf of all the victims. The text, as it were, erupts. There is a change in tone, which makes explicit what was previously implicit, that is, that he is working on (at least) two fronts at once: the philosophical and the political:

> When the guilty are fat, well nourished, enriched by the economic miracle, forgiveness is a sinister pleasantry. No, forgiveness is not made for that; forgiveness is not made for the pigs and their sows . . . In order for us to forgive, should they not come and ask us for forgiveness? Have they ever asked for forgiveness? . . . Why would we forgive those who regret so little and so rarely their monstrous infamy? . . . From the day after the massacre convenient indulgence modestly enveloped the crime in silence and forgetting, forgiveness has become derisory; in future [*désormais*] forgiveness is a farce.[23]

This farcical forgiveness, what he also calls "buffoonery," is as the sinister double to the spontaneous sublimely mad forgiveness delimited over the previous 150 pages. It resonates with Baudelaire's *ennui*.[24] He repeats word for word the same position in the polemical text *Pardonner?*, which was written in 1965 on the occasion of the public debate that took place in France concerning whether statutes of limitations should be applied to the prosecution of crimes against humanity.[25] In the polemical text, however, he announces in addition the following: "Forgiveness has died in the death camps [Le pardon est mort dans les camps de mort]. Our horror for what properly speaking the understanding cannot conceive would suffocate pity from its birth . . . if the accused could make us feel pity."[26]

FORGIVENESS HAS DIED IN THE DEATH CAMPS

As Jankélévitch acknowledges in the preface to *Pardonner?* (written in 1971), the announcement that forgiveness has died in the death camps seems to contradict the central thesis of *Forgiveness* (1967), which, as noted above, is that forgiveness is an unconditional obligation arising from the duty of love. In *Pardonner?*, Jankélévitch does not specify whether the death of forgiveness is simply a consequence of the failure on the part of the great majority of the Nazis to acknowledge responsibility for what happened, or whether forgiveness in this exceptional instance *and henceforth* is radically impossible—indeed immoral—*even with a sincere and genuine repentance on the part of the Nazi perpetrators and collaborators*, among whom Jankélévitch counts the German (and Austrian) people in their entirety—or almost. If forgiveness has died in the death camps, it would mean not only that this particular crime, the *Shoah*, is radically unforgivable but that it has destroyed the very possibility of forgiveness in general, such that in future forgiveness of any fault or crime appears as a sinister double of itself, as a farce or buffoonery. The Shoah, he seems tp suggest, has killed forgiveness.

Before analyzing whether such a thesis is at all defensible and what it may imply politically, for example, in terms of a thesis of history, it is useful to read Jankélévitch's thesis, not in terms of the "integrity" of his thought, but of the contradictions, tensions, and abysses to which his thought bears witness. It would be reductive to read Jankélévitch's thesis on the death of forgiveness in isolation from what he wrote elsewhere on this topic. The forgiveness, which in *Pardonner?* has died in the death camps, is in all probability the same forgiveness whose structure Jankélévitch has scrupulously delimited in *Forgiveness*, which was published two years *after* it.[27] Why would he write a philosophical meditation analyzing the conditions under which forgiveness takes place, after he has announced that forgiveness is dead?

To this question there are at least two responses. On the one hand, one can say that *Forgiveness* is a book of mourning: a monument in memory of something that no longer exists, that has perhaps never existed. On the other hand, *Forgiveness* is an expression of the refusal or impossibility to mourn: to accept the death of forgiveness that Jankélévitch had previously announced, as if the hyperbolical ethics of love, which enjoins forgiveness even of the unforgivable, could not be murdered even by the Nazis. These two responses, I would argue, do not exclude one another. One may not believe in the existence of forgiveness, and yet at the same time affirm that a thought or dream of forgiveness is indestructible.[28] There is, as mentioned above, an unresolved contradiction (of which Jankélévitch is fully aware) between an unconditional thought of forgiveness or love, for which in principle nothing is unforgivable, and the thesis that forgiveness has died in the death camps. In the case of the death camps—which for him is not a case but an irreparable wound of history—there would be an impossibility of another order to that which is reserved to forgiveness as an ultimate recourse; a nonunderstanding incommensurable with the nonunderstanding that forgiveness should, according to Jankélévitch, always accommodate. It is at this point that Jankélévitch introduces the concept of "the inexpiable." The crimes of the Nazis are inexpiable not only in the sense that they are beyond apology and remorse but also because they exceed the possibility of a proportional punishment. For this reason, the penalty is almost indifferent. It is impossible to forgive, not only because it is impossible to punish in a proportional manner but also because beyond a certain limit it is impossible to know who to accuse, who to blame: "One can do nothing. It is impossible to bring this immense mountain of miserable ash back to life. There is no way to punish the criminal in a way that is proportionate to his crime, for next to the infinite all finite magnitudes tend to be equal; in such a way that the penalty becomes almost indifferent; what happened is literally *inexpiable*. One no longer even knows who to put the blame on or whom to accuse."[29] Like Hannah Arendt, Jankélévitch presumes that forgiveness must be the correlate of the possibility of punishment.[30] Everything can be forgiven except that which puts into question the human power to forgive as such. For Jankélévitch, it is because the crimes of the Nazis are inexpiable that they are radically unforgivable. For Derrida, on the other hand, the inexpiable opens the possibility of another thought of forgiveness, beyond the measure of human power, the sacredness of the love of men, and the possibility of proportional punishment.[31] What if, rather than the love of men, the hyperbolical ethics of forgiveness were to be grounded in the otherness of the other? Could the otherness of the other henceforth be considered to be sacred? Or would the sacred itself then have to be rethought (that is, no longer along the lines of the intact, the immune, the unscathed, the phallic, and the fetish)?[32]

If at the limit one no longer knows on whom to put the blame or whom to accuse, if the crime is no longer *on a human scale*, then this would, it seems, have consequences for fraternal sympathy, or in other words, specular self-identification with the other as the sine qua non of forgiveness in Jankélévitch's understanding. If I can scarcely conceive of what you have done, if it exceeds, damages, perhaps irreparably, my image of a human being, then how can I identify myself as a (virtual) agent—or victim for that matter—of what has happened? Or if, on the contrary, it *is* possible (all too possible) to identify myself in relation to this crime, would such self-identification not amount to consenting to inconceivable devastation?

To interpret another (I believe more essential) dimension of the impasse: before the absolutely monstrous size of the crime, how is it possible to delimit the responsibility? The model of forgiveness that Jankélévitch proposes presumes that in principle one knows whom to accuse, and therefore whom to forgive—and for what. The Shoah is not simply one event. Moreover, it cannot be separated from a vast history of anti-Semitism in Europe dating back as far as the Middle Ages. While it is possible to attribute responsibility in an unambiguous fashion to individuals who were actively involved, beyond them, however, where does the responsibility end? With the Nazis themselves and their collaborators throughout Europe; the bystanders (German and non-German) who watched and did nothing, the victims themselves perhaps (who in many cases didn't see—or want to see—before it was too late); the U.S. State Department, who it seems also knew from as early as August 1942, and obstructed rescue efforts, etc.?[33] Beyond this level of complexity (which is enormous), how to measure, for example, the responsibility of European thought, of Christianity (and its history of anti-Semitism, both Protestant and Catholic), and finally the unprecedented use of modern means of communication, transport, and the invention of industrial processes for the purpose of mass murder? Is the machinery of death here simply a tool at the disposal of a wicked human agency, or does such machinery have an agency of its own with which it is necessary to contend?[34]

If forgiveness has died in the death camps, then one would presume that this is because fraternal sympathy is hopelessly inadequate given the measure and complexity of the crime. The mirror, in which humanity reflects itself and in so doing recalibrates and repairs itself through the reciprocal exchange of expressions of remorse and offers of forgiveness, has been—it would seem—irreparably broken. And yet, this might be an overly hasty judgment, for even if Jankélévitch is unable to offer fraternal sympathy ("Our horror for what properly speaking the understanding cannot conceive would suffocate pity from its birth"), he nonetheless cannot help but make an appeal for it—not from the "Jews" but from the "Germans": "To ask for forgiveness! We have long been waiting for a word, a single word, a word of understanding and sympathy . . . we have hoped for it, this *fraternal* word! Certainly, we were not expecting our forgiveness to be implored . . . But we would have received words of understanding with gratitude, with tears in our eyes."[35] This appeal for sympathy and understanding mirrors that of so many victims of massive injustices. What in 1971 is scandalous for Jankélévitch is the lack of empathy for the victims of the Shoah manifest in all the forms of self-justification and denial in the decades following the end of World War II. He reads the *coldness*—the apparent indifference—not only of the Nazis themselves but also of the German peoples in general (in the name of whose racial supremacy, Jankélévitch recalls, the crime was committed) as a sign of complicity in the slaughter and a refusal to assume responsibility for its consequences.[36] And yet, if there is (or was or has been) such an empathic failure, can this not *also* be read as a human—all too human—defense against something that is too threatening? Or is, on the other hand, empathic failure in some measure unavoidable if, as Jankélévitch says, what has happened truly exceeds "our" powers of comprehension?

At this point it is necessary to mention that Jankélévitch ignores—like almost all those who have spoken of this crime—the victims of other groups targeted by the genocidal violence of the Nazis, in particular, the Sinti and Roma people. No Sinti or Roma were called to testify at the Nuremberg trials, and no one came forth to testify on their behalf, although scholars estimate that between 70 percent and 80 percent of the Romani population in Europe were annihilated between 1939 and 1945. The Romani name for this event is little known: *Porrajmos* (the Devouring). This name invites us to think that there is a bestial element of the Nazi crimes. According to the *Oxford English Dictionary*, "devouring" is associated with predatory behavior.[37] It also recalls the psychoanalytic concept of incorporative identification mentioned above, the process by which the other is assimilated or "swallowed." Up until the present there has been little attention paid to Sinti or Roma survivors or their relatives.[38] Indeed, the same is also true of the victims of operation T4, the systematic killing of the mentally ill and the handicapped, most often in prototypes of the killing centers that were later constructed in occupied Poland—and with many of the same personnel.[39]

Jankélévitch's appeal for fraternal sympathy and understanding makes clear that the self-identifying mirror is as much a prerequisite for the one who asks for forgiveness as for the one who forgives. As noted above, whoever sincerely asks for forgiveness must in a preliminary manner acknowledge a resemblance with the one who accuses them, such that if they were in the accuser's place they would also complain of a wrong done to them. Only by identifying with the other can the accused, as it were, accuse themselves, say *mea culpa*, and in so doing expiate the fault through confession and remorse. Self-accusation on the part of the accused signifies (or at least is supposed to signify) at once the accused's recognition of the fault and his/her dissociation from who they were when they committed it. It is strange, although perhaps not impossible to understand, that Jankélévitch should ask for expiation of a crime that he recognizes is inexpiable.

"I MYSELF HAVE NOT KILLED ANY JEWS. HAVING BEEN BORN GERMAN IS NOT MY FAULT."

Nine years later, a young German wrote to Jankélévitch in response to the publication of *Pardonner?*[40] The letter contests the notion of collective guilt, while nonetheless confessing to a sense of responsibility (for a fault that the signatory has not himself committed). The letter begins as follows:

> I myself have not killed any Jews. Having been born German is not my fault, or my doing. No one asked my permission. I am completely innocent of Nazi crimes; but this does not console me at all. My conscience is not clear [*Je n'ai pas la conscience tranquille*], and I feel a mixture of shame, pity, resignation, sadness, incredulity, revolt. I do not always sleep well.[41]

The letter also goes on to invite Jankélévitch to visit him in Germany:

> If ever, dear M. Jankélévitch, you pass through here, knock on our door and come in. You will be welcome. And be assured my parents will not be there. No one will speak to you of Hegel, or of Nietzsche, or of Jaspers, or of Heidegger or of any of the other great Teutonic thinkers. I will ask you about Descartes and Sartre. I like the music of Schubert and Schumann. But I will play a record of Chopin, or if you prefer Faure and Debussy . . . Let it be said in passing: I admire and respect Rubinstein; I like Menuhin.[42]

As mentioned above, Jankélévitch was a musician and a lover of music. He had written several books on the subject. His response to the author of the letter, Wiard Raveling, makes clear that what was awaited has finally arrived:

> I am moved by your letter. I have waited for this letter for thirty-five years. I mean a letter in which the abomination is fully assumed and by someone who had no part in it [*n'y est pour rien*]. This is the first time I have received a letter from a German, a letter that was not a letter of more or less disguised self-justification. You alone, you the first and no doubt the last, have found the necessary words outside the pious clichés . . . There is no mistaking it. Thank you.[43]

And in response to Raveling's invitation to visit him in Germany:

> No, I will not come to visit you in Germany. I will not go that far. I am too old to inaugurate this new era. Because for me it is a new era all the same. For which I have waited too long. But you are young, you do not have the same reasons as I. You do not have this uncrossable barrier to cross [*cette barrière infranchissable à franchir*]. It is my turn to say to you: When you come to Paris, do as everyone does, knock on my door, we will sit down at the piano.[44]

Raveling recounts that he visited Jankélévitch in Paris only once, that everything took place very cordially, but that Jankélévitch "systematically avoided" returning to these questions. Even in the correspondence that followed.

The fraternal word, which was painfully awaited and joyously received, was to all appearances not enough for "forgiveness" to be offered or to take place between the two men. However, the allusion on both sides to music, to music played and listened to together, to the sharing of music, is significant to the extent that it designates a realm beyond words which is perhaps required by forgiveness (if it is truly something that happens only between two singular individuals, an event irreducible to any form of generalization or universalization).

It is certainly possible to read Jankélévitch's refusal to go to Germany, or to discuss the questions further, in short to reach some sort of reconciliation on the issue, as a fault on his part. *There was in all probability nothing more that the young man could have done.* In Hegelian terms, Jankélévitch, like Wiesenthal, is in the position of the "hard heart" that stubbornly refuses to break: the spirit that indignantly refuses to offer or receive the word of reconciliation. And yet, it is possible to read Jankélévitch's response in another way. Precisely because the young man reaches the limit of his capacities, one can say that his relationship to the unforgivable events of the past has a chance to deepen. Jankélévitch's resistance permits an experience of finitude, of powerlessness *to be shared* with the young man. It is, one may argue, only on this basis that a forgiveness worthy of the name may perhaps one day be possible.

In his exemplary reading of this scene, Jacques Derrida approves, gives reason to Jankélévitch's resistance to Raveling, which he reads not simply as a refusal, but as the consequence of two incompatible discourses or logics crossing one another: one of reconciliation, the other of the irreconcilable. If forgiveness has died in the death camps, then this death of forgiveness (like all deaths) will have to be mourned, and mourned precisely through forgiveness, through a work of memory and reconciliation by future generations that Jankélévitch in fact welcomes as a positive development, "a new era for which I have waited too long." On the other hand, however, under the pretext of being "too old to inaugurate this new era," he gives to understand that such mourning—even when it takes place—will and must remain impossible, the death of forgiveness being the testimonial trace of an unhealable wound of history.

Even though Jankélévitch wrote to Raveling: "But you are young . . . You do not have this uncrossable barrier to cross," this affirmation is belied by what later happened between them. For the impossible insists. The barrier will not be any more crossable for the young man or for the generations to come—even if it will necessarily be experienced differently. Jankélévitch's response to Wiard Raveling recalls the irony of Kafka's famous answer to his friend Max Brod in 1920: "an infinite amount of hope, only not for us" (*unendlich viel Hoffnung–, nur nicht für uns*).[45] Despite appearances, Kafka's response need not be read in an exclusively negative sense, that is, as an unambiguous truth, which would lead to inertia. Inasmuch as the response is not without irony (even humor perhaps), the meaning is haunted by a double attitude: a living and sustaining of the contradictions without attempting to reconcile them.[46]

Jacques Derrida speaks of a "great paradigmatic lesson for us at the heart of Jankélévitch's letter": "One senses the unaltered conviction, unalterable, that even when forgiveness of the inexpiable will have taken place, in the future, in the generations to come, it will not have taken place, it will have remained illusory, inauthentic, illegitimate, scandalous, equivocal, mixed with forgetting (even when its subjects are and believe themselves to be sincere and generous)."[47] What Derrida writes here should not, it seems to me, be read as a denigration of the noble and necessary work of reconciliation, and in particular the courage of attempts such as Wiard Raveling's to build a bridge across an abyss. It is rather that attempts at reconciliation should be undertaken on the basis of the acknowledgment of a fundamental powerlessness and impossibility. This acknowledgment might be translated as *an interdiction on hope.* The impossibility here is several-sided. On the one hand, the impossible is indeed an infinitely intractable limit, which cannot be overcome. And yet, on the other hand, this intractable limit is productive of desire, indeed of the highest, most insane desire. (It is in this sense that the impossible is also a chance, a gift.) On the other hand again, however, the limit is not presentable; it does not present itself as such in the present. ("Even when forgiveness of the inexpiable will have taken place, it will not have taken place, it will remain illusory, illegitimate, scandalous, equivocal, mixed with forgetting.") In its most essential dimension the impossibility of forgiveness does not appear simply as an uncrossable barrier, for forgiveness is not an indivisible concept.

If "forgiveness of the inexpiable" is impossible in the senses that I have suggested, then it bears an essential similarity with death and dying, thinking in particular of what Maurice Blanchot's *Le pas au-delà* (*The Step Not Beyond*) gives to read of this relation.[48] If death is not foreign to forgiveness, then the formulation "death of forgiveness" must also be read in the subjective genitive: death is not something that happens to forgiveness from the outside, but belongs to it intrinsically. Against the implication of Jankélévitch's thesis, the death of forgiveness therefore would not be something that the disaster of the Shoah, the Holocaust, the Porrajmos, the Final Solution simply causes to happen, but more modestly gives us to think about.

The first consequence of this is that the contradictions and impasses to which Jankélévitch bears witness would not be restricted to the exceptional character of the Shoah, but can be extended to all "crimes against humanity" and indeed to any crime or fault at all against the other as other. The inexpiable would be the most everyday thing in the world; it would not be restricted to the massive injustices of history. Would one then be driven to say that there is no such thing as forgiveness? There has never been forgiveness? Even when forgiveness is believed to have happened, it never really happens, because it is not identical to itself? Yes, perhaps.

The second consequence is marked in the brackets of the quotation from Derrida above: "forgiveness of the inexpiable will not have taken place . . . (even when its subjects are and believe themselves to be sincere and generous)." If death belongs to forgiveness, then forgiveness necessarily exceeds the power and capacity of a subject, that is, of a human being understood as a ground or *subjectum*.[49] There will be a remainder of the unforgivable, even if the subjects concerned do not know about it or deny it. Beyond a certain point they are powerless, even when well intentioned. As impossible, forgiveness belongs to a metonymic chain that would include alterity, death, madness, writing, irony, and perhaps even stupidity.[50]

The critical point seems to be the insufficiency of a Judeo-Christian conceptualization of forgiveness as something that may be presumed to take place if sincerely asked for and generously offered. The hardness of this thought is to give, as it were, only on the condition that everything is first taken away: only if it is *thought* as truly impossible, as a radical experience of powerlessness, is there today a chance for impure forgiveness—as something yet to be invented, for something poetic to take place. Forgiveness is this ultimate recourse, which perhaps opens onto a new dimension of not exclusively "human" relations, or otherwise is a guarantee that can sanction the worst injustices.

THE "PRIVILEGE" GIVEN TO THE SHOAH

Jankélévitch's thesis of the death of forgiveness in the Nazi extermination camps during World War II raises the question of the "privilege" given to this event over other comparable crimes against humanity. This is both a political and ethical question that should not be passed over in silence, as if it went of itself, in good conscience. One would perhaps today have to ask forgiveness for speaking about the Shoah, when apparently so much has already been thought, said, and seen; and so little of other genocides. Or is one rather inevitably held to secrecy in respect of this, in the sense that it marks a sacrificial decision that in the last analysis cannot be accounted for and justified?[51]

The word "genocide" was first employed in a printed article in November 1944. In an article written six months later, the inventor of the term, Raphael Lemkin, wrote the following: "The crime of the Reich in wantonly and deliberately wiping out whole peoples is not utterly new in the world. It is only new in the civilized world as we have come to think of it. It is so new in the traditions of civilized man that he has no name for it."[52] There is, Derrida argues, by definition, no archive of the secret. "The secret," he wrote one day, "is the very ash of the archive."[53] Lemkin's gesture, whose necessity scarcely needs to be underlined, consists firstly in reading the ash of the archive, the traces of what has not simply been repressed, but so radically erased that there remains no memory intact, no name to keep the memory of the crime in its specificity. By inventing the word "genocide" (from the Greek *genes*, meaning tribe or race, and the Latin *cide*, meaning killing), he memorializes the victims of the Holocaust, but in such a way that in future and retrospectively it will be possible to identify other victims at other times and in other places, victims of the same (if not identical) injustice.

Lemkin situates the novelty of the "crime of the Reich" not in relation to history but in relation to how "civilized man" sees and understands himself, that is, the self-reflecting mirror of fraternalist universalism. Beyond this mirror, Lemkin seems to suggest, the crime is invisible: it has no name. Today one must ask what crimes—as yet unrecognized—remain unseen beyond the mirror of genocide or "crimes against humanity."

In 1981 the American composer Steve Reich first recorded *Tehillim* for voices and ensemble. While on a totally different register, Steve Reich's gesture resonates with that of Raphael Lemkin in that it relates itself to what has been absolutely lost, beyond memory, that is, the oral tradition among Jews in the West for the singing of the Psalms of the Old Testament. While based on the study of cantillation, no Jewish themes were used for any of the melodic materials. These derive from Balinese Gamelan Ganbang and no doubt also from the composer's absorption of West African drumming. However, the rhythm of the music is derived directly from that of the Hebrew text. In this regard, *Tehillim* ("Psalms," literally "Praises") is reminiscent of *Different Trains* (1988), where the melodic speech patterns of recorded witnesses provide the musical material for musical instruments. *Tehillim* was cocommissioned by West German Radio, Cologne; South German Radio, Stuttgart; and the Rothko Chapel in Houston.

Conclusion

Forgiveness as a Jewish Joke

[T]hese two Jews will have forgiven each other, but without saying so to each other. They have at least spoken to each other, even if they have not spoken forgiveness. They have told each other—in silence, a silence of innuendo (*sous-entendu*) where misunderstanding can always find space to reside—that forgiveness granted does not signify "reconciliation" (Hegel) nor "work itself," "the deep work of time."

—Jacques Derrida, "Hostipitality"

It is no doubt significant that on the sole occasion (to my knowledge) where Derrida provides an affirmative characterization of what forgiveness is or might be, it is by means of the interpretation of a joke. Forgiveness is a joke perhaps: an object of ridicule and scepticism; or, following Freud's famous argument, a mechanism by which repressed psychic energy, for example, aggressive or sexual urges, are discharged without fear of social sanction:

> Two Jews, long-time enemies, meet at the synagogue, on the Day of Atonement [*le jour du Grand Pardon*]. One says to the other [as a gesture, therefore, of forgiveness—J. D.]: "I wish for you what you wish for me." The other immediately retorts: "Already you're starting again?"[1]

This joke was reported by Theodore Reik.[2] Derrida recounts the joke in at least two texts: first, in the course of a session dated 12 February 1997, of his seminar entitled "Hostipitality"; and, second, in a eulogy he gave for Sarah Kofman, which was first published in the same year.[3] Kofman herself had cited the same joke at the conclusion of her book: *Pourquoi rit-on? Freud et le mot d'esprit* (*Why Do We Laugh? Freud and Wit*).[4] In his eulogy for her, Derrida recalls that they must have told the joke to one another, probably while eating together. Derrida allies his thinking of forgiveness to Sarah Kofman, both to the work and the woman, whose "incisive, singular and unappeasable suffering I simply could not bear." She was "a great friend," but it was "an impossible friendship, impossible right up to the end, we often blamed one another. She would make fun of me."[5]

One can well imagine Derrida might have found Kofman making fun of him to be "unforgivable." That she exposed him (and others) for decades to her unappeasable suffering was perhaps also difficult to forgive, even while (or because) such suffering was in all probability not entirely foreign to him. In recounting this joke in the wake of her suicide, Derrida allows us to think that he is seeking forgiveness from Sarah Kofman and/or granting it to her. He does not explicitly say so. I would suggest that he could not say so explicitly if he is to be faithful to his own thought, which demands that forgiveness, if there is any, must remain unavowed, unavowable, if it is not to be reduced to an economy of exchange.[6] Through and beyond death, he dreams rather of mad, complicitous laughter between them:

> You see, you start again, you don't want to forgive me, even on the Day of Atonement, but me too, "me" neither, we are in accord, we will forgive each other nothing, it is impossible, let us not forgive each other, agreed [*d'accord*]? And then comes the complicitous burst of laughter, the mad laughter, laughter becoming mad, demented laughter [*le rire dément*, also the laughter denies, refutes].[7]

If such laughter were forgiveness, one would have to say that it is an *invention* in both senses of the word. It is something that has been made up, a fiction, but as such it brings something new into the order of what already exists or is otherwise possible or imaginable. Forgiveness, if there is any, *dreamexists*.[8] Undoubtedly, one reason why Derrida defines forgiveness as forgiveness of the unforgivable is because he believes that it must be an invention. Above all else perhaps he wishes to keep open the possibility that forgiveness brings something new into the order of what already exists, what is currently believed to be possible or imaginable: "Nothing is given in advance for an act of forgiveness, no rule, no criterion, no norm. It is chaos at the origin of the world."[9]

If forgiving the unforgivable is not, as it appears to be, a cold and formal contradiction, but, as he says, "a tragedy of compassion and intersubjectivity,"[10] then it must be bound to an experience, an appeal from the other, and especially, of the other's name. For Derrida one such name for forgiveness would be Sarah Kofman, uniquely, whose suicide on the date of Nietzsche's 150th birthday left him, he confessed, unable to speak:

> Since the death of Sarah—and what a death—it has been impossible for me to speak as I knew I wanted to, impossible to speak *to her, to* her, as one does without pretending to friends who have disappeared, impossible also to speak *of* her, as other friends, who are also mine, have known how to do—and have done so well, and were right to do. I thus had to try to relearn everything, and I am still at it.[11]

Elsewhere in the course of an interview bearing the title "Passages: From Traumatism to Promise," Derrida put forward the thesis: "A philosophical discourse that would not be provoked or interrupted by the violence of an appeal from the other, from an experience that cannot be dominated, would not be a very questioning, very interesting philosophical discourse . . . It has to 'deal' [*traîte*] so to speak, with the traumatism."[12] For a philosophical discourse to be genuinely questioning, genuinely interesting, it must, *on the one hand,* allow itself to be provoked and interrupted by an experience it cannot master. On the other hand, however, it also has to "deal with" this experience, "treat" (*traîte*) it in some way. Tempting as it may be, it is never enough not to "deal with" a traumatism. It is quite possible that Derrida was furious with Sarah Kofman for committing suicide. In so doing, she had left him with a great deal of what is called survivor guilt. For decades he had been her mentor, as well as her close colleague and friend, and yet, as he is careful to note, she had always protested: "'Protestation' will have been I now realize . . . the privileged mode of our face-to-face encounters."[13] Protested against what or who exactly? He does not say, but in proximity to the word he does not fail to mention sexual difference, a topic which undoubtedly will have haunted their personal and professional exchanges: "We will touch upon the veil of modesty that it lays out or barely lifts over sexual difference . . . Sarah Kofman knew this, she thought it, I believe, and analyzed it—but she protested . . . against this movement to which, like, all of us, and from the very first day, she had to succumb."[14] In a very circumlocutory manner, as a circumfession one might say, Derrida mentions the word "guilt" in relation to Kofman's "incisive, singular and unappeasable suffering," as well as avowing in a conditional mode that he might still blame her for *his* suffering: "even if I were still to blame her for my suffering, at least it would be her, and her alone, who would be implicated, and that is my first concern here."[15]

In this context, that of a eulogy, bearing witness to a close friend's singularity and uniqueness would be more important than trying to master one's negative feelings or ambivalence. Derrida did not fail to mention that they had made many scenes before one another. As if to mark the exasperation and difficulty this caused him, he adds: "When it comes to scenes, I have to say that I'll never be able to make as many as she; I'll never catch up."[16] By implication, committing suicide on Nietzsche's 150th birthday was the last in a long line of such public scenes. It may have made him so angry with her that he found it impossible to speak in the kind and generous way that one is generally expected to speak of close friends who have died. Moreover, he preserved the trace of this silence by not giving a title to his remarks, which were published simply as ". . . . .". Among the many eulogies Derrida gave for his dead friends and colleagues (Kofman was not the only one to commit suicide), this decision not to give a title, or to give a nontitle, was a unique gesture. The ". . . . ." may indeed have been a way to testify to his inability to speak about and/or to Sarah in the way he wanted. However, it may also have been a way to draw attention to the singular and infinite silence that accompanies every suicide. One day in a seminar in Paris when answering a question about the suicide of Walter Benjamin, I remember he said that unless one is in the mind of the person who has gone at the exact time(s) in which the decision was made, one can never know exactly what made them do it or if it could have been prevented.[17] When later he comes to recount the joke about the two Jews in the synagogue on the Day of Atonement, he adds in parentheses (a signal the point is very important) that the decision of one longtime enemy just to speak to the other is *already* a gesture of forgiveness.

From chapter 1, one can recall that the narrator in Simon Wiesenthal's *The Sunflower* does not only not respond to the SS man's request for forgiveness, he says nothing to him at all and leaves the room in silence. And yet, despite this resolute decision, the narrator very quickly feels a sense of dissatisfaction, guilt, or responsibility that obliges him *in the wake of the other's death* not to just leave it at that. In Wiesenthal, as in Derrida, there is an injunction "to treat" (*traîte*) silence and traumatic memory, or as one translator has suggested, "to deal with" it. Derrida's innovative contribution to this "treatment" is the thought that in just speaking about silence and traumatic memory, some forgiveness is already inscribed. Forgiveness is a "treatment of memory" (*traîtement de mémoire*).[18] After citing the joke at the conclusion of Kofman's book *Why Does One Laugh?* (*Pourquoi rit-on?*), he speaks as if to Sarah, "as one does without pretending to friends who have disappeared." As if by a kind of internal displacement, he would seem to do the very thing he previously said that he could not do: "I will thus venture to say this . . . to address this to you as if to Sarah, to Sarah in me. Allegorically, what these two Jews come to experience and what makes us laugh is the radical impossibility of forgiveness. A Jew, a Jew from time immemorial, and especially in this century, . . . is put to the test of the impossibility of forgiveness."[19]

This last sentence is remarkable. Without using the word "anti-Semitism," it interprets and thinks anti-Semitism as "the test of the impossibility of forgiveness"—a test to which the Jews will have been put from time immemorial, and especially during the century of the Holocaust. Anti-Semitism tests not only the Jews' ability to forgive but also—and probably much more importantly—the ability *to be forgiven*. Such would be the immemorial double bind: "as if it were because the Nazis treated the being of their victim, the Jew, as an inexpiable crime (it is not forgivable to be Jewish), that they behaved in a way that was itself inexpiable, beyond all possible forgiveness."[20]

Both Kofman and Derrida, like millions of others during the twentieth century, will have found themselves in this immemorial double bind. Growing up in French-colonized Algeria, Derrida indeed suffered from anti-Semitism. He was expelled in 1942 from Ben Aknoun high school and also had his French citizenship withdrawn. As he later emphasized, this decision was made at the time without the intervention of any Nazi. It was taken solely by the governing body of French Algeria, in the form of the governor general, as if he and they were just waiting for the opportunity to do it. As a consequence of the expulsion, Derrida suffered at the time anti-Semitic insults from other children at the school and also in the street. The wound in him caused by these events, he avowed, never healed. Later he was enrolled in Maimonides high school, where the Jewish professors of the region, who were also excluded, regrouped to form a place of instruction. The experience of being expelled from school and then thrown into a makeshift school of all those who had been excluded left him, he said, with a feeling of *not belonging* either to the Jewish community or to the non-Jewish community: "a double suffering, a divided cruelty."[21]

While Sarah Kofman's experience in some respects resembles Derrida's, it was much more difficult. After her father, Berek Kofman, a rabbi of a small synagogue in the Eighteenth District of Paris, was arrested in 1942 and deported to Auschwitz, the family went into hiding. "Saved" by a woman whom she calls "Mémé" who hid her and her mother in her home until the liberation, she was obliged to pass as her daughter. Changing one home for another, she was torn between a Jewish and a Christian upbringing. She was baptized in a Christian ceremony, her name changed.[22] In a short autobiographical text, "Damned Food," she testified about her symptomatic resistance as a child to eating. This intensified while in hiding with Mémé, when she received contradictory imperatives as to what she should or was allowed to eat from two competing mothers (Christian and Jewish). This took place at a time when there was very little and sometimes nothing to eat at all. The text concludes: "Put in a real double bind, I could no longer swallow anything and vomited after each meal."[23]

When after Kofman's suicide Derrida comes to reread her work (as a gesture already of forgiveness perhaps) he rediscovers his copy of "Damned Food" with a dedication to him from her in 1980 "in the hopes of *Eating* together."[24] Six years later in the copy she gave him of *Pourquoi rit-on? Freud et le mot d'esprit* he discovered that she wrote: "For Jacques and Marguerite, recalling the good Jewish jokes we once peddled at table, and hoping we can do it again one day."[25] As a memory and also a promise for the future, both he and she at different times, across death, recall a moment of joy that they had shared together while eating and laughing, "peddling," as she put it, Jewish jokes. Peddling, in French "*le colportage*," bears on the transport of merchandise for selling as well as transmitting widely to many people. In the section entitled "Peddling: The Economic Necessity of the Third" in the book on laughter by Kofman named above, she stops to consider for a moment the word "peddling" (*colporter*) as a particularly welcome translation of the German "*zutragen*" in a passage from Freud on the speedy circulation of a new joke:

> Etymologically, the word peddling (*colporter*) means "to carry on one's neck." As the peddler circulates merchandise on his neck from town to town, the joke [*le mot d'esprit*] travels from mouth to mouth and what it peddles, scattering euphoria and laughter around it, is the good news of a victory [*la bonne nouvelle d'une victoire*], which relieves necks [*cous et nuques*], for it delivers them from the weight of society's yoke. Everyone yearns for this deliverance for ordinarily each of us can only bear society's yoke at the cost of a great psychic expenditure.[26]

Following Freud, Kofman compares the circulation of a new joke to that of a military victory. However, she adds that the joke is "good news" (*bonne nouvelle*), subtly implying that for her the joke is also a harbinger of redemption. Derrida's eulogy to Kofman invites us to think that as adults, wounded children put to the test of the impossibility of forgiveness, peddling jokes would have been their way, an affirmative, dare I say, joyful way of nourishing themselves, of deciphering their anxiety and managing their unconscious. Kofman concludes her book about laughter with the joke reported by Theodor Reik to commemorate the date when the book was completed, 25 September, which happened to coincide with Yom Kippur, the Day of Atonement.[27] As a way to say good-bye to her and resist that his ambivalence toward her should have the last word, Derrida would have inventively recalled, as Kofman herself had done, the scene of them peddling Jewish jokes together at table while laughing complicitously, madly, and denyingly (*le rire dément*).

LOVING PAUL DE MAN

In the joke itself, it is worth underlining that the two Jewish speakers wisely avoid making any statements in the absolute about forgiveness. They do not state that forgiveness is impossible. Rather, they say it to one another *allegorically*: "I wish for you what you wish for me"; "Already you're starting again." An allegorical reading of the joke is ineluctable because what the two speakers admit to and what makes them laugh is not said. Commenting on allegory in Paul de Man, Derrida wrote: "Allegory is not just one form of figurative language among others; it represents one of language's essential possibilities . . . the possibility of always saying something other than what it gives to read, including the scene of reading itself."[28] For a thinking and practice of forgiveness, allegory is probably indispensable, for it stands in the way of forgiveness appearing as a statement of fact or object of presentable knowledge. Derrida will argue that if there is forgiveness [asked for or granted], it may only take place to the measure in which it remains "undecidably equivocal, by which I do not mean ambiguous, shady, twilit, but heterogeneous to any determination in the order of knowledge, of determinate theoretical judgment, of the self-presentation of an appropriable sense [*de la presentation de soi d'un sens appropriable*]."[29] On one occasion, however, Derrida confessed to having allowed himself to dismiss this exigency and make a statement of an onto-theological kind about forgiveness, that is, one that implied that he knew, like God one imagines, what is and is not forgivable. This was notably with reference to Paul de Man.

De Man had been Derrida's close friend and colleague right up to de Man's death in 1983. This is probably saying too little. De Man had been a brilliant, uniquely powerful voice for what came to be known as "deconstruction" in or, as Derrida also suggested, as America.[30] Shortly after de Man's death in 1983, Derrida gave a very moving set of lectures dedicated to the memory of de Man and his work, which were later published under the title *Memoires for Paul de Man*.[31] When de Man's wartime journalism was discovered four years later, Derrida found himself once again in a double bind—put to the test of the impossibility of forgiveness. De Man had told him nothing of the period of his life during which he had published articles in a collaborationist newspaper in Belgium—at least one of which was undeniably anti-Semitic. This article, entitled "The Jews in Contemporary Literature" ("Les Juifs dans la littérature actuelle"), contained the following sentences: "[A] solution of the Jewish problem that would aim at the creation of a Jewish colony isolated from Europe would not entail, for the literary life of the West, deplorable consequences. The latter would lose, in all, a few personalities of mediocre value and would continue, as in the past, to develop according to its great evolutive laws."[32] In the first essay Derrida published following the discovery of de Man's wartime journalism, he ventured to write (and indeed underline) that what de Man had done was "unforgivable" (*impardonable*). After quoting the passage from de Man given above, Derrida wrote:

> Will I dare to say "on the other hand" in the face of the *unforgivable* [*impardonable*] violence and confusion of these sentences? What could possibly attenuate the fault? And whatever may be the reasons or the

> complications of a text, whatever may be going on in the mind of its author, how can one deny that the effect of these conclusions went in the sense and the direction of the worst? In the dominant context in which they were read in 1941, did not their dominant effect go unquestionably in the direction of the worst? Of what we now know to have been the worst?" (translation modified)[33]

This passage was, Derrida believed, the only time in his life he had employed the word "unforgivable" publicly to condemn anyone's actions. He later sought to justify himself by saying that in the context of the vehement debate that arose following the discovery of de Man's wartime journalism, he did not wish to be "accused of blindness to the gravity of de Man's offences" on the basis of his known friendship for him. Furthermore, by employing the word "unforgivable" he wished to underline that no one had the right to forgive a collaborator unless one is directly its victim, that is, "those who perished in the camps, or those who were persecuted by German or Belgian Nazis."[34]

Nonetheless, despite these cogent self-justifications for what was undoubtedly written at a very difficult moment, he ultimately confessed that he felt wrong to have used the word "unforgivable" to describe the actions of his close friend, who being dead could no longer defend himself. He even felt the need somehow to ask for forgiveness: "I blame myself still today for having written this word and it is up to me to somehow ask for forgiveness . . . For it is a way of saying in the absolute that what de Man did is unforgivable, and this I cannot say of anything or anyone."[35] It is arresting and thought-provoking that Derrida should have used the highly charged word "unforgivable" uniquely to describe the actions of one who was most important to him, who was not Jewish, and about whom he wrote hundreds of pages both before and after the discovery of the wartime journalism (much more, one might add, than he ever wrote about Sarah Kofman). In the same article in which he stated that what de Man had done was unforgivable, he wrote again testifying to his feelings: "Nothing in what I am about to say . . . will heal over the wound I right away felt when, my breath taken away, I perceived in it what the newspapers have most frequently singled out as recognized anti-Semitism . . . [one] that would have come close to urging exclusions, even the most sinister deportations."[36] As Benoit Peeters notes in his biography of Derrida, it was around the same time (1941–42) in which de Man published articles in a collaborationist newspaper in Belgium that Derrida had been expelled from Ben Aknoun high school in Algeria.[37] In both cases, Derrida spoke of a wound that has not healed, a formulation very close to the one he reserved to describe the Holocaust itself: "History continues on the background of [*sur fond de*] an interruption of history, in the abyss, rather, of an infinite wound, which, in its very scarring, will have to remain an open and unsuturable wound. In any case it is in the zone of hyperbole, of aporia and paradox that we should often have to stand or move in this reflection on forgiveness."[38] In chapter 1, I suggested that one might tentatively inscribe Simon Wiesenthal's narrative *The Sunflower* within a long and painful history of Jewish fascination with—even love for—the gentile, "Christian" other. No doubt, Derrida's friendship with Paul de Man might also be inscribed in such a history, even if in a deconstructive spirit one should distrust the self-evidence of the oppositions Jew/gentile and Jew/Christian. Like the narrator of *The Sunflower*, Derrida's actions bear witness to a surplus of responsibility that does not allow itself to be satisfied with pregiven rules, codes, norms, axioms—be they Jewish or gentile, sacred or secular, theist or atheist. As testimony perhaps of his enduring difficulty to understand his friend and the impossibility to put "the affair" behind him, much later Derrida wrote two long essays, "Typewriter Ribbon: Limited Ink (2)" (2001) and "Le Parjure, perhaps" (2002), on excuses, perjury, and forgiveness in relation to the work and character of Paul de Man.[39] What Derrida may have owed uniquely to Paul de Man, and to their mutual injuries toward one another, is, I would argue, also encrypted in his thinking of forgiveness. If labeling a person or act "unforgivable" is itself, according to Derrida, a fault, then what sense does the concept "to forgive the unforgivable" have? How can Derrida's concept be applied to anything if the moment one labels something or someone unforgivable, one has already committed a wrong?

Maybe the answer lies in interpreting the concept of forgiveness in a different way. If there were such a thing as forgiveness, it would require as a condition that the place of the unforgivable be left empty and/or unspoken. No definition of the unforgivable should be presupposed nor any definite criteria given as to how it could be judged. Only by resisting translation of the injury into a statement of an ontotheological kind (such as "this is unforgivable," or even at the limit, "this is wrong"), only by questioning the necessity of such a translation, can giving and forgiving continue to be possible. As Blanchot argues in *The Writing of Disaster*: "By accusing, by stating the injury, the wrong becomes irredeemable [*irremissible*]."[40] From this point of view, the concept of "forgiving only the unforgivable," "the worst of the worst," may—even must—be interpreted *as an allegory*, that is, as a way of saying something else than what it gives to read. Evacuating the place of the unforgivable can be read, on the one hand, as a gesture of forgiveness for Paul de Man on his behalf (since he was and is still, believe it or not, dead); and, on the other hand, as a request for forgiveness from him for having one day used the word "unforgivable" to describe in his absence what he had done.

FORGIVENESS INSCRIBED IN THE VERY FIRST SPEECH ACT

As noted above, in just speaking to the other, especially one's enemy on the Day of Atonement, there is, Derrida believes, already a gesture of forgiveness. Not in the sense of a consummated act, certainly, but of a *promise*, the performative force of which is not diminished by it not being able to be realized or kept: "Even if a promise could be kept, this would matter little. What is essential here is that a pure promise cannot properly take place, in a proper place, even though promising is inevitable as soon as we open our mouths—or rather as soon as there is text."[41] Both Derrida and de Man interpret all speech acts as having a priori the structure of a promise. Much later, in resonance with this affirmation, Derrida put forward the idea that every speech act (be it speaking, listening, reading, or writing) inscribes some forgiveness both asked for and granted: "Somewhere I wrote that as soon as I write, I am asking for forgiveness, without of course knowing what will happen. But forgiveness is inscribed in the very first speech act. I cannot perform what I would like to perform. That is why things happen."[42] The thought of "forgiveness [as] inscribed in the very first speech act" is, I would suggest, Derrida's *most important contribution* to the subject of forgiveness within the Abrahamic tradition.

Because to my knowledge he does not elaborate further on this thought, I will attempt to reconstruct an account of why he puts it forward on the basis of his earlier work on speech act theory in "Signature Event Context" (1971). When I speak to the other, *what never happens* is that I speak to the other as such in the living present, because every speech act in order to function must be repeatable, or as he says, "iterable."[43] Because of this iterability, there is always some uncontrollable mechanicity, an "essential drifting" (*dérive essentielle*), which "cuts [the speech act] off from all absolute responsibility, from *consciousness* as the authority of the last analysis": "This essential drifting, due to writing as an iterative structure cuts off from all absolute responsibility, from *consciousness* as the authority of the last analysis, writing orphaned, and separated at birth from the assistance of its father, is indeed what Plato condemned in the *Phaedrus*. If Plato's gesture is, as I believe, the philosophical movement par excellence, one realizes what is at stake here."[44] Derrida argues that the characteristics that the history of Western philosophy has generally identified as specific to writing are valid for all speech acts, for any marking practice and therefore for all experience: "For me every experience is, in a certain way, an experience of trace and writing."[45]

Because iterability is irreducible, every speech act always implies some non-self-identity and nonpresence. What happens is never identical with what one wishes to make happen. As a consequence, every speech act (or act *tout court*) implies, whether explicitly voiced or not, some forgiveness asked for and granted for this non-self-identity, this nonpresence, this inability to act as such in accordance with one's desire or intention. This asked-for and granted forgiveness is not the decision of a subject but takes place, as it were, before there is a subject, if indeed there has ever been one in the sense of a self-sufficient *basis or support* (in Latin, *subjectum*, in Greek *hypokeimenon*) which subtends our experiences and representations, such as the *ego cogito* (Descartes), the transcendental unity of apperception (Kant) or the self-positing I (Fichte).[46] Memorably, Geoffrey Bennington glosses Derrida's thesis about the inability to perform what one would like to perform in the following terms: "What makes it possible for a performative to be brought off 'happily' necessarily includes the possibility of recitation outside the 'correct' context; this necessary possibility means that it is never completely happy."[47] I have often asked myself if there is something idiomatically Jewish in this deconstruction of the performative utterance as "never completely happy," as a priori cut off from its roots.[48] One could, following the entire metaphysical tradition from Plato to Austin, denigrate this condition, interpret it as secondary and derived, as an accidental, even dangerous deficiency in relation to full presence and being rooted in a home, a lineage, a tradition. On the other hand, however, accepting this deconstruction as ineluctable could also provoke a certain laughter and compassion. While Derrida hesitated to identify the place from which he writes as Jewish ("I am one of those marranos who no longer say they are Jews even in the secret of their own hearts"),[49] he nonetheless held onto the Jewish joke (l'histoire juive) as a way of dreaming and reading *not only forgiveness, but also peace and life*—all three of which he thought together one day, as if in a leap of faith:

> This paradoxical agreement in the compassion that I imagine or dream between two Jews in the synagogue—is it not peace? Yes, it is peace, it is life: at bottom, this is the great forgiveness [*le grand pardon*], if there is one . . . And what is more comical than the great forgiveness as test and ordeal of the unforgivable? What is more alive, what better reconciliation? What an art of living![50]

What to make of these big words, "forgiveness," "peace," "life," suddenly brought together in a quasi-equivalence of the colon and the "is"? "Life: at bottom this is *le grand pardon*," implying, of course, that every day is and/or should be a day of atonement, which is also to say, a day of remembrance. (The French language renders the Day of Atonement, Yom Kippur, as "le Jour du Grand Pardon.")[51] In an interview he gave to *Le Monde* shortly before he died, Derrida confessed that he did not know how to die and that according to a great philosophical tradition this amounted to saying that he not know how to live: "No, I never learned-to-live. Absolutely not! Learning to live ought to mean learning to die . . . Less and less in fact. I have not learned to accept death."[52] Yet in the passage quoted above, without claiming to possess any such knowledge, he dares to dream or imagine "an art of living" in "this paradoxical agreement in the compassion . . . between two Jews in the synagogue." In this dreamed-of art of living, it would be mistaken to think of "*le grand pardon*" as a sublime, momentous, or enlightened act of courage or endurance, but really as something very comical. The comedy could certainly be interpreted in the sense of something light and not worthy of being taken seriously, but at the same time, like all good comedy, also as the vehicle of saying what cannot be said otherwise. By not attempting to say exactly what they mean to say to one another, by keeping a certain silence, these two longtime enemies reconfirm and are faithful to the *nonpresence*, the impossible forgiveness that is promised, Derrida thought, in the very gesture of speaking to one another on the Day of Atonement. Not only in deciding to speak to the enemy but also in speaking *allegorically* to him and/or her, would give forgiveness and laughter more rather than less chances of taking place. Why? Because it keeps the door open. There would be an allegorical way of speaking to the other which would allow what cannot be said nonetheless in a certain way to be heard. Why does Derrida link humor and complicitous laughter to forgiveness? Perhaps because in such laughter there is both a release of aggression and a momentary disarmament which in a discreet, inexplicable way *may* change something. "People," Simon Wiesenthal said, "who have laughed together do not want to kill one another anymore."[53]

A KIND OF COMPASSION

When speaking of the two Jews at the synagogue on the Day of Atonement, Derrida emphasizes not only comedy and laughter but also compassion, as indicated above. Perhaps the two enemies will have experienced some compassion for one another in the mutual confession that forgiveness between them is impossible. This compassion would be, Derrida thought, the precondition of a kind of forgiveness that filters through unconsciously. At least in one respect, this is reminiscent of Hegel's reading of forgiveness, which imagines a reciprocal recognition of two self-consciousnesses who identify with one another.[54] The reciprocal recognition between the two Jews who meet at the synagogue is, as it were, the shadow of the speculative economy of forgiveness: a confession of endless fraternal hate rather than infinite fraternal love. It is not the word of reconciliation (*Wort der Versöhnung*) but "inexpiable war and blame (of) one another, as if in a mirror."[55] And yet, Derrida seems to suggest only in the *silent* avowal of this inexpiable war and blame of one another does any forgiveness worthy of the name have a chance: "The test and ordeal that these two Jews undergo . . . is the radical impossibility of forgiveness. And yet . . . in this impossible, and commonly endured impossible forgiveness, in this common non-forgiveness, this mutual non-forgiveness, these two Jews, face to face (or without a third), experience, perhaps, a kind of compassion. Perhaps. And perhaps a kind of forgiveness filters unconsciously through this compassion, supposing that an unconscious forgiveness were not nonsense."[56] The repeated use of the word "perhaps" in this prophetic announcement of forgiveness is not a sign of tentativeness or irresolution but must be related to what he writes elsewhere of the arrival of the event and of the friendship to come.[57] In the passage quoted above the word "perhaps" is elevated, exalted even, for it corresponds to "the regime of a possible whose possibilization must prevail over the impossible."[58] For

Derrida, *the impossible does not have the last word.* Prevailing over the impossible is a thinking and saying of "perhaps," of the dangerous perhaps, which, in the passage cited above, is forgiveness of the unforgivable.[59] This forgiveness must be imagined to be unconscious, for if it were conscious it would enter into a circuit of economic exchange.

ANOTHER MODE OF TRANSMISSION

Reading Derrida's allegory of forgiveness, in particular, the kind of compassion of which he speaks, I cannot help but imagine the intonations of the two Jewish voices and perhaps also the look on their faces when they speak to one another. Were they smiling? Eleven years prior to the lecture in which he recounted and analyzed the joke about forgiveness, he was asked in an interview about his Jewish upbringing and inheritance. In this context, he also spoke memorably of nonconscious paths of transmission:

> The paths of this inheritance have to be extremely complicated to be passed along neither by genes, nor by a thematics, nor by language, nor by religious instruction. It can follow other trajectories. So what are they? It is very difficult to improvise an answer, but one can imagine that a community cut off from its roots can, by way of non-conscious paths, communicate with . . . a certain manner of managing its unconscious [*gérer son inconscient*], of reading, deciphering, living its anxiety [*inquiétude*]. All of this may give rise to a certain relation to the world, a certain attitude that compels [*pousse*] one to write in this way or that. I know I am giving a very inadequate answer concerning these trajectories, but it is the direction of these very singular trajectories that one must look in order to pose the question. That is, neither in the direction of religion, nor themes, nor language, nor content, but of another mode of transmission.[60]

It is very challenging to comment on a passage that so obviously touches on what is very intimate and difficult to speak of. Nonetheless, or perhaps for this very reason, I believe it is of extreme interest and importance. From a political point of view, this passage dismisses both religious and ethnic definitions of who and/or what is Jewish. It dismisses the traditional Halakhic Law of maternal inheritance (and orthodox conversion), the anti-Semitic definitions imposed by the Nuremberg Laws of 1935 as well as the secular apparently "inclusive" definitions of the current Israeli Law of Return, which include people of Jewish ancestry (children and grandchildren regardless of maternal lineage) but exclude those who may have converted to another religion. Derrida refuses to answer for the singularity of his Jewish inheritance, or Jewish inheritance in general, in terms of anything that would be manifest, public or supposedly identifiable, such as a language, thematics, content, genetic code, religious instruction, or conversion. It passes in a hidden way; its paths of transmission are "nonconscious." With regard to the direction he feels necessary to pose the question, he improvises a kind of half response that would somehow be true both for him as well as for others. The response is marked by an ellipsis (" . . . ") and a request for forgiveness ("I know I am giving a very inadequate answer"), making me wonder to what extent both of these might be facets of whom and/or what he is seeking to answer for. The response is preceded by "one can imagine," which makes clear that what follows would not be in the realm of anything that could be proven.

Among the very singular trajectories of this "other mode of transmission," one would have to include the relative specificity of a sense of humor and especially the laughter it produces.[61] The phrase "a certain way of managing one's unconscious" (*gérer son inconscient*) is noteworthy, even surprising, for it implies a *dominant* attitude toward the unconscious and even surprisingly a certain success. Elsewhere, Derrida does not hesitate to mark the unique success of the Jewish religion on a world scale and of "the small 'Jewish people'" whose unheard-of survival and resistance to attempts at extermination and demographic disproportion is, he believes, without historical analogue:

> There is more than one way of interpreting the unheard-of survival of the small "Jewish people" and the global extension [*rayonnement mondiale*] of its religion, single source [*source unique*] of the two monotheisms, which share in a certain domination of the world and of which, in dignity at least, it is the equal. There are a thousand ways of interpreting its resistance to attempts at extermination as well as to a demographic disproportion, the like of which is not known [*dont on connaît aucun autre exemple*].[62]

In making this claim Derrida lays himself open to the charge of Jewish exceptionalism, that is, the thesis that the Jews have a thoroughly unique historical position and role.[63] One can note that he does not claim that the

Jewish people have suffered more than other persecuted minorities or even that they have survived the longest. He considers the resistance of the Jews to be exceptional. No other people would have resisted attempts at extermination and demographic disproportion in a comparable way and, by implication at least, with the same success. Derrida is careful, of course, to put the category "Jewish people" in quotation marks, for to speak of this people as if they have existed as a single, unified, strictly identifiable group is arguably already to fall back into a thinking which can be called metaphysical and/or ontotheological—what Philippe Lacoue-Labarthe might have termed the restitution of a subject of history.[64] Like the German people, the "Jewish people" is a fiction, a dreamexistence. Thinking in such terms should at least be juxtaposed with the sketch given above of Jewish inheritance as "another mode of transmission," which is "passed along neither by genes, nor by a thematics, nor by language, nor by religious instruction." And yet, Derrida seems willing to take the risk of being accused of metaphysics or ontotheology and, what is perhaps related, Jewish exceptionalism, because he is worried about the survival of the Jews to come. For their sake, immediately following the passage above he asks a series of questions, which amount to nothing less than a prophetic warning:

> But what will come of this survival the day (already arrived, perhaps) when worldwidization [*mondialisation*] will be saturated? Then, "globalization," a term so frequently encountered in American English will perhaps no longer allow the surface of the human earth to be segmented into micro-climates, those historical, cultural, political micro zones, little Europe and the Middle East, in which the "Jewish people" had such great difficulty surviving and bearing witness to its faith. "I understand Judaism as the possibility of giving the Bible a context, of keeping this book readable," says Levinas. Does not the worldwidization of demographic reality and calculation render the probability of such a "context" weaker than ever and as threatening for survival as the worst, the radical evil of the "final solution"?[65]

It would be naïve to think that the only threat to the "Jewish people" today is the spread of anti-Semitism and, inseparable from it, the possibility of another Shoah. Threatening not only to the Jews but also to the survival of *every distinct culture and minority* today is "the worldwidization of demographic reality and calculation," which tends to reduce all regional and cultural specificity to a single "worldwide-latinized" idiom of political, juridical and economic exchange (see chapter 2). And yet, if it is true that this worldwidization threatens every culture and minority, it would pose a specific threat to the "Jewish people" or, more specifically, to Judaism, which, following Levinas, Derrida interprets as "the possibility of giving the Bible a context, of keeping this book readable." "As the unique source of the two monotheisms, which share in a certain domination of the world," Judaism would have a singular responsibility for giving the Bible the possibility of such a context. Perhaps it is in this sense that Derrida considers the resistance of the "Jewish people" to be exceptional, above and beyond their survival in the face of immemorial anti-Semitism. As Sigmund Freud recalled in 1938, and again in 1939, through the voice of his daughter Anna: "The nation's political misfortune taught it to value as its true worth the one possession that remained to it—its literature [*ihr Schriftum*]. Immediately after the destruction of the Temple in Jerusalem by Titus, the Rabbi Jochanan ben Zakkai asked permission to open the first Torah school at Jabneh. From that time onwards, the Holy Writ [*die heilige Sprache*] and intellectual concern with it were what held the scattered people [*das versprengte Volk*] together."[66] In the epoch of the (self-)deconstruction of Christianity, what will become of the "Jewish people" and their literature (*ihr Schriftum*)? In the microclimates of little Europe and the Middle East, it will have still always been possible to reinvent a "context" for the Holy Writ and the intellectual concern with it, even if these were places where the Jews lived for centuries under the constant threat of expulsion and annihilation. As both Freud and Heine attest, whenever they had to flee or hide, the scattered people always took their literature (*Schriftum*) with them and in so doing could bear witness to their faith even, if necessary, in secret, and indeed even when they could no longer read the Holy Writ and their only access to it was through (often inexact and anti-Semitic) translations or, dare I say, jokes. This, it should be noted, is a major difference concerning the survival of the "Jewish people" when compared with that of indigenous cultures such as the "Aboriginal people" of Australia, whose Holy Writ is inscribed in the land itself. When robbed of their land, they cannot so easily reinvent a "context" to guard what is most precious to them.[67]

With the globalization of demographic reality and calculation, however, Derrida believes the probability of such a "context" for the "Jewish people" also to be weaker than ever, that is, weaker paradoxically than during the centuries of demographic disproportion and extermination. Moreover, there is no evidence to suggest that he believed that the establishment of the State of Israel has in any way increased the probability of such a "context." Indeed, almost the contrary. Derrida took great interest in the apocalyptic concern raised by Gershom Scholem in his letter to Franz Rosenzweig in 1926 about the "actualization" (*Aktualisierung*) of biblical Hebrew, that is, the project, intrinsic to Zionism, of biblical Hebrew's modernization and transformation to the needs of everyday communication. This project was already under way from the beginning of the twentieth century. Derrida ends his fascinating essay on Scholem's letter by citing Stephane Mosès, who translated the letter into French and first brought it to Derrida's attention.

To say that the Torah is a divine text signifies that it is infinitely open "to interpretation. The day when 'the ancient names and seals'—today buried away in the unconscious of secular culture—will emerge anew into the light of day, no one can say how they will be re-interpreted. But the risk is great, according to Scholem, of seeing their return, after a long period of collective repression, take the form of an anarchic explosion of uncontrolled religious forces."[68] I would like to suggest that Derrida's elaboration of the concept of unconditional (as heterogeneous to conditional) forgiveness, of forgiveness of the unforgivable, can and should be read as in favor of the possibility of giving the Bible such "a context," of keeping this book readable in the course of worldwide-latinization, worldwide Christianization, in which he claims "the very dimensions of forgiveness tend to be effaced . . . and with it all measure and conceptual limitation."[69] Even though Derrida does not claim to speak "as a Jew" and, moreover, never declared biblical Hebrew to be one of his languages, in a singular way I would argue his work is concerned with the survival of the "small 'Jewish people.'" Without ever saying that he simply belongs to this people, he lays claim to "another mode of transmission," which is "passed along neither by genes, nor by a thematics, nor by language, nor by religious instruction." What can be said about such a "context" in relation to his elaboration of the concept of forgiveness can also be said of his concept of unconditional (as heterogeneous to conditional) hospitality,[70] as well as what he writes of sacrificial responsibility and the secret in Kierkegaard's *Fear and Trembling*,[71] and further, the envisaging of another Abraham after a parable from Kafka.[72] Not to mention the disseminative reinscriptions of his "secret" name, "*Elie*" (Elijah), the name of his circumcision: "(*eh! lis* [eh! read], *et lie* [and link], *élit* [elects], *et lit* [and read], *et l'I, elle y, l.I., l'Y* at the end of the double session)."[73] While he recognizes that in its origins the word "deconstruction" is more closely related to Christianity than to Judaism or Islam (he often notes that Heideggerian deconstruction [*Destruktion*] refers back to Luther's [*destruuntur*]), he testifies that "what is important to me, since always, would be a deconstruction of *this* deconstruction, of this "Christian" landscape of deconstruction."[74]

From the point of view of forgiveness, a rigorous concept is necessary, because it provides a measure, or what he calls, following Heidegger, a *dimension*[75] in relation to which one can judge abuses of the value of forgiveness, notably, those which make it the ally of the drive for closure and normalization. Without an appeal to a rigorous concept of forgiveness on unconditional grounds, it is impossible to denounce such abuses, which unjustly condemn the "Jewish people" among others for not feeling permitted and/or able to forgive, or which reduce forgiveness to a therapy of mourning, a necessary means for individuals or nations to "move on" from wrongdoing and trauma. If there were such a thing as forgiveness, it would have to be something else, another experience entirely, one which would not rely in the first instance on a subject's supposed power. By insisting above all on the distinction between the two orders (the conditional and the unconditional, knowledge and decision), which he recognizes are yet indissociable from one another, Derrida seeks to give measure and conceptual limitation to the Abrahamic values of law, hospitality and forgiveness in the course of worldwide-latinization (*mondialatinisation*): "We find here again the distinction between the two orders (indissociable but heterogeneous), which has preoccupied us since the beginning of this interview."[76]

THE ARAB, THE JEW

When Derrida utters the word "peace" in relation to forgiveness, he is perhaps also thinking about the so-called "peace process." It appears he will have said very little, almost nothing about it, other than expressing clearly the hope for a "political invention" in relation to the despair that recent events have not attenuated:

> I am among those who await this "political invention" in Israel, among those who call for it in hope, today more than ever because of the despair that recent events, to mention only them, have not attenuated

> (for example, though these are just examples from yesterday and today, the renewed support of colonial "settlements" or the decision by the supreme Court authorizing torture, and, more generally, all the initiatives that suspend, derail, or interrupt what continues to be called, in this manner of speaking, the "peace process").[77]

In reading and recounting a Jewish joke about forgiveness on the Day of Atonement, it is quite possible that Derrida is also speaking about what he elsewhere calls, in a footnote from an essay on denials, "the Jew, the Arab":

> If one day I had to tell my story, nothing in this narrative would start to speak of the thing itself if I did not come up against this fact: for lack of capacity, competence or self-authorization I have never been able to speak of what my birth, as one says, should have made closest to me: the Jew, the Arab.
>
> This small piece of autobiography confirms it obliquely. It is performed in all of my foreign languages: French, English, German, Greek, Latin, the philosophic, metaphilosophic, Christian, etc.[78]

If Derrida's thinking is predicated on a nonfinite experience of "lack of capacity, competence or self-authorization," if this is the basis on which he thinks many, if not all, of his keys concepts, (forgiveness, gift, invention, hospitality, democracy to come, messianism without messiah, reading, etc.), then by his own suggestion they should all be linked to that about which he apparently says nothing, that is, "the Jew, the Arab." As if the folds of this singular "avoidance" were a cryptic name for what he calls the thing itself (without quotation marks). One awaits a reading to come, which will follow the folds of this avoidance in, or rather, as the Derridean text.[79] As Jill Robbins has astutely pointed out with relation to the essay cited above on avoidance and denials: "In a manner rigorously consistent with the logic of negative theology, Derrida speaks of the Jewish and Islamic traditions by not speaking about them. He refers to these other traditions as 'an internal desert,' an "immense place left empty," and within his essay, he speaks of Heidegger in place of this place."[80] The reference to Heidegger in this context is not accidental, of course. Derrida's "avoidance" with regard to what he calls "the Arab, the Jew" in a certain way recalls that of Heidegger, who one day during a seminar in 1951 announced: "If I were yet to write a theology, as I am sometimes tempted to do, the word 'being' ought not to appear there."[81] In the essay cited above "How to Avoid Speaking: Denials," Derrida reads Heidegger in the following terms: "With and without the word being, he wrote a theology with and without God. He did what he said it would be necessary to avoid doing. He said, wrote, and allowed to be written exactly what he said he wanted to avoid. He was not there without leaving a trace of all these folds."[82] Derrida's thinking of forgiveness, particularly in its most innovative aspect, that is, that which reads forgiveness as inscribed in the very first speech act, would not be possible without Heidegger's thought, especially, that of the "*Zusage*": Heidegger's reading of the deployment of language as a grant, promise, or pledge (*Zusage*).[83] If Derridean deconstruction is a deconstruction of Heideggerian (and by extension, Lutheran) deconstruction, of this "Christian," intrinsically anti-Semitic landscape of deconstruction, then it can and should be read as an immense test of the impossibility of forgiveness. If Derrida wrote hundreds of pages about Paul de Man and Maurice Blanchot (who both had dalliances with anti-Semitism), he wrote thousands of pages about Heidegger, the path through whose meditation he memorably said is "uncircumventable" (*incontournable*).[84] Since the recent publication of the Black Notebooks (2014), it is difficult to deny that Heidegger's anti-Semitism is of another order to that of Maurice Blanchot or Paul de Man. Beyond being only complicit with that of the Nazis, for whom the Jews were still a "people" or a "race" to be exterminated, Heidegger links his philosophical anti-Semitism to what he calls "the history of Being," which is not reducible to that of any given entity (such as a race or people): "The question of the role of world Jewry (*Weltjudentum*) is not a racial question, but the metaphysical question about the kind of humanity that, without any restraints, can take over the uprooting of all beings from being as its world-historical 'task.'"[85] In the final pages of this book it is scarcely possible in any seriousness to analyze the terrible passages from the Black Notebooks which bear witness to an anti-Semitism at once indissociable from that of the Nazis, but in certain respects even more radical and extreme (if such were possible). By allying anti-Semitism to his reading of Western metaphysics and the ontological difference, Heidegger gave to anti-Semitism a philosophical depth and radicality well beyond that of the other Nazi ideologues for whom he had contempt.[86] As Jean-Luc Nancy has convincingly argued, Derrida was not unaware that Heidegger did in his way share the anti-Semitism popularized by the Nazis in Germany during the 1930s, despite the efforts Heidegger and many of his readers had made to conceal it.[87] However, Derrida did not know of the passages from Heidegger's private Black Notebooks, which were first published in German a decade after Derrida's death. About these Black Notebooks, Nancy writes with probity:

> One must ask oneself why Heidegger had excluded from all his published texts the claims made in his private notebooks concerning what Peter Trawny, their editor, very rightly named "historial anti-Semitism" [*antisémitisme historial,* Peter Trawny's formulation in German is *seinsgeschichtlicher Antisemitismus,* anti-Semitism of the history of Being][88] . . . To [this] question, one can sketch a provisional response: Heidegger excluded all mention of anti-Semitism (and anti-Judeochristianity) from his writings because he knew in so doing it would commit him to establishing that anti-Semitism must play a structural role in the thought of the destiny of the West, which could put this thought into an impasse (*dans l'embarras*). In avoiding this [ ] enterprise, Heidegger showed that he could not or did not dare to take the risk–despite himself, as it were, even while he would guessed the inconsistency of so doing. He touched therefore a limit of his thought.

Nancy then goes on to draw out the consequence of his argument:

> Is this limit not still ours, if we think little or badly the fundamental—spiritual as Lacoue-Labarthe would say—constitution of anti-Semitism in the West?[89]

In the very specific terms in which Derrida insists that the question of Jewish inheritance should be posed, "passed along neither by genes, nor by a thematics, nor by language, nor by religious instruction," what would be the Jewish specificity of the joke about forgiveness, if there were any? If as its elementary condition of possibility a trace must be repeatable, "iterable," as Derrida says, outside of its supposedly original context, then any specificity, be it Jewish or otherwise, is never pure or absolute, but only ever regional and relative, such as, for example, the references in the joke to the synagogue on the Day of Atonement and indirectly the Talmudic law whereby faults toward one's fellow human beings can be forgiven by God only if they have been forgiven beforehand by those who have been sinned against. Could today or tomorrow the same joke be told by a Jew and a Palestinian and yet still provoke laughter?

Yes, I would venture to say that perhaps it could, but only if both were sensitive to this *other mode of transmission*, which is linked in laughter to acceptance of and compassion for the impossible. And yet, given this is a *Jewish* joke, whose transmission for Derrida is taken as the exceptional condition for peace and forgiveness, even life, would this not in the context of the Middle East "peace process" amount inevitably to a prioritization and hierarchalization of one side over the other? Yes, in all likelihood, that is true. And perhaps this is a limit of Derrida's thought, unless one imagines that in deconstructing itself in humor, Jewishness is or will be something more and other than the name, identity, and privileged possession of an identifiable group of people, be they victimized, victimizing and/or both.

THE FORGIVENESS TO COME

No doubt the historical event that goes under the name of the Holocaust (among others) will have also been passed along through nonconscious paths of transmission. I daresay today more than ever these paths remain to be read and reread with great care and tact. The dreamed-of forgiveness between two "Jews," who are perhaps "Germans" and/or "Arabs," on the Day of Atonement will not take place in any present but only in a future anterior dreamexistence. Derrida writes: "These two Jews will have forgiven one another." The messianic temporality of this dreamed-of forgiveness must be juxtaposed to that forgiveness analyzed in chapter 4 in the scene between Wiard Raveling and Vladimir Jankélévitch: "One senses the unaltered conviction, unalterable, that even when forgiveness of the inexpiable will have taken place, in the future, in the generations to come, it will not have taken place, it will have remained illusory, inauthentic, illegitimate, scandalous, equivocal, mixed with forgetting (even when its subjects are and believe themselves to be sincere and generous)."[90] This foreseeable but illusory, illegitimate, equivocal "forgiveness" of the future is also what Jean Améry calls "the monstrosity of the natural time sense" (*das Ungeheure und Ungeheuerliche des natürlichen Zeitgefühls*), against which he deems it necessary to revolt, even as he recognizes in despair the powerlessness of this revolt.[91] As is true for Derrida, Jankélévitch, Wiesenthal, and so many others who lived through the twentieth century, Améry recognizes the great danger of the "natural time-sense," which is, one might say, the common enemy of so many thinkers and survivors:

> Your question about the date, the signature and the generation, lead me to think, with some horror that perhaps, in two or three generations, all this will have been relativized, if not forgotten, and that the Shoah will find its place as one episode, among so many others, of the murderous violence within humanity: there have been other genocides before or after, the Bible is full of horrifying violence, of nations who destroy one another. So one knows that perhaps, in the future, this will be, if not erased or forgotten, at least classed, relativized by being classed.[92]

If one were to juxtapose this foreseeable and yet horrifying "forgiveness" of the future with that dreamed of between the two speakers in the joke, one may identify two different temporalities: the first corresponding to an inexorable movement of history, which will lead to relativization and normalization, and ultimately forgetting of the *inassimilable character* of the horrors of the past; and the second, more prophetic, messianic, an interruption of history—"the forgiveness to come" ("*à venir*").[93] Contrary to appearances, "the forgiveness to come" does not refer to any foreseeable forgiveness that may happen in the future but rather to the impossibility of any foreseeable forgiveness as transmitted by the laughter and compassion of a joke. This joke is "an unfathomable story, a story that seems to stop on the verge of itself, a story whose development consists in interrupting itself, in paralysing itself in order to refuse itself all *avenir*."[94]

In the gap between "forgiveness" of the future (*avenir*) and forgiveness to come (*à venir*), one can also distinguish two different experiences of the impossible: one in which it is suppressed and forgotten, and the other in which it is welcomed unconditionally—even celebrated in a certain way. In the suppression and forgetting of the impossible, there is, Derrida suggests, no chance of forgiveness or gift worthy of the name. One might be tempted to write "no chance of 'authentic' forgiveness." But rather than referring to authenticity, Derrida repeatedly says "worthy of the name." This not only implies distance from a certain reading of Heidegger but also lays emphasis on the call for another way of speaking, for a renewal of respect for the promise of language and, in particular, of the name. "Worthy" should probably be read in the Kantian sense of dignity (*Würde*), as that which is not reducible to any market price.[95]

"Forgiveness to come" may also be read in an erotic sense, recalling the often concealed, uncanny relationship between erotic attachment and forgiveness to which both Hannah Arendt and Nietzsche testify, as was indicated briefly in the introduction. Because in Derrida's understanding forgiveness cannot be enacted in the present as such by two parties who consciously agree to forgive one another; the event of forgiveness, if there is any, is *inseparable from the desire and longing for forgiveness.* Forgiveness is a longing, which can have—perhaps always has—some eroticism attached, recalling René Char's magnificent thesis about "the poem" as "the realized love of desire remained desire."[96] One keeps open the possibility of forgiveness more faithfully by refusing to reconcile or forgive in any conventional, that is, metaphysical or ontotheological sense. If it happens, it must each time invent its language and its secret.

In the final words of her eulogy for Jacques Derrida, Hélène Cixous laid emphasis on Derrida's care and respect for language: "'Someone [*un type*] who pays attention to what he says,' he told me one day of Heidegger as also of himself. Attention to what he says."[97] The forgiveness Derrida has perhaps shown and learned from reading Heidegger, through the extreme care he has taken to read him (more than anyone in the twentieth century, one might well argue), would be echoed by the care he recognizes that Heidegger himself takes in his published texts: "'One never gets bored with Heidegger,' he says, 'a guy [*un type*] who pays attention to what he says,' he laughs."[98] How to read the trace of this laughter, which Cixous took great care to record? Could one imagine such laughter as the trace of a joke shared between them? Shortly after, while still echoing Derrida, Hélène Cixous writes in her own name:

> One never gets bored with any Jacques Derrida, I say. It is the able-to-pay attention to what you say that excludes boredom . . . the guy who pays attention to what he says is someone who pays attention to the other; to where he puts his words down. Carefulness, compassion, love.[99]

Sometimes I ask myself if scholarship has no higher purpose and justification than the transmission of this commitment to pay attention to the other by paying attention to what one says, and perhaps also sometimes to laugh. If protestation were the privileged mode of spoken exchanges between Derrida and Sarah Kofman, between Derrida and Hélène Cixous there was, there dreamexisted, an assent without reserve. A celebrated scholar in her own right, for many years Cixous faithfully listened and recorded what

Derrida said to her. She also recorded his dreams, believing in how important they will have been.

In his eulogy for Jacques Derrida, Samuel Weber, a close friend who wrote extensively about Freud's analysis of the joke (*der Witz*),[100] suggested an association between Jewish jokes and what Derrida, following Heidegger, in a long footnote of *Of Spirit* called *die Zusage.*[101] *Die Zusage* (in French, *le gage*) is the quasi-originary pledge—the commitment or promise both *of* and *to* language—to which we must have already assented before we pose any question about the essence of language. *Die Zusage* is the advance (in both senses) of language, its condition of having being already both addressed and entrusted to us "before" we speak. Speech cannot not be a (re)confirmation of this prior pledge of and to language. In his essay entitled "The Nature of Language" ("Vom Wesen der Sprache"), Heidegger went so far as to characterize thinking itself, before all questioning, as a listening to this pledge ("Das Denken [ist] ein Hören der Zusage").[102]

Weber precedes his seemingly mad but, for me, very thought-provoking suggestion linking the Heideggerian *Zusage* to Jewish jokes, by arguing that one of the particularities of such jokes is that, generally speaking, they are not directed against the other, as, for example, Belgian jokes in France and Polish jokes in Germany, but rather against the one who speaks. In Jewish jokes the speaker may allow themselves to be laughed at—a gesture which could well be interpreted as a sort of compassion towards all involved. In the same eulogy, Weber recalled Derrida's wish to reread Heidegger in a way that would give place to laughter, as if the permission to laugh were one of the un-thoughts, the highest gifts of Heidegger's thought. Samuel Weber writes:

> Such [Jewish] jokes, and especially the laughter that they release, for me seem to be associated with what [Derrida] calls the "grant" [*le gage*] in a long footnote in *Of Spirit.* In this reading of Heidegger, Jacques Derrida goes beyond or behind the questioning attitude or posture, which had been for Heidegger "the piety of thought," to discern a promise "in language—and therefore in *a particular* language [*une langue*]." This promise refers to a "grant," which "precedes language," without "being foreign to it." In this note, he proposes a re-reading of Heidegger on the basis of the "grant" and its "call" (*Zusage*).[103]

Inasmuch as Derrida suggests (even in the very recounting of the joke about the two Jews in the synagogue) that for him speaking and/or listening to the other is *already* a gesture of forgiveness, it seems clear that he understands forgiveness in terms of this pre-original grant or promise (*Zusage*), what he elsewhere names following Nietzsche, Joyce, and a few others, the "yes" or "yes, yes."[104] On what basis then could one think an alliance between Jewish humor and especially the laughter that it releases, and this quasi-originary "yes" or "yes, yes" of thought and language? The answer lies perhaps in what Jewish humor in its regional specificity retains of the prophetic and the messianic: the experience of unspoken compassion in the shared recognition of the impossible, in unconscious forgiveness perhaps and/or forgiveness to come. Perhaps.

> "What could the old lady have said? Does she perhaps know when we will get out of here? Or when they are going to slaughter us?"
>
> "Nobody knows the answers to those questions. But she said something else, something that we should perhaps think about in times like these. She thought that God was on leave [*daß Gott auf Urlaub sei*]." Arthur paused for a moment in order to let the words sink in. "What do you think of that, Simon?" he asked. "God is on leave."
>
> "Let me sleep," I replied. "Tell me more when He gets back." ("*Erzähl weiter, wenn Er wieder zurück ist.*")
>
> "For the first time since we had been living in this stable I heard my friends laughing, or had I merely dreamt it?"[105]

Afterword

What an Art of Living!

Dear Professor,

Part of me would love to be finished with this book and move onto the next chapter of my life. Not finishing holds me back, etc. But, as you know from wherever you are, there's no being finished with this . . . You didn't like to talk too much about the Holocaust, reminding people that much of what is usually said about it is not specific to it, and that one need not to refer to this event to make many of the same arguments about memory, responsibility, testimony, and so on. Provocatively, you even used the word "holocaust" a few times (without a capital letter) to describe things that apparently had nothing to do with it, like the burning of love letters and the gift.[1] And yet, you admitted that you were a man of your time and that if you spoke, for example, of survival and incineration as elementary structures of experience and "forgiveness of the unforgivable," the Holocaust was naturally what people thought of, and you too, at least for the time being.[2]

No doubt you were in a way, yet to be analyzed, inscribing the historicity and finitude of your thought—and its chances to come.

When I first heard you speak about forgiveness, pure forgiveness no less, I was a little shocked. It came to me as an impermissible thought, not that you said anything about it directly, but you spoke of two Jews of the twentieth century, a French man and a German woman, both of them nonbelievers. I remember it like yesterday. Arendt, of course, I had heard of, but not the other one. It took me a long time to learn even how to spell his name. Shortly after the war you recounted that he thought that forgiveness was possible, but then sixteen years later, absolutely not: "Forgiveness died in the death camps," he said. I liked the sound of this guy who dared to be inconsistent. But then you said something that really triggered me: the younger Jankélévitch was more on the side of the future than the older one. So *you* think forgiveness is possible? That made me very angry. Your daughter, dare I say, wasn't allowing any questions. So I was kind of stuck with it.

I spent some time in Berlin, as many do these days. It's easy to travel, especially if you're lucky enough to have a grant. But still I had to go. I met a man called . . . *felicis, felicitas*: the lucky one. Fateful you could say. A dancer. He invited me to a house in Poland and something happened there of an erotic character mixed with violence. Then I came back with a mad certainty that this is the "topic" I wanted to explore. There was no talking me out of it. Everybody advised me against it. Or nearly. Not your daughter. Whenever anyone asks me what I'm writing about, what "the book" is on, and I try to tell them, they immediately think that it has something to do with my family. But this is terrible also in a way . . . People think they know you (or at least I imagine they do) as one with some kind of disability, who can't help but talk about that interminably. I know it's a strong word, especially in English: dis-ability. But what some activists today call "ableism," or the able-centrism of Western culture and philosophy, hasn't that also been one of your most insistent concerns?

Forgive me for writing to you like this. Forgive me also for writing so much about your work. People will think asking for forgiveness is a rhetorical ploy. Well, yes and no. Perhaps it's hubris to think that one has the permission to ask for forgiveness. If it's truly forgiveness, maybe one can't know if one is asking for it. I tend to think that that's probably also true. In your opening remarks one day at Cerisy-la-Salle, you said to your friends, your close readers: "For what you have given me during these ten days, I not only thank you. I forgive you." Now that was audacious. Recalibrating almost immediately, you added: "But who can authorize himself to forgive? Let's say I ask pardon for you, of you yourselves, for you yourselves."[3]

I get into difficulties from talking too much about your work. And I feel guilty about it. Like a *shoah,* dare I say, it should be kept quiet. Shhh. I think people don't want to hear me talk about you all the time. Your friend Levinas said once: "When I read him, I always recall the exodus of 1940 . . . everything is deconstructed and devastated."[4] *Entre nous,* was that some kind of Jewish joke? I remember how you shuddered when you saw me one day at NYU in 2002. I think you were feeling guilty. But still it was nice you remembered me, and no doubt what happened and didn't happen between us. "You are not dis-empowered enough," your daughter would say to me.

Forgive me, but I would also like to speak to Sarah, uniquely. Professor Kofman? Do you remember I was your student when you left us? People teased me at the time, saying I must have driven you to it. I laughed uncontrollably when I first heard. Suicide is an occupational hazard they never tell you about when you first begin your studies. Much later during a performance in Berlin, I felt I had to tell them what I thought forgiveness was—how it dreamexists (in) my life, beyond, as it were, scholarship. Certainly it has to do with humor, the economy of "pleasure given by the superego, the forgiveness that it in some sense grants . . . since, thanks to these 'gifts,' the diminished 'I' finds itself if not euphoric, at least lifted back up (*regonflé*)."[5] To give the audience some idea, I told them a story about the laughter that arrived in me one night when I couldn't do what I wanted to do, which happened to be writing:

"It was a Saturday evening and I was faced with the decision, do I go out and have a good time? Or do I stay home and work? I thought, Well, okay, I'll stay at home and work; it'll be a good idea; I haven't done enough work. Seven o'clock, eight o'clock, nine o'clock, ten o'clock, eleven o'clock, I was all alone, and I wasn't working. It was too late to go out. I felt rather sad about this. I felt my evening was shot. I hadn't gone out to have a good time, and I hadn't worked. And my superego was becoming very aggressive. I started to hate myself. It got worse and worse. So I thought, all right, I'll just lie down and breathe. Usually a good strategy, because it calms you down, helps you concentrate. So I lay down and started breathing. No, it didn't work. I got only more and more depressed. Then while I was lying down trying to breathe, I had a thought. And the thought was, 'I'm depressed,' or more likely, it was, 'you're depressed, so what?' And then after a moment I laughed. It's hard to explain. It's something seemingly very banal. I kind of said 'so what' to my situation. And then I laughed. I associate that with forgiveness. It wasn't a conscious act. It wasn't something done for the purpose of feeling better. It was just breaking with the whole logic of you work or you play; you do one or the other for some sort of return, for something to come back to you. What I was doing, nothing was coming back to me, and I laughed. It so happened very shortly afterward that I found myself working. But that wasn't the point. After I laughed, I was still depressed. It wasn't as if the evil disappeared, but something changed, swerved you might say, very slightly. I think that's what I mean by forgiveness. It's not a conscious act. It's not me saying: 'I'm sorry, would you forgive me?' And you saying, 'Yes, I'll forgive you' or remaining silent. It's more unexpected, more enigmatic and mysterious." Not without pain, searing pain, like death. But it's not death. Why not call it life? Of course, I know I can't presume to tell you what forgiveness is or what it really means, or even at the limit what I mean. It's always tempting to fill the gap, especially at the "end." Please forgive me. I was not laughing at myself. It was laughing at a certain logic to which I found "I" had been submitted, as when with Bataille you spoke so beautifully one day of laughing at philosophy (at Hegelianism),[6] a certain audacity of hopelessness rather than hope. Very close, I imagine, to the one that drives you to kill, but rather opens you with laughter or tears.

Sydney, 14 August 2016

Acknowledgments

First, I thank Dimitris Vardoulakis for insisting that I publish this book and for introducing me to Tom Lay, acquisitions editor at Fordham University Press, who has supported me throughout. Much of this book was written during the period 2006–9, while I had the good fortune to live and study in New York City and Berlin. This was made possible with support from the Graduate School of Arts and Sciences at New York University, the Leo Baeck Institute in New York, the German Academic Exchange Service (DAAD), and the Free University of Berlin.

Avital Ronell, Jean-Luc Nancy, Geoffrey Hartman, Werner Hamacher, Bruce Gardiner, Irmela von der Lühe, Ulrich Baer, Paul Fleming, Melinda Cooper, Magdalena Zolkos, Avril Alba, Jill Scott, Dennis Klein, Sebastian Job, Nicola Jungsberger, Dasniya Sommer, Natalia Jerzmanowska, and Felix Ruckert have each in singular ways motivated and accompanied this research along the aporetic paths it has taken. For generously proofreading drafts and helpful suggestions I also thank Wayne Stamp and Robyne Conway.

The love of my family goes beyond words: my parents, Marlene and George Banki; my sister, Dallis Wilkes; Sammy and Brett; and the memory of my grandfather Tibor Berger.

Notes

Preface

1. "It is therefore . . . a structural element in the realm of human affairs, that men are unable to forgive what they cannot punish and that they are unable to punish what has turned out to be unforgivable" (Hannah Arendt, *The Human Condition* [Chicago: U of Chicago P, 1998], 241).

2. One of the inspirations of this book was attending Avital Ronell and Jacques Derrida's "Seminar on Violence and Forgiveness" at New York University in the fall of 2002. Rather than simply reproducing the title of his seminar in Paris, "Le pardon et le parjure" ("Forgiveness and Perjury"), Derrida began by recognizing the necessity of Ronell's insistence on thinking violence and forgiveness together. For reasons given in chapter 2, I will be following Derrida's use of the term "worldwidization" as the translation of the French *mondialisation,* rather than the more familiar "globalization."

3. Primo Levi, *The Voice of Memory: Interviews, 1961–1987,* ed. Marco Belpoliti and Robert Gordon, trans. from the Italian by Robert Gordon (New York: New Press, 2001), 111.

4. Primo Levi, *The Reawakening* (1965; New York: Touchstone, 1995), 197.

Introduction: To Forgive the Unforgivable

1. Ingeborg Bachmann, *The Book of Franza and Requiem for Fanny Goldmann,* trans. Peter Filkins (Evanston: Northwestern UP, 2010), 130; Ingeborg Bachmann, *Das Buch Franza/Requiem für Fanny Goldmann* (Munich: Piper, 1995), 126. The novel fragment was first published in 1979 under the title *Der Fall Franza.* Hereafter cited as *The Book of Franza and Requiem for Fanny Goldmann,* with the first page number referring to the English version; the second to the German.

2. "She no longer knew how to put her reasons into a sentence that would make sense, for the reason could not be made available [der Grund war nicht

flüssig zu machen], in no speech" (*The Book of Franza and Requiem for Fanny Goldmann*, 129/125, translation modified).

3. See Sigrid Weigel, *Ingeborg Bachmann. Hinterlassenschaften unter Wahrung des Briefgeheimnisses* (Vienna: Zsolnay, 1999), 13–15. See also Sigrid Weigel, "Secularization and Sacralization, Normalization and Rupture: Kristeva and Arendt on Forgiveness," trans. Mark Kyburz, *PMLA* 117.2 (2002): 323.

4. Bachmann, *The Book of Franza and Requiem for Fanny Goldmann*, 134/128

5. The name "Franza" resonates with the name "Franz Kafka." At the end of *A Hunger Artist* (1924), at the moment where the hunger artist is about to die from self-imposed starvation, he also makes a strange request for forgiveness, which is interpreted as a sign of insanity: "'Forgive me, everybody' ['Verzeiht mir alle'], whispered the hunger artist; only the overseer, who had his ear to the bars, understood him. 'Of course,' said the overseer, and tapped his forehead with a finger to let the attendants know what state the man was in, 'we forgive you' ['wir verzeihen dir']" (Franz Kafka, *Erzählungen, Taschenbuchausgabe in 8 Bänden*, ed. Max Brod [Frankfurt: Fischer, 1989], 199).

6. Jean Améry, "Resentiments," from *Jenseits von Schuld und Sühne* (*Beyond Guilt and Atonement*), translated into English by Sidney Rosenfeld and Stella P. Rosenfeld as *At the Mind's Limits: Contemplations by a Survivor on Auschwitz and Its Realities* (Bloomington: Indiana UP, 1980), 75, 80; Jean Améry, *Werke Band 2* (Stuttgart: Klett-Cotta, 2002), 138. Ingeborg Bachmann was familiar with the work of Jean Améry. She referred to his essay "Über die Tortur" ("On Torture") in "Drei Wege zum See" ("Three Paths to the Sea") (see *Ingeborg Bachmann, Gesamtausgabe*, ed. Christine Koschel, Inge von Weidenbaum, und Clemens Münster [Munich: Piper, 1995], 2:421). Survivors of torture and other atrocities cite the Améry quote above as an accurate and exemplary testimony of their experience (see, for example, "Spokes in the Wheel: An Account of Torture," *Tikkun* 22.3 [May/June 2007]: 36–39; and Imre Kertész, "Who Owns Auschwitz?," trans. John Kay, *Yale Journal of Criticism* 14.1 [2001]: 268–69).

7. Ingeborg Bachmann, *Das Buch Franza/Requim für Fanny Goldmanm*, 131/126.

8. Jacques Derrida, *Apories: Mourir—s'attendre aux limites de la vérité* (Paris: Galilée, 1996). See also Rodolphe Gasché, "L'expérience aporétique aux origines de la pensée: Platon, Heidegger, Derrida," trans. Georges Leroux, in *Études Françaises* 38.1–2 (2002): 103–21.

9. "When talking about this book *weiter leben* in German or *Still Alive* in English to German audiences, I was invariably confronted with the anxious question whether I could 'forgive.' It was not clear whether I was to forgive the perpetrators or all Germans . . . How can I 'forgive' the murder of my teenage brother when I have had my life, and he didn't get to have his? And perhaps the

adult I am now cannot forgive even in the name of the child I was then. This was not a free decision, I would explain: it was simply not in my power to grant the kind of absolution that is implied in the plea or demand for forgiveness" (Ruth Klüger, "Forgiving and Remembering," *PMLA* 117.2 [March 2002]: 311).

10. Sarah Kofman, "Shoah (or Dis-grace)," in *Selected Writings,* ed. Thomas Albrecht et al. (Stanford: Stanford UP, 2007), 245–46. Sarah Kofman, "Shoah (ou la Dis-Grâce)," *Les Nouveaux Cahiers* 95 (Winter 1988–89): 67.

11. G. W. F. Hegel, *Elements of the Philosophy of Right,* ed. Allen W. Wood, trans. H. B. Nisbet (Cambridge: Cambridge UP, 1991), 325; G. W. F. Hegel, *Werke,* vol. 7, *Grundlinien der Philosophie des Rechts,* ed. Eva Moldenhauer and Karl Markus Michel (Frankfurt: Suhrkamp, 1970), 282.

12. "The deed still subsists, but only as something past, as a fragment, as a corpse. That part of it which was bad conscience has disappeared, and the remembrance of the deed is no longer that conscience's intuition of itself; in love, life has found life once more" (G. W. F. Hegel, "The Spirit of Christianity and Its Fate," in *On Christianity: Early Theological Writings,* trans. T. M. Knox [New York: Harper Torchbooks, 1961], 239).

13. Kofman, "Shoah (or Dis-grace)," 245–46.

14. By "Holocaust," I refer to the project of extermination of the Jewish, Sinti, and Roma peoples, the physically and mentally handicapped, and other targeted groups (including homosexuals and Jehovah's Witnesses) during World War II. Thought-provokingly, there are several names for the Nazi project of extermination, each, as it were, implying a different reading: the Greek *Holocaust* (wholly burnt offering); the Hebrew *Shoah* (annihilation) and *Churban* (devastation); the lesser-known Romani *Porrajmos* (the Devouring), and the Nazi *Endlösung* (Final Solution). It is as if no one name were able to name what has happened. "The Holocaust has often consisted in an attempt to erase the names, to erase the proper names, not only to put people to death, but also the archive . . . the first gesture was to restore, to gather, and to keep the names, as if the names were really the very thing that the extermination was aimed at. So, at the same time identity and memory, the possibility of calling" (Jacques Derrida, "An Interview with Professor Jacques Derrida," Shoah Resource Center, the International School for Holocaust Studies, 10, online, www.yadvashem.org).

15. Ruth R. Kok, *Statutory Limitations in International Criminal Law* (Cambridge: Cambridge UP, 2007), 37–61.

16. On the critical role played by Simon Wiesenthal in the comparatively late decision of the West German government to abolish statutory limitations for crimes against humanity, see Hella Pick *Simon Wiesenthal: A Life in Search of Justice* (Boston: Northeastern UP, 1996), 206–11. See also Vladimir

Jankélévitch, "Pardonner?," in *L'imprescriptible* (Paris: Éditions du Seuil, 1986). On Ingeborg Bachmann's public statements in favor of the abolition of statutory limitations, see Hans Höller, *Ingeborg Bachmann* (Hamburg: Rowolt, 1995); and also Simon Wiesenthal, *Verjährung? 200 Persönlichkeiten des öffentlichen Lebens sagen nein: Eine Dokumentation* (Frankfurt: Europäische Verlagsanstalt, 1965).

17. Kok, *Statutory Limitations in International Criminal Law*, 115.

18. Jacques Derrida, "Le siècle et le pardon," in *Foi et savoir* (Paris: Éditions du Seuil, 2007), 127; Derrida, *On Cosmopolitanism and Forgiveness*, trans. Mark Dooley and Michael Hughes (London: Routledge, 2001), 53, translation lightly modified, italics mine.

19. "On Forgiveness: A Roundtable Discussion with Jacques Derrida," in *Questioning God*, ed. John D. Caputo et al. (Bloomington: Indiana UP, 2001), 55–56.

20. Immanuel Kant, "Die Streit der Fakultäten," in *Immanuel Kant's Sämmtliche Werke*, ed. Karl Rosenkranz und Friedrich Wilhelm Schubert (Leipzig: Leopold Voss, 1938), 10:339–57. Derrida had undertaken an extended reading of this text in "Mochlos: or, the Conflict of the Faculties," in *Logomachia: The Conflict of the Faculties*, ed. Richard Rand (Lincoln: U of Nebraska P, 1992), 1–34.

21. I will return to this in chapter 3, in "The Self-Evidence of the Logic . . ." section.

22. "Here the signified always already functions as a signifier. The secondarity that it seemed possible to ascribe to writing alone affects all signifieds in general, affects them always already, the moment they *enter the game*. There is not a single signified that escapes, even if recaptured, the play of signifying references that constitute language . . . This, strictly speaking, amounts to destroying the concept of 'sign' and its entire logic" (Jacques Derrida, *Of Grammatology*, trans. Gayatri Chakravorty Spivak [Baltimore: Johns Hopkins UP, 1997], 7; Jacques Derrida, *De la grammatologie* [Paris: Éditions de Minuit, 1967], 16).

23. Kant, "Die Streit der Fakultäten," 10:351.

24. When he visited Yad Vashem in Jerusalem, Derrida admitted that "when I speak of forgiveness, of hospitality, it is always by reference to this event [i.e., the Shoah]" ("An Interview with Professor Jacques Derrida." Shoah Resource Center, 4). And yet, as an idea, forgiveness is not reducible to any particular historical event. "Idea" should, I argue, be read as "Idea in the Kantian Sense" derived from the readings of Edmund Husserl that Derrida undertook in the 1960s. The "Idea in the Kantian sense" is posthistorical or post-temporal: "totally open, opening itself . . . the most powerful structural *a priori* of history,

the very birth of history and the sense of becoming in general . . . structurally genesis itself" (Jacques Derrida, *L'écriture et la différence* [Paris: Seuil, 1967]; English translation by Alan Bass, *Writing and Difference* [Chicago: U of Chicago P, 1978]. 250/267). For an excellent reading of "the Idea in the Kantian Sense" in Derrida, see Leonard Lawlor, *Derrida and Husserl: The Basic Problem of Phenomenology* (Bloomington: Indiana UP, 2002). See also Paola Marrati, *Genesis and Trace: Derrida Reading Husserl and Heidegger*, trans. Simon Sparks (Stanford: Stanford UP, 2005).

25. Derrida, "Le siècle et le pardon," 111, 119–20; Derrida, *On Cosmopolitanism and Forgiveness*, 45, 36, translation modified. I will return to the motif of the madness of forgiveness in chapter 4, in the "Tensions and Contradictions in Forgiveness" section.

26. Jankélévitch, "Pardonner?," 50–53.

27. This prohibition can be found, for example, in Rabbinical Judaism: "God's forgiveness, however extensive, only encompasses those sins which man commits directly against Him, "*bein adam la-Makom*." Those in which an injury is caused to one's fellow man, "*bein adam le-havero*," are not forgiven until the injured party has himself forgiven the perpetrator . . . In rabbinic thought, only the offending party can set the wrong aright and only the offended party can forgo the debt of the sin" (Rabbi David Rosen, "The Concept of Forgiveness in Judaism," online, www.rabbidavidrosen.net). See also Dan Cohn-Sherbok, *Judaism: History, Belief, Practice* (London: Routledge, 2003). For more on this prohibition, see chapter 1 of this volume, "Must Forgiveness Be a Speech Act?"

28. "After the war priests, philanthropists, and philosophers implored the world to forgive the Nazis . . . The priests said indeed that the criminals would have to appear before the Divine Judge and that we could therefore dispense with earthly verdicts against them, which eminently suited the Nazis' book. Since they did not believe in God they were not afraid of Divine Judgment. It was only earthly justice that they feared" (Simon Wiesenthal, *The Sunflower: On the Possibilities and Limits of Forgiveness* [New York: Schocken, 1998]). Cf. Donald Shriver, *An Ethic for Enemies Forgiveness in Politics* (Oxford: Oxford UP, 1995).

29. "In the spirit of *ubuntu*, the central concern is the healing of breaches, the redressing of imbalances, the restoration of broken relationships and a search to rehabilitate both the victim and the perpetrator who should be given the opportunity to be reintegrated into the community, which he has injured by his offense" (Desmond Tutu, *No Future without Forgiveness* [New York: Image, 2004], 55). Mark Sanders has suggested that Tutu's reference to *ubuntu* displaces the meaning of the concept of forgiveness: "It is no longer simply

Christian, or even religious . . . not simply unconditional or conditional, but the very condition of possibility for human-being" (Mark Sanders, *Ambiguities of Witnessing: Law and Literature in the Time of a Truth Commission* [Stanford: Stanford UP, 2007], 96–97).

30. *Forgiving Doctor Mengele*, a film by Cheri Pugh and Bob Hercules, First Run Features, 2005; hereafter cited as FDM. The quotations that follow from Eva Mozes Kor and her family have been transcribed from the documentary.

31. Eva Mozes Kor's taboo-breaking gesture has been given consideration in at least one recent study on forgiveness in relation to the Holocaust (see Hanna-Barbara Gerl-Falkovitz, *Verzeihung des Unverzeihlichen? Ausflüge in Landschaften der Schuld, der Reue und der Vergebung* [Dresden: Bibliotek der Unruhe und des Bewahrens, 2006], 3; see also Eva Mozes Kor and and Mary Wright, *Echoes from Auschwitz* [Terre Haute: CANDLES, 1995]).

32. For more information, see www.candlesholocaustmuseum.org.

33. Like many Holocaust survivors, Eva Mozes Kor testifies in an idiom that does not always obey the norms and conventions of English grammar. This is a delicate and complex issue that I will not explore here, except to note that it sometimes adds to the strength of her testimony. "Things are done to us; we have no power over it." She could have said: "We have no power over the things that are done to us," but then the pause, or rather, the abyss between these two statements would be inaudible. For more on the aporias of testimonial speech, see Jacques Derrida, "Demeure: Fiction and Testimony," in *The Instant of My Death,* trans. Elizabeth Rottenberg (Stanford: Stanford UP, 2000), 41–43; and Shoshana Felman and Dori Laub, *Testimony: Crises of Witnessing in Literature, Psychoanalysis, and History* (New York: Routledge, 1992).

34. Jacques Derrida, *H. C. for Life, that is to say . . .* , trans. Laurent Milesi and Stefan Herbrechter (Stanford: Stanford UP, 2006), 157. See also Hélène Cixous, *Insister of Jacques Derrida,* trans. Peggy Kamuf (Stanford: Stanford UP, 2006), 142. I will come back to this important concept in chapter 2, and also in the conclusion.

35. Friedrich Nietzsche, *The Genealogy of Morals,* trans. Walter Kaufmann and R. J. Hollingdale (New York: Vintage, 1989), 72–73; Friedrich Nietzsche, *Kritische Studienausgabe,* vol. 5, ed. Giorgio Colli and Mazzino Montinari (Berlin: Deutscher Taschenbuch Verlag de Gruyter, 1988), 309.

36. Ibid. Eva Mozes Kor announced that she had forgiven Josef Mengele after his death in Bertioga, Brazil, in 1979 had been confirmed beyond doubt by DNA testing of his corpse in 1992.

37. Jean-Francois Lyotard, *The Differend: Phrases in Dispute,* trans. Georges Van Den Abbeele (Minneapolis: U of Minnesota P, 1989), 106. What happens when Nazism is interpreted as "a mad dog," which for Lyotard designates

what is beyond philosophical engagement, refutation and rational dismissal? Well, the first thing one could say is that if Nazism is a mad dog, then philosophical rationality and engagement is itself not safe. It can also be bitten and become rabid. Philosophy is not simply beyond Nazism. It can be infected. (In this regard, how can one not think of Heidegger?) Lyotard is not the only philosopher who links Nazism to animals. During a tirade against the possibility of forgiveness of the Holocaust, Jankélévitch, for example, also wrote: "No, forgiveness is not for swine and their sows. Forgiveness died in the death camps" (Jankélévitch, "Pardonner?," 51; Jankélévitch and Hobart, "Shall We Pardon Them?," 555). Cf. Jean-François Lyotard *Heidegger and "The Jews"* trans. Andreas Michel and Mark S. Roberts (Minneapolis: U of Minnesota P, 1990); and Jacques Derrida, *The Animal That I Therefore Am,* trans. David Wills (New York: Fordham UP, 2008).

38. "Can we become more humane and overcome our resentments without needing to consign our trespassers to the realm of parasites, worms or little insects we disdain to crush? Derrida sees this as the fundamental question of forgiveness, since 'a forgiveness worthy of its name,' as he puts it, 'would be a forgiveness without power . . . without sovereignty'" (Michael Ure, "The Politics of Mercy, Forgiveness and Love: A Nietzschean Appraisal," *South African Journal of Philosophy* 26.1 [2007]: 64).

39. Derrida, "Le siècle et le pardon," 107–8; trans. Mark Dooley and Michael Hughes, *On Cosmopolitanism and Forgiveness,* 31–32, translation modified.

40. Eva Mozes Kor's understanding of forgiveness is in this sense not incompatible with that of Hannah Arendt, who claims that forgiveness as "the undoing of what was done" is necessary in human relations in order to preserve our capacity to act. Arendt was, however, reluctant to extend her concept of forgiveness to "radical evil," i.e., "to offences which transcend the realm of human affairs and the potentialities of human power, both of which they radically destroy whenever they make their appearance" (Arendt, *The Human Condition,* 240–41).

41. What is not mentioned in the documentary is that Münch was later twice indicted, first for comments made in an interview with *Der Spiegel* in 1998, and later in France as a consequence of derogatory statements about the Roma and Sinti during an interview with the French radio *France-Inter* in 2001. Although he was acquitted by the Bavarian justice ministry due to "progressed dementia" for the comments made in the *Der Spiegel* interview, for the comments about the Sinti and Roma he was convicted for "incitement of racial hatred" and "belittlement of crimes against humanity."

42. In *The Wanderer and His Shadow* (1879) Nietzsche writes: "Finally, he will refrain from revenge in the not uncommon case that he loves the

perpetrator: he will thus lose honour in the perpetrator's eyes, to be sure, and will perhaps become less worthy of being loved in return. But to renounce even all claim to love in return is a sacrifice which love is prepared to make if only it does not have to hurt the beloved being: this would mean hurting oneself more than any sacrifice hurts" (Friedrich Nietzsche, *Human All Too Human: A Book for Free Spirits,* trans. R. J. Hollingdale [Cambridge: Cambridge UP, 1996], 318; Friedrich Nietzsche, *Kritische Studienausgabe,* vol. 2, ed. Giorgio Colli and Mazzino Montinari [Berlin: Deutsche Taschenbuch Verlag de Gruyter, 1988], 567). "Only love has the power to forgive . . . by reason of its passion, [it] destroys the in-between which relates us to and separates us from others as long as its spell lasts . . . only love is fully receptive to *who* somebody is, to the point of being always willing to forgive him whatever he may have done" (Arendt, *The Human Condition,* 242–43).

43. Dan Bar-On, *Fear and Hope: Three Generations of the Holocaust* (Cambridge: Harvard UP, 1995); Dan Bar-On, *Legacy of Silence: Encounters with Children of the Third Reich* (Cambridge: Harvard UP, 1989); Dan Bar-On, *The Indescribable and the Undiscussable. Reconstructing Human Discourse after Trauma* (Budapest: CEU Press, 1999).

44. In chapter 1, in the section "The Speculative Economy of Christian Confession," I will return to some of Hegel's major texts on forgiveness: *The Phenomenology of Forgiveness* and *The Spirit of Christianity and Its Fate.* Hegel's thinking of forgiveness (both as asked for and granted) is grounded in the capacity of the self-conscious subject to recognize itself in the other.

45. Derrida in response to John Milbank, "On Forgiveness: A Roundtable with Jacques Derrida," in *Questioning God,* 69. On the gaze of the cat as infinitely other, see Jacques Derrida, *L'animal que donc je suis* (Paris: Galilée, 2006), 18–32.

46. Compare Nietzsche's characterization of "*the last men*" in *Thus Spoke Zarathustra*: "'We invented happiness'—say the last human beings, blinking. / They abandoned the regions where it was hard to live: for one needs warmth. One still loves one's neighbor and rubs up against him: for one needs warmth . . . One is clever and knows everything that has happened, and so there is no end to their mockery. People still quarrel but they reconcile quickly—otherwise it is bad for the stomach. / One has one's little pleasure for the day and one's little pleasure for the night: but one honors health. / 'We invented happiness' say the last human beings, and they blink" (Friedrich Nietzsche, *Thus Spoke Zarathustra,* trans. Adrian Del Caro [Cambridge: Cambridge UP, 2006], 10; Friedrich Nietzsche, *Kritische Gesamtausgabe,* pt. 6, vol. 1, ed. Giorgio Colli and Mazzino Montinari [Berlin: Walter de Gruyter, 1968], 13–14).

47. Jacques Derrida, *Béliers: Le dialogue ininterrompu: Entre deux infinis, le poème* (Paris: Galilée, 2003); translated by Thomas Dutoit as "Rams," in *Sovereignties in Question: The Poetics of Paul Celan* (New York: Fordham UP, 2005), 74/160. Unlike Dutoit, I have translated *mélancolie* as "melancholia" rather than "melancholy" to underline the pathological aspect.

48. "In mourning it is the world which has become poor and empty; in melancholia it is the ego itself." "When the work of mourning is completed the ego becomes free and uninhibited again" (Sigmund Freud, "Mourning and Melancholia" [1917], in *The Standard Edition of the Complete Psychological Works of Sigmund Freud,* ed. James Strachey [London: Hogarth, 1953–74], 14: 244–45; Freud, *Gesammelte Werke,* 10:430–31). For a rethinking of the distinction between mourning and melancholia, see Nicolas Abraham, "The Shell and the Kernel: The Scope and Originality of Freudian Psycho-analysis" (1968), in Nicolas Abraham and Maria Torok, *The Shell and the Kernel: Renewals of Psychoanalysis,* vol. 1, ed. Richard T. Rand (Chicago: U of Chicago P, 1994), 79–99.

49. Jean Améry, "Resentiments," in *At the Mind's Limits: Contemplations by a Survivor on Auschwitz and Its Realities* (Bloomington: Indiana UP, 1980), 138.

50. "He writes: 'We are finally sick and tired of hearing again and again that our fathers killed six million Jews. How many innocent women and children did the Americans murder with their bombings, how many Boers did the British murder in the Boer War?' This protest confronts us with a moral vigor that is sure of its cause. One scarcely dares to object that the equation "Auschwitz = Boer internment camp" is faulty moral mathematics" (ibid., 75–76). Recalling the words of Thomas Mann: "No matter how terrible Communism may at times appear, it still symbolizes an *idea* of man, whereas Hitler-Fascism was not an idea at all, but depravity [*Schlechtigkeit*]" (ibid., 31). Consider also his position on Nazi torture and sadism: "Torture was no invention of National Socialism. But it was its apotheosis . . . The Nazis tortured, like others, because by means of torture they wanted to obtain information important for national policy. But in addition they tortured with the good conscience of depravity [*Schlechtigkeit*]" (ibid.). As is also true for Derrida, for Améry the worst evils are done with the self-certainty of good conscience.

51. For a critical reading of Améry's ethics of *ressentiment,* see chapter 1 of this volume, "The Survival of the Question" section.

52. See chapter 3 of this volume, "The Self-Evidence of the Logic . . ." section.

53. For Freud, "normal" mourning is work (*Trauerarbeit*). As such, it implies from its beginning a *telos* or end.

54. I have decided not to include a reading of Paul Celan's famous *Todtnauberg* (1970), which testifies to Celan's meeting with Martin Heidegger in his

hut in the Black Forest in 1967. Several contemporary readings of the poem, including that of Derrida, have questioned the priority given to the theme of the poet's disappointed expectation and have focused rather on the motif of the gift of the poem as of a forgiveness asked for, granted and/or to come. I feel I have nothing to add to these fine studies. See, for example, James K. Lyon, *Paul Celan and Martin Heidegger: An Unresolved Conversation* (Baltimore: Johns Hopkins UP, 2006); Axel Gellhaus, *Paul Celan bei Martin Heidegger in Todtnauberg* (Marbach am Necker: Literaturhaus Museum, 2002); and Derrida, "To Forgive: The Unforgivable and the Imprescriptible," in *Questioning God*, 36–37.

55. "We desire a fragment of human history and one, indeed, that is drawn not from past but future time" (Kant, "Die Streit der Fakultäten," 10:339).

1. The Survival of the Question: Simon Wiesenthal's The Sunflower

1. Simon Wiesenthal, *Die Sonnenblume: Eine Erzählung von Schuld und Vergebung* (Frankfurt: Ullstein, 1998), hereafter cited as SB. The text appeared in English translation as Simon Wiesenthal, *The Sunflower: On the Possibilities and Limits of Forgiveness* (New York: Schocken, 1998), hereafter cited as SF. Throughout this essay, I quote from the English translation and modify it where it is misleading. When modifying or when the German text is not translatable without remainder, I also include the German in brackets. I cite page numbers from both editions.

2. "Whether or not you are an agnostic or a believer, I do not know, but your problem belongs to the realm of guilt and atonement . . . [Your] problem is a *theological* one, and as such it does not exist for me because I am an atheist who is indifferent to and rejecting of any metaphysics of morality. I think that this is not about individual forgiveness or individual intransigence [*Unversöhnlichkeit*] . . . Since I see the question of forgiveness only in political terms, I must abstain either from approving or condemning your behavior . . . Politically, I do not want to hear anything about forgiveness. For one simple reason, what you and I went through must *not happen again, never, nowhere.* Therefore I refuse any reconciliation with criminals" (SB 219–20; SF 107–8).

3. I quote the passage in German in full, as parts of it do not appear in the English translation: "Hätte ich, hätte überhaupt jemand, ihm verzeihen sollen, verzeihen dürfen? Aber die Welt von Heute verlangt von uns, daß wir auch denjenigen verzeihen, die uns durch ihre Haltung immer wieder provozieren. Sie verlangt von uns, daß wir einen Schlußstrich ziehen, als sei nichts Wesentliches geschehen. Und viele von uns, die in jener grauenvollen Zeit gelitten haben und die sich manchmal noch in ihren Gedanken jener Hölle verhaftet fühlen, sind vor diesem Verlangen nach Verzeihen verstummt. Diese Frage

wird alle Prozesse überleben und auch dann noch aktuell sein, wenn die Verbrechen der Nazis längst einer fernen Vergangenheit angehören. Deshalb richte ich sie an Menschen, von denen ich glaube, daß sie etwas zu sagen haben. Sie soll als Aufruf dienen. Denn das Geschehen, das sie hervorgebracht hat, kann sich wiederholen" (SB 107–8).

4. For a critique of the notion of performative utterances, see Jacques Derrida, "Signature, Event, Context," in *Margins of Philosophy*, trans. Alan Bass (Chicago: U of Chicago P, 1986). See also Werner Hamacher, "Afformative, Strike," trans. Dana Hollander, *Cardozo Law Review* 13.4 (December 1991).

5. Some readings resist this temptation. See, for example, Elisabeth de Fontenay in Simon Wiesenthal, *Les fleurs de soleil* (Paris: Albin Michel, 2004), 199–213. For an appraisal of the different responses in English, see John K. Roth, "Who Needs Forgiveness? Further Thoughts on the Moral Dilemma Posed by Simon Wiesenthal's *The Sunflower*," in *Anti-Semitism: The Generic Hatred: Essays in Honor of Simon Wiesenthal*, ed. Michael Fineberg et al. (London: Vallentine Mitchell, 2007), 165–76.

6. Ruth Klüger: "How can I 'forgive' the murder of my teenage brother when I have had my life, and he didn't get to have his? And perhaps the adult I am now cannot forgive even in the name of the child I was then. This was not a free decision, I would explain: it was simply not in my power to grant the kind of absolution that is implied in the plea or demand for forgiveness" (Ruth Klüger, "Forgiving and Remembering," *PMLA* 117.2 [March 2002]: 311). In response to Wiesenthal, Primo Levi wrote: "You did right . . . But, of course, nothing is resolved through this refusal, and it is understandable that you were left with doubts" (SB 143; SF 191).

7. "Les fautes de l'homme envers Dieu sont pardonnées par le Jour du Pardon; les fautes de l'homme envers autrui ne lui sont pas pardonnées par le Jour du Pardon, à moins que, au préalable, il n'ait apaisé autrui" (Michna Yoma [85a–85b] qtd. in Emmanuel Levinas, *Quatre lectures Talmudiques* [Paris: Éditions de Minuit, 1997], 29). "The faults of man toward God are forgiven by the Day of Atonement; faults towards one's fellow man are not forgiven by the Day of Atonement, unless the fellow man has been appeased beforehand" (translation mine).

8. "Guilt [*Schuld*] can never be discharged by another person, so far as we can judge according to the justice of our human reason. For this is no transmissible liability which can be made over to another like a financial indebtedness [*Geldschuld*] (where it is all one to the creditor whether the debtor himself pays the debt or whether someone else pays it for him); rather is it the most personal of all debts, namely a debt of sins [*Sündenschuld*], which only the culprit can bear and which no innocent person can assume even though

he be magnanimous enough to wish to take it upon himself for the sake of another" (Immanuel Kant, *Religion within the Limits of Reason Alone* [1793], trans. Theodore M. Greene and Hoyt H. Hudson with John R. Silber [New York: Harper Torchbooks, 1960], 67, translation modified). "I don't want the mother to embrace the oppressor who threw her son to the dogs! She dare not forgive him! Let her forgive him for herself, if she will, let her forgive the torturer for the immeasurable suffering of her mother's heart. But the sufferings of her tortured child she has no right to forgive . . . [T]oo high a price is asked for harmony" (Fyodor Dostoyevsky, *The Brothers Karamazov*, trans. Constance Garnett [New York: Lowell, 1969], 269).

9. This is Jacques Derrida's position (see J. Derrida, "On Forgiveness: The Unforgivable and the Imprescriptible," in *Questioning God,* ed. John D. Caputo, Mark Dooley, and Michael J Scanlon [Bloomington: Indiana UP, 2001], 45–46).

10. Maurice Blanchot, *L'écriture du désastre* (Paris: Gallimard, 1980), 89. See also Sara Guyer's reading of this passage in "The Pardon of the Disaster," *SubStance* 35.1 (2006): 85–105.

11. "The person who forgives . . . does not profit from the advantageous position that his innocence confers upon him, he does not keep for himself this privilege of alone being infallible, impeccable and irreproachable, and he renounces every monopoly that he may have upon this position, he sacrifices therefore [*il fait le sacrifice*] a very brief and precarious superiority which perhaps is due to chance" (Vladimir Jankélévitch, *Philosophie morale* [Paris: Flammarion, 1998), 1146]; Vladimir Jankélévitch, *Forgiveness,* trans. Andrew Kelly [Chicago: U of Chicago P, 2005], 161–62).

12. I will explore this possibility further below.

13. "I knew how the story would end. My own country had been occupied by the Germans for over a year and we had heard of similar happenings in Bialystok, Brody, and Gródek. The method was always the same. He could spare me the rest of his gruesome account" (SB 48; SF 41).

14. "The encounter with him was a heavy burden on me, his confession had profoundly disturbed me [*mich im Innersten aufgewühlt*]" (SB 63; SF 55). One may juxtapose the SS man's address with that of Pope Jean-Paul II in the year 2000. In Rome, and later in Jerusalem before the Western Wall, the pope addressed his repentance for the violence and intolerance of those in the Catholic Church *to God,* with the Jewish people as a witness. For the role of the Vatican *Curia*, and in particular, Alois Hudal (the German bishop in Rome), in helping Nazis escape to South America after the war, see Hella Pick, *Simon Wiesenthal: A Life in Search of Justice* (Boston: Northeastern UP, 1996), 127–28. For the pontiff's historic address, see "Liturgy of Repentance"

in *Catholic Teaching on the Shoah* (Washington: United States Catholic Conference, 2001).

15. The term "speculative" is employed here in both senses: economic and philosophical.

16. Simon Wiesenthal, *Les fleurs de soleil,* trans. Denise Meunier (Paris: Stock, 1969). The first German edition appeared a year later: Simon Wiesenthal, *Die Sonnenblume* (Hamburg: Hoffman and Campe, 1970).

17. Simon Wiesenthal outright rejected the thesis of collective guilt as a fundamental principle of his work. He justifies this decision in the following terms, which are worth citing at length: "To begin with: Even though I have not spoken my prayers in the language of the Bible since childhood, I am deeply aware of the moral value of biblical subject matter. In the story about Sodom and Gomorrha Abraham wrestles with God saying, if there are only ten just individuals, or nine, or eight, or seven—then don't destroy them. God answers: There are no just individuals. Abraham's struggle here was a struggle against collective guilt. Nothing that stands in the Bible is accidental, and I recognized that I must reject the idea of collective guilt. Secondly: We Jews have been the victims of the collective guilt theory for 2000 years, and we have stood up against it. Why should contemporary Jews, who were not alive 2000 years ago, be held responsible for the death of Jesus on the cross? These two considerations have led me to consistently stand up against collective guilt with respect to the Germans, the Austrians, or other nationalities for more than 40 years. My work in the Documentation Center is aimed at pointing out individual guilt and it thus stands as the categorical antithesis to collective guilt" (qtd. in Maria Sporrer and Herbert Steiner, *Simon Wiesenthal: Ein unbequemer Zeitgenosse* [Vienna: Orac, 1992], 66–67).

18. G. W. F. Hegel, *Phänomenologie des Geistes* (Hamburg: F. Meiner, 1988), 345; G. W. F. Hegel, "The Beautiful Soul, Evil and Its Forgiveness," in *The Phenomenology of Spirit,* trans. A. V. Miller (Oxford: Clarendon, 1977), 405.

19. For more on the fundamental role that Hegel gives to language as *Logos* throughout the phenomenology, see Jean Hyppolite, *Genèse et structure de la phénoménologie de l'esprit de Hegel* (Paris: Aubier, 1946), 1:146; 226–27.

20. In an important early theological text, "The Spirit of Christianity and Its Fate," Hegel also treats the dialectic of the remission of sins. There he writes: "Before the law the criminal is nothing but a criminal . . . but because punishment does not come from an alien law, since on the contrary it is from man that the law and the right of fate first arise, a return is possible to the original situation, to wholeness. For the sinner is more than a sin existent, a character that has committed a crime [*eine Persönlichkeit habendes Verbrechen*], he is a man, crime and fate are in him. He can return to himself again" (G. W. F.

Hegel, *Frühe Schriften* [Frankfurt: Suhrkamp, 1986], 353–54; G. W. F. Hegel, *Early Theological Writing,* trans. T. M. Knox [Philadelphia: U of Pennsylvania P, 2011], 238).

21. Hegel, "The Beautiful Soul, Evil and Its Forgiveness," 407. In "The Spirit of Christianity and its Fate," Hegel makes the same point even more vividly: "The deed [*Tat*] still subsists, but only as something past, as a fragment, as a corpse [*tote Trümmer*]. That part of it which was a bad conscience has disappeared, and the remembrance of the deed is no longer that conscience's intuition of itself; in love, life has found life once more" (Hegel, *Early Theological Writings,* 238–39). *Der Geist des Christentums,* ed. Werner Hamacher (Frankfurt: Ullstein, 1978), 451–52.

22. Hegel, *Early Theological Writings,* 240, translation modified

23. Pick, *Simon Wiesenthal: A Life in Search of Justice,* 78.

24. "I admit I had some pity [*Mitleid*] with the fellow" (SB 92, SF 83); "Vorhin habe ich noch etwas wie Mitleid mit dem Sterbenden empfunden" (SB 54).

25. "*emporter le paradis économiquement*" (Charles Baudelaire, *La Fausse Monnaie,* see J. Derrida, *Donner le temps 1: La Fausse Monnaie* [Paris: Galilée, 1991]).

26. Pick, *Simon Wiesenthal: A Life in Search of Justice,* 223.

27. Elisabeth de Fontenay in Wiesenthal, *Les fleurs de soleil,* 201.

28. Charles Baudelaire, "Au lecteur," in *Fleur du mal* (Paris: Gallimard, 2002).

29. Pick, *Simon Wiesenthal: A Life in Search of Justice,* 78.

30. Jacques Derrida, "Il n'y a pas le narcissisme," in *Points de suspension: Entretiens* (Paris: Galilée, 1992), 222–23; Jacques Derrida, *Points: Interviews 1974–1994,* ed. Elizabeth Weber, trans. Peggy Kamuf (Stanford: Stanford UP, 1995), 209.

31. Speaking of this gesture, Derrida says: "I believe that, on the contrary out of respect for the Shoah, it is a way of rethinking ethics, politics, philosophical discourse on the basis of categories that seem to us most appropriate to the Shoah." A study yet to be undertaken would be required to analyze what is at stake in this gesture, which is important not only for the reading of Derrida, but more generally. Derridean categories such as the cinder, living on (*survivance*), testimony and forgiveness (of the unforgivable) are, on the one hand, valid par excellence for designating the Shoah. On the other hand, they could be articulated in the same way had there been no Shoah, for they designate elementary structures of experience and communication. The same is true for categories such as trauma, persecution, "Thou shalt not kill" in the philosophy of Emmanuel Levinas, as Derrida in the same interview does not fail to

point out. Everything happens as if to keep the memory of the uniqueness of the Holocaust, it was necessary to accept and even hasten the disappearance of the simulacrum of "the Holocaust" as a unique, intact, "sacred," that is, unscathed signifier or signified. See "An Interview with Professor Jacques Derrida" (recorded at Yad Vashem in Jerusalem in 1998, www.yadvashem.org). In the afterword I return to this.

32. One day Jacques Derrida memorably resumed this aneconomical exigency in the following terms: "Pour que ça gagne, il faut que ça se perde. On peut dire que ça gagne, tout en restant sur le côté de ce qui se perde." ("For it to win, it must lose itself. One can say that it wins, and yet remain on the side of what loses itself.") This was said during an international conference, "Passions de la littérature avec Jacques Derrida," which I attended at the Université Catholique de Louvain from 24 to 29 July 1995. It was in response to a debate that arose concerning whether to accentuate the "neither nor" (*ni . . . ni*) or the "both . . . and" (*et . . . et*). For Derrida, the "neither . . . nor" is prior.

33. Vladimir Jankélévitch, "Le pardon," in *Philosophie morale*, 997–1148. See also Alain Gouhier, "Le temps de l'impardonable et le temps du pardon selon Jankélévitch," in *Le Point Théologique, Forgiveness,* proceedings of the colloquium organized by the Centre Histoire des Idées, Université de Picardie, ed. Michel Perrin (Paris: Beauchesnes, 1987). I will return to the hyper-ethical in the thought of Jankélévitch in chapter 4.

34. Wiesenthal's other autobiographical novel, *Max und Helen* (Frankfurt: Ullstein, 1981), also contains dream reports and is attentive to the question of unconscious motivations.

35. Jacques Derrida, "Force of Law: the Mystical Foundations of Authority," *Cardozo Law Review* 11.919 (1990): 944.

36. While in the death block at Mauthausen: "I realized that I only had a few days to live, or at best a few weeks and yet I remembered the SS man again and his confession. His eyes were no longer completely hidden; they looked at me through small hole in the bandages. There was an angry expression in them. He was holding something in front of me—the bundle that I had refused to accept from the nurse. I must have screamed" (SB 87; SF 78).

37. It is estimated that more than 1,100 Nazi war criminals were bought to trial, thanks to Wiesenthal's work for more than sixty years in the Dokumentationszentrum in Vienna. During the celebration of his ninetieth birthday, Wiesenthal asked his audience please not to make a hero out of him ("Bitte, macht aus mir keinen Helden"). The reason for this, one can argue, is that, more than his achievements, his life and work bear witness to religious, ethical, and political aporias and the silences that accompany them. For more information, see Simon Wiesenthal, *Antisemitism: The Generic Hatred: Essays in Memory of*

Simon Wiesenthal (United Nations Educational Scientific and Cultural Organization; Verbe et Lumière-Vigilance, 2007); and *I Have Never Forgotten You: The Life and Legacy of Simon Wiesenthal*, documentary video directed by Richard Trank and Marvin Hier [Simon Wiesenthal Center, 2007]).

38. "I thought of my own mother who would never write me another letter. Five weeks previously she had been dragged out of a ghetto in a raid" (SB 35; SF 29).

39. "Das versöhnende Ja . . . ist der erscheinende Gott mitten unter ihnen, die sich als das reine Wissen wissen" (Hegel, *The Phenomenology of Spirit*, 409). The manifestation of God at the conclusion of the dialectic of evil and its forgiveness marks the transition from the sphere of morality to that of religion, of which Christianity is highest moment, superseding Judaism.

40. "An uncanny feeling [*unheimliches Gefühl*] overcame me. I did not know whether this unreal scene was actuality or dream. Here was I in the ragged clothes of a concentration camp prisoner in the room of the former Dean of Lemberg High School—now a military hospital—in a sickroom which must be in reality a death chamber [*Sterbezimmer*]" (SB 32; SF 34). And again after the meeting: "Suddenly I was assailed by a doubt as to the reality of all this. Had I actually been in the Dean's room that day? It all seemed to me doubtful and unreal as our whole existence in those days . . . it could not have been all true; it was a dream induced by hunger and despair [*Verzweiflung*] . . . it was too illogical—like the whole of our lives" (SB 75–76; SF 76). The meeting itself is designated as ghostly: "Again and again my thoughts returned to that ghostly encounter [*gespenstischen Begegnung*]" (SB 64; SF 64).

41. Sigmund Freud, *Der Mann Moses und die monotheistische Religion* (Frankfurt: Fischer, 1999), 164; Sigmund Freud, *Moses and Monotheism*, trans. Katherine Jones (London: Hogarth, 1939), 147.

42. I will return to the hypothesis of forgiveness as a consequence of a certain laughter—or dream of laughter—in the book's conclusion: "Forgiveness as a Jewish Joke."

43. Jacques Derrida, *Demeure: Fiction and Testimony*, trans. Elizabeth Rottenberg (Stanford: Stanford UP, 2000), 29–30. For a detailed meditation on the political and philosophical dilemmas posed by testimony, see Jean-Francois Lyotard, *The Différend: Phrases in Dispute* (Minneapolis: U of Minnesota P, 1988); and Avital Ronell, "The Differends of Man," in *Finitude's Score: Essays for the End of the Millennium* (Lincoln: U of Nebraska P, 1998), 255–68.

44. For this reason, the book burnings also, which took place all over Germany at the beginning of Hittlerism, must also be understood related to the Holocaust (see "An Interview with Professor Jacques Derrida," Shoah Resource Center, The International School of Holocaust Studies, online, www.yadvashem.org).

45. "Le monde, ce n'est ni l'univers, ni le cosmos. Même quand saint Paul a parlé de *cosmos* pour designer le monde Chrétien, il affectait le mot de *cosmos* d'une nouvelle signification signifiant l'ordre de créatures, de la fraternité des hommes comme prochain, etc. . . . quand on dit mondialisation il faut se rappeler cette mémoire qui est à la fois théologique et philosophique et le mot de globalization perd la référence à cette mémoire-là" ("Philosophie et mondialisation," Rencontre de Jacques Derrida et Etienne Balibar, in *Philosophie, Philosophie* [Revue des Etudiants de Philosophie Paris] 8.7 [2007]: 21, translation mine). For more on the motif of the "deconstruction of Christianity" and the thesis of worldwidization (*mondialisation*) as Christianisation, see chapter 2 of this volume, "The Worldwidization of Forgiveness . . ." section.

46. Jean Améry, "Resentiments," in *At the Mind's Limits: Contemplations by a Survivor on Auschwitz and Its Realities* (Bloomington: Indiana UP, 1980), 75, 80. At the conclusion of his famous essay "On Torture," Améry makes another decisive reference to the "world": "Whoever has succumbed to torture can no longer feel at home [*heimlich*] in the world. The shame [*Schmach*] of destruction cannot be erased. Trust in the world, which already collapsed in part at the first blow, but in the end, under torture, fully, will not be regained . . . One who was martyred is a defenseless prisoner of fear. It is *fear* that hence-forth reigns over him. Fear—and also what is called resentments. They remain, and have scarcely a chance to concentrate into a seething, purifying thirst for revenge" (ibid., 40).

47. J. L. Austin, *How to Do Things with Words* (Oxford: Clarendon, 1969). See also John R. Searle, *Speech Acts* (Cambridge: Cambridge UP, 1969).

48. Améry, "Resentiments," 81. The same anti-Hegelian revolt against history is also discernable in Améry's meditation on suicide, and in particular, in his contestation of what he calls "the logic of life": "It's nice to assume that the housemaid or Pavese or Celan would have been saved and taken into therapy, that all three would have unanimously proclaimed they had only been deranged for a moment, and that now everything is fine. Forgiven, forgotten . . . But what does this prove? Really just that fact that, after successful therapy, they are different people, but not that they became better and more respectable ones. Here is the place, I think, to put a stop to temporality and historicity" (Jean Améry, *On Suicide: A Discourse on Voluntary Death*, trans. John D. Barlow [Bloomington: Indiana UP, 1999], 10–11).

49. "Fifty years after liberation, I, Eva Mozes Kor, in my name only hereby give amnesty to all Nazis who participated directly or indirectly in the murder of my family and millions of others, because it is time to forgive, but not to forget. It is time to heal our souls" (Eva Mozes Kor in *Forgiving Doctor Mengele*; see introduction to this volume).

50. On the concept of "hostipitality," see the conclusion of this volume. "Any ethics that is not aware—or does not run the risk—of its exposure to the *an-* or *un*-ethical disqualifies itself and is, in that sense, unethical" (Hent de Vries, *Philosophy and the Turn to Religion* [Baltimore: Johns Hopkins UP, 1999], 71).

51. William Shakespeare, *Hamlet, Prince of Denmark*, ed. Philip Edwards (Cambridge: Cambridge UP, 2003), 249 (act 3, scene 4). Hamlet is speaking to his mother, Queen Gertrude.

52. "The children of Nazi victims and the children of the Nazi perpetrators live side by side in Germany and Austria; they have no choice but to coexist. How can we find a way of living together so that we will never again have a generation growing up either as victims or as perpetrators? I believe that there is no other solution than to examine closely at the past, over and over again [uns immer wieder mit der Vergangenheit auseinanderzusetzen], and to learn from it (Simon Wiesenthal, from a lecture given at the Symposium "Überleben der Shoah," Wiener Rathaus, November 1997, online, www.simon-wiesenthal-archiv.at).

53. Albert Speer's response to the narrative consists in recounting the details of a meeting he had with Simon Wiesenthal on May 20, 1975. At the conclusion of the meeting, Wiesenthal gave him a copy of *Die Sonnenblume.* The meeting was preceded by a six-month correspondence between the two men. It appears that Wiesenthal was indeed willing to forgive Albert Speer, if forgiveness amounts to saying: "For me, Herr Speer, you are a new-born baby." What was important for Wiesenthal was that Speer was unwilling to submit his conscience entirely to a logic of calculation on the future and self-interest. This is what Wiesenthal said about him: "I said to him, 'I was at your trial, I saw your defense counsel's despair when you suddenly said you wanted to account not only for yourself and what you had done, but also for the actions of the government of which you had been a member. Without this testimony, you would have gotten ten years at the time; however, if everything we now know from available documents and other sources, had already been disclosed then, you would have been sentenced for life or even to death. But,' I told him, 'our legal system would be absolutely meaningless, if someone who admitted his guilt and served his sentence were not allowed to make a new beginning. For me, Mr. Speer, you are a new-born baby'" (from a lecture given at Technischen Universität Wien, June 1988, online, www.simon-wiesenthal-archiv.at). The critic Lawrence Langer has suggested that Albert Speer functions for Wiesenthal as a substitute for the SS man to whom the narrator had remained silent (see Laurence L. Langer, *Preempting the Holocaust* [New Haven: Yale UP, 2000], 179).

54. "Even the most humble and commendable discussions of atonement, guilt, and forgiveness—whether they concern spiritual atonement, material reparations, or restitution in general—are necessarily haunted and threatened by the unstated presumption that the other side is capable of participating and listening" (Ulrich Baer, "The Hubris of Humility: Günter Grass, Peter Schneider, and German Guilt after 1989,"*Germanic Review* 80 [Winter 2005]: 53). Elsewhere Baer speaks of the willingness and capacity to listen as the "imaginary *Vorgriff*, or implicit mental projection, that renders an appeal for forgiveness possible" (ibid., 51). The reference to the imaginary, the phantasm, indicates that this projection or fundamental presupposition not need be "real," present or well-grounded in order to be effective. This recalls what Hélène Cixous calls "dreamexistence" (*rêvexistence*).

55. "The survivor's guilt for the death of the other, this forgiveness asked *a priori* by the living as survivor—this is what, making us *a priori* guilty for the death of the other, transforms this death into something other than a natural death: forgiveness begged confesses guilt and transforms the death of the other into a murder . . . My own are the victims of murder, those who do not die of a natural death, since, actively or passively, I feel I have lent my hand to their death. This is also what one calls love . . . One also finds in Blanchot and Levinas this thought of death that is always a murder" (Jacques Derrida, "Hostipitality," in *Acts of Religion,* ed. Gil Anidjar [London: Routledge, 2002], 384).

56. As a final thought, I would also like to suggest that *The Sunflower* could also be for Wiesenthal's mother, Rosa, which in Latin is the name of a flower. After the war, the narrator supposedly meets the SS man's mother in Stuttgart. In an act of compassion, about which he is also later conflicted, he does not tell her who her dead son was and shatter her faith in his inherent goodness.

2. Reading Forgiveness in a Marrano Idiom: Jacques Derrida

1. See Elazar Barkan and Alexander Karn, "Group Apology as an Ethical Imperative," in *Taking Wrongs Seriously: Apology and Reconciliation* (Stanford: Stanford UP, 2006); and Elazar Barkan, *The Guilt of Nations: Restitution and Negotiating Historical Injustices* (New York: Norton, 2000).

2. Other notable recent studies include Danielle Celemajor, *The Sins of the Nations and the Ritual of Apologies* (Cambridge: Cambridge UP, 2009); M. Gibney, *The Age of Apology: Facing up to the Past* (Philadelphia: Pennsylvania UP, 2008); and Andrew Schaap, *Political Reconciliation* (New York: Routledge, 2005). Many of these studies have been guided by the thought of Hannah Arendt.

3. "La dimension même du pardon tend à s'effacer au cours de cette mondialisation, et avec elle toute mesure, toute limite conceptuelle" (Jacques Derrida,

"Le siècle et le pardon," interview by Michel Wieviorka, *Le monde des débats*, December 1999, 10–17).

4. Derrida prefers to use term "Abrahamic" to designate an idiom of apology, reconciliation, and forgiveness, which is the shared inheritance of the three great monotheistic religions Judaism, Christianity, and Islam. However, it is clear that what he is most concerned with is the Jewish and in particular, Christian appropriations of this idiom (see Jacques Derrida, *The Gift of Death*, trans. David Wills [Chicago: U of Chicago P, 1995]).

5. Jacques Derrida, "On Forgiveness," in *On Cosmopolitanism and Forgiveness*, trans. Mark Dooley and Michael Hughes (London: Routledge, 2001), 31. A striking contemporary example of the "worldwidization of forgiveness" is recent apologies from the Zen community in Japan for complicity with the Japanese military during World War II—complicity which included giving justification to policies of invasion and colonization; and in particular, "spiritual education" to kamikaze pilots prior to their missions. Significantly, these public apologies, which acknowledge a submerged and largely unknown history, were issued shortly after September 11, 2001 (see Brian Diazen Victoria, *Zen at War* [London: Rowman and Littlefield, 200; and *Zen War Stories* [London: RoutledgeCurzon, 2003]).

6. Consider, for example, critical readings of the work of the Truth and Reconciliation Commission in South Africa, such as Heidi Grunebaum, "Talking to Ourselves 'among the Innocent Dead': On Reconciliation, Forgiveness, and Mourning," *PMLA* 117.2: (2002): 306–7; and Mahmood Mamdani, "Reconciliation without Justice," in *Religion and Media*, ed. Hent de Vries and Samuel Weber (Stanford: Stanford UP, 2001), 376–88.

7. Derrida resists translating "*mondialisation*" as globalization because of the particular resonances of "world" (*mundus*) rather than globe, cosmos or universe, even though "*mondialisation*" is *also* the French translation of globalization. The significance of the reference to world or *mundus* in the term *mondialisation* is that it keeps the memory of a Christianization of the Greek: "Le monde, ce n'est ni l'univers, ni le cosmos. Même quand saint Paul a parlé de *cosmos* pour designer le monde Chrétien, il affectait le mot de *cosmos* d'une nouvelle signification qui signifiant l'ordre de créatures, de la fraternité des hommes comme prochain, etc . . . quand on dit mondialisation il faut se rappeler cette mémoire qui est à la fois théologique et philosophique et le mot de globalization perd la référence à cette mémoire-là" ("Philosophie et mondialisation," Rencontre de Jacques Derrida et Etienne Balibar, 21). Cf. Jean-Luc Nancy, *La création du monde ou la mondialisation* (Paris: Gallilée, 2002), 21. See also J. Derrida, "Above All, No Journalists!," in *Religion and Media*, 67–68.

8. For Derrida's concept of dissemination, see, for example, "Signature, Event, Context" (particularly the section "Writing and Telecommunication"), in *Margins of Philosophy*, trans. Alan Bass (Chicago: U of Chicago P, 1986), 311–21.

9. Derrida, "Le siècle et le pardon," 21.

10. "What is important is not the Christian marks, so numerous and so visible, that the West bears, and for which the cross is an abbreviation (*abrégé*). What is important is, on the contrary, that Christianity is present even where-and perhaps especially where-it is no longer possible to recognize it . . . [A] certain conception of "human rights," as well as a certain determination of the relationship between politics and religion, comes straight out of Christianity" (Jean-Luc Nancy, *Dis-Enclosure: The Deconstruction of Christianity,* trans. Bettina Bergo, Gabriel Malenfant, and Michael B. Smith [New York: Fordham UP, 2008], 33).

11. For a critical reading of the concept of the worldview, see Martin Heidegger, "The Age of the World Picture," in *The Question Concerning Technology and Other Essays,* trans. William Lovitt (New York: Harper Torchstone, 1977).

12. Nancy, *Dis-Enclosure: The Deconstruction of Christianity*, 36. The thesis of atheism as realized Christianity is related to the formulation of Marcel Gauchet adopted by Nancy, "Christianity is the religion of religion's exit" ("*Christianisme est la religion de la sortie de la religion*"). On the noncontradiction between atheism and faith, see also "Epoché and Faith: An Interview with Jacques Derrida," in *Derrida and Religion: Other Testaments,* ed. Yvonne Sherwood and Kevin Hart (New York: Routledge, 2005), 36–38.

13. Derrida, "Epoché and Faith: An Interview with Jacques Derrida," 33. In the same interview, Derrida makes the point that the word "deconstruction" is more closely related to Christianity than to Judaism or Islam, inasmuch as it refers to Heidegger's *Destruktion* and to Luther's *destruuntur*: "But the fact that it is literally linked to Christianity does not mean that Christianity is more deconstructive than other religions." Again Nancy goes further: "we must say that deconstruction . . . is itself Christian. It is Christian because Christianity is, originally, deconstructive, because it relates immediately to its own origin as to a slack [jeu], an interval, some play, an opening in the origin" (Nancy, *Dis-Enclosure: The Deconstruction of Christianity*, 149).

14. Simon Wiesenthal, *The Sunflower: On the Possibilities and Limits of Forgiveness* (New York: Schocken, 1998), 107–8; Simon Wiesenthal, *Die Sonnenblume: Eine Erzählung von Schuld und Vergebung* (Frankfurt: Ullstein, 1998), 219–20.

15. Several recent studies in political science have attempted to use Améry's work to rethink responses to debates about transitional justice and reparation,

most notably Thomas Brudholm, *Resentment's Virtue: Jean Améry and the Refusal to Forgive* (Philadelphia: Temple UP, 2008). See also *On Jean Améry: Philosophy of Catastrophe*, ed. Magdalena Zolkos (Lanham, MD: Lexington, 2011); and Thomas Brudholm, "The Justice of Truth and Reconciliation," *Hypatia: A Journal of Feminist Philosophy* 18 (Spring 2003): 186–96. Brudholm's book argues for the ethical defensibility of the emotion of anger under certain circumstances and for a particular reason. The book is divided into two parts, of which the second focuses on Jean Améry and his work. Brudholm makes a persuasive and compelling account that urges readers not simply to assume that forgiveness is the obvious best course. Negative emotions and attitudes (involved in surviving and remembering atrocity), he argues, need a fairer hearing. This is a position to which I am deeply sympathetic. It is not at all incompatible with Derrida's thought, inasmuch as he insists on the ethical necessity of the inability and refusal to mourn (see the introduction to this volume). However, as Jean Améry himself recognized, the ethics of resentment (*ressentiment*) he puts forward will be overcome by the forces of what he termed "the natural time-sense" (*naturliches Zeitbewußtsein*), which will inevitably lead to relativization and normalization, and ultimately forgetting of the horrors of the past. As is true for Derrida, Jankélévitch, Wiesenthal, and so many others who lived through this period of history, Améry recognizes the great danger of the "natural time-sense," which is, if you like, the common enemy of all these thinkers and survivors. Against Améry, however, I believe that there is a possibility of resistance to the "natural time-sense," which can be found *from within* the Abrahamic heritage and the value of forgiveness, which comes from it. Up to the very end, Améry subscribes to an antireligious vigilance, which leads him outright to dismiss the value of forgiveness as belonging to the sphere of guilt and atonement (*Schuld und Sühne*). I argue rather that it is necessary and more affirmative in the light of the Holocaust to rethink the conditions under which forgiveness is called for and supposedly takes place.

16. The designation "metaphysical" is understood here with reference to Heidegger's determination of the history of Western thought as the forgetting of the difference between being (*Sein*) and beings (*Seinende*). This forgetting speaks out, for example, in the understanding of God as an existing or absolute being which is present as an essence or substance (*ousia*). Indeed it speaks out in any interpretation of being which is grounded and guaranteed by a presence (Idea, *ens summum*, Subject, Will). The term "metaphysical" should also be related to Derrida's rereading of Heidegger's ontological difference in terms of the phonocentrism, logocentrism, phallocentrism, and finally, carnophallogocentrism of the history of Western thought. See, for example, Derrida, *De la grammatologie* [Paris: Éditions de Minuit, 1967]; and "'Eating Well' or the

Calculation of the Subject: An Interview with Jacques Derrida," in *Who Comes after the Subject?*, ed. E. Cadava, P. Connor, and Jean-Luc Nancy (New York: Routledge, 1991), 96–119. For the ontological difference, see Martin Heidegger, introduction to *Being and Time,* trans. John Macquarrie and Edward Robinson (Oxford: Basil Blackwell, 1978). Cf. Jean-Luc Nancy's exegesis of Derrida's formulation "the closure of metaphysics," in "Ouverture," in *La déclosion: La déconstruction du Christianisme* (Paris: Galilee, 2005), 16.

17. "Belief or faith has no place in thought" (Martin Heidegger, "Der Spruch des Anaximander," qtd. in Jacques Derrida, "Faith and Knowledge: The Two Sources of 'Religion' at the Limits of Reason Alone," in *Religion,* ed. Gianni Vattimo and Jacques Derrida, trans. David Webb et al. (Stanford: Stanford UP, 1998). See also the exclusion of theology from philosophy as fundamental ontology in paragraph 3 of *Being and Time,* 28–31.

18. Hent de Vries speaks of "the irreducibility of the theologico-political" (see Hent de Vries, *Religion and Violence: Philosophical Perspectives from Kant to Derrida* [Baltimore: Johns Hopkins UP, 2002], 353).

19. Derrida, "Epoché and Faith: An Interview with Jacques Derrida," 33.

20. From the film *D'ailleurs, Derrida,* directed by Safaa Fathy, 1999.

21. Following Benveniste, Derrida recalls that, within the Latin sphere, the origin of *religio* has been the subject of two competing but nonetheless commensurate readings: *relegere* (supported by Cicero): "bringing together in order to return and begin again"; and *religare* (Lactantius and Tertullian): "linking religion to the *link,* precisely, to obligation, ligament, and hence to obligation, to debt, etc." "Whatever side one takes in this debate, it is to the ellipse of these double Latin foci that the entire modern (geo-theologico-political) problematic of the "return of the religious" refers. Whoever would not acknowledge either the legitimacy of this double foci or the Christian prevalence that has imposed itself globally within the said Latinity would have to refuse the very premises of such a debate. And with them, any attempt to *think* a situation in which, as in times past, there will perhaps no longer exist, just as once it did not yet exist, any common Indo-European term for "religion" (Jacques Derrida, "Faith and Knowledge: The Two Sources of Religion within the Limits of Reason Alone," in *Acts of Religion*, ed. Gil Anidjar [London: Routledge, 2002], 36–38).

22. Cf. Hélène Cixous, *Insister: A Jacques Derrida* (Paris: Galilée, 2006).

23. Derrida, "Faith and Knowledge," 66. Note: the word "*Pâques*" in French can mean both Passover and Easter (see Samuel Weber, "Once and For All," *Grey Room* 20 [2005]: 113–14).

24. Jacques Derrida, "Circumfession," in *Jacques Derrida,* trans. Geoffrey Bennington (Chicago: U of Chicago P, 1999), 72.

25. *D'ailleurs, Derrida,* directed by Safaa Fathy, 1999.

26. I say presumably, because, as Yirmiyahu Yovel has noted in his study of Marranism, Judaism was guarded only in a "fragmentary and distorted manner." Information about it was often gleaned from "polemical works against it, the Latin Vulgate and other Christian sources." The residual Judaism of Marranism was, according to Yovel, a hybrid mixture of religions, "fraught with Christian symbols and categories," making it appear both Christian and Jewish, and neither (Yirmiyahu Yovel, *Spinoza and Other Heretics,* vol. 1, *The Marrano of Reason* [Princeton: Princeton UP, 1989], 15–39). See also Yirmiyahu Yovel, *The Other Within: The Marranos: Split Identity and Emerging Modernity* (Princeton: Princeton UP, 2008).

27. Yovel, *Spinoza and Other Heretics,* 1:15–39.

28. For Arendt, forgiveness is a mode of action, which corresponds to a new beginning: "Handeln als Neuanfangen entspricht der Geburt des Jemand, es realisiert in jedem Einzelnen die Tatsache des Geborenseins" (Hannah Arendt, *Vita activa oder Vom tätigen Leben* [Munich: Piper, 1999], 217).

29. See Derrida's interpretations of a Jewish joke recounted by Theodor Reik in Derrida, "Hostipitality," 397–98; and also Jacques Derrida ". . . . .," *Les cahiers du Grif,* no. 3 (Paris: Descartes and Cie, 1997), 131–65. In the chapter of his memoirs entitled "How to Deal with Opponents," the Nazi hunter and Holocaust survivor Simon Wiesenthal makes the observation that "people who have once laughed together do not want to kill one another anymore" ("Menschen, die einmal miteinander gelacht haben, wollen einander nicht mehr umbringen") (Simon Wiesenthal, *Recht nicht Rache* [Frankfurt: Ullstein, 1988], 424). For more on this, see the conclusion of this volume.

30. Jacques Derrida, "On Forgiveness: Roundtable Discussion with Jacques Derrida," in *Questioning God,* ed. John D. Caputo, Mark Dooley, and Michael J Scanlon (Bloomington: Indiana UP, 2001), 56.

31. Jacques Derrida, "Marx and Sons," in *Ghostly Demarcations: A Symposium on Jacques Derrida's Specters of Marx,* ed. Michael Sprinker (London: Verso, 1999), 262.

32. "For manifestly you have long been aware of what you mean when you use the expression "*being*" [*wenn ihr den Ausdruck 'seiend' gebraucht*]. We, however, who used to think we understood it, have now become perplexed [*in Verlegenheit gekommen*]." This epigram from Plato's Sophist opens *Being and Time* (see Heidegger, *Being and Time,* 19).

33. The term "symptom" is loosely employed here as referring to a formation, which testifies to an unconscious conflict.

34. "The only possible pardon is really the impossible pardon . . . I don't believe the pardon defined in that way rightly belongs in the public, political, juridical, or even ethical field. Which is why its secret is so serious and

important an issue" (Jacques Derrida, "Others Are Secret Because They Are Other," in *Paper Machine,* trans. Rachel Bowlby [Stanford: Stanford UP, 2005], 161). See also Jacques Derrida, "Literature in Secret: An Impossible Filiation," in *The Gift of Death* 2nd ed., trans. David Wills (Chicago: U of Chicago P, 2008), 121–29.

35. Derrida, "Others Are Secret Because They Are Other," 160–61.

36. Derrida, "Hostipitality," 385–86.

37. Cf. the Freudian concept of the fetish, which draws its durability from the tension created by contradictory ideas: "In very subtle instances both the disavowal and the affirmation of castration have found their way into the construction of the fetish itself . . . a fetish of this sort, doubly derived from contradictory ideas is especially durable" (Sigmund Freud "Fetishism" [1927], in *The Standard Edition of the Complete Psychological Works of Sigmund Freud,* 21:152–59). See also Derrida's proposal of a general economy of fetishism in *Glas,* trans. John P. Leavy and Richard Rand (Lincoln: U of Nebraska P, 1990).

38. Jacques Derrida, "Psyche: Inventions of the Other," trans. Catherine Porter, in *Reading de Man Reading,* ed. Wlad Godzich and Lindsay Waters (Minneapolis: U of Minnesota P, 1989), 60.

39. Maurice Blanchot and Jacques Derrida, *The Instant of My Death/ Demeure: Fiction and Testimony,* trans. Elizabeth Rottenberg (Stanford: Stanford UP, 2000), 83.

40. J. Derrida, lecture given at Columbia University, October 2002.

41. The quotation marks around the term "logic" are Derrida's. See, for example, "As if it were possible, 'within such limits,'" in *Paper Machine,* 89.

42. Ibid., 82.

43. See Jacques Derrida, *Given Time,* trans. Peggy Kamuf (Chicago: U of Chicago P, 1992).

44. Ibid., 25.

45. "Das überunmöglichste ist möglich" (Angelus Silesius *Cherubinischer Wandersmann*). *Das Überunmöglichste* can mean both the most impossible or the more than impossible. See J. Derrida, "Post-Scriptum: Aporias, Ways and Voices," in *Derrida and Negative Theology,* ed. Harold Coward and Toby Foshay (Albany: State U of New York P, 1992), 290–91. Silesuis's formulation recalls Heidegger's formulation about death.

46. Jacques Derrida, "To Forgive: The Unforgiveable and the Imprescriptible," in *Questioning God,* ed. John D. Caputo, Mark Dooley, and Michael J Scanlon (Bloomington: Indiana UP, 2001), 25.

47. Desmond Tutu claimed that forgiveness (in the sense of reconciliation) "is not just personally rewarding. It is a political necessity." (Desmond Tutu, *God Has A Dream: A Vision of Hope for Our Time* (New York: Doubeday, 2004)

51. "Reconciliation is practical politics." And Jankélévitch: "We have hope for it, this fraternal word! Certainly, we were not expecting our forgiveness to be implored . . . But we would have received words of understanding with gratitude, with tears in our eyes" (Vladimir Jankélévitch, "Shall We Pardon Them?," *Critical Inquiry* 22.3 [Spring 1996]: 49). See chapter 4 of this volume, "Forgiveness Has Died . . ." section.

48. Jacques Derrida, "Fichus, Frankfurt Address," in *Paper Machine*, 168, translation modified; Jacques Derrida, *Fichus, Discours de Francfort* (Paris: Galilée, 2002).

49. "'Politik des Traums,' das ist keine Politik von Träumern oder für Träumer. Der Traum, von dem ich spreche, ist der Traum des Denkens, nicht das gegenwärtige kollektive Phantasma von Sicherheit, Patriotismus oder Rache. Ein Krieg, wie er jetzt vorbereitet wird, kann nicht allein die Antwort sein. Der Traum wäre zu sagen: Erfinden wir etwas anderes" (translation mine) (Jacques Derrida, "Niemand ist unschuldig," interview by Ulrich Raulff, *Süddeutsche Zeitung,* 24 September 2001).

50. "Changed into the deformation of their essence, 'war' and 'peace' are taken up into an erring [*Irrnis*], and disappear into the mere course of the escalating manufacture of what can be manufactured [*Machen von Machbarkeiten*], because they have become unrecognizable with regard to any distinction. The question of whether there will be peace cannot be answered not because the duration of war is unfathomable, but rather because the question already asks about something which no longer exists, since war is no longer anything which could terminate in peace" (Martin Heidegger, "Überwindung der Metaphysik," qtd. in Jacques Derrida, *Politics of Friendship,* trans. George Collins [London: Verso, 1997], 248–49).

51. In his famous sketch, Kant designated perpetual peace as a "sweet dream," i.e., that which does not exist in the present. In her reading of Kant's sketch, Avital Ronell writes: "The problem that Kant faces in the entire essay involves the deflection of perpetual peace from its semantic hole in the graveyard: could there be a movement of peace that is unhitched from the death drive? Must the duty we have toward peace have as its background music that radical tranquility which resonates with 'rest in peace'? If Kant can only draw a philosophical sketch of peace, this is because his leanings push him toward the edge of undecidability where absolute peace, like war, means you're dead" (Avital Ronell, "Support Our Tropes," in *Finitude's Score: Essays for the End of the Millennium* [Lincoln: U of Nebraska P, 1998], 286).

52. Jacques Derrida, "Choreographies," *Diacritics* 12.2 (Summer 1982): 76–77.

53. Jacques Derrida, *H. C. for Life, that is to say . . .*, 157.

54. Derrida, *Glas*, 217. "Philosophical discourse is not only governed by the phantasmatic (either originary or derived), but, more seriously, can no longer be assured of possessing a philosophical concept of the phantasm, a knowledge that would control what is at issue in this word . . . What happens if the absolute phantasm is co-extensive with absolute knowledge? It should be possible to demonstrate . . . that the philosophic is the phantasmatic" (Jacques Derrida, "Between Brackets 1," in *Points: Interviews 1974–1994*, 23).

55. Jacques Derrida, "The University without Condition," in *Without Alibi*, trans. Peggy Kamuf (Stanford: Stanford UP, 2002), 204–5.

56. Jacques Derrida, *The Ear of the Other: Otobiography, Transference, Translation*, ed. Christine V. McDonald, trans. Peggy Kamuf (New York: Schocken, 1985), 115.

57. Derrida, *H.C. for Life, that is to say . . .*, 157.

58. J. Derrida, "As If It Were Possible, 'Within Such Limits,'" in *Paper Machine*, 96.

59. J. Kristeva, "Forgiveness: An Interview," *PMLA* 117.2 (March 2012): 283, 290.

60. Jacques Derrida, On "Forgiving the Unforgivable," European Graduate School, online, www.egs.edu, italics mine.

61. Jacques Derrida, "Not Utopia, the Im-possible," in *Paper Machine*, 131.

3. Crimes against Humanity or the Phantasm of "We, Men"

1. In a similar vein, Pheng Cheah argues that "the task and challenge of the humanities today in relation to globalization may be to question [the] precomprehension of the human and, somewhat perversely, even to give it up." And later in the work: "we commonly oppose the human to inhuman forces that oppress and degrade humanity . . . The aporias of development, however, indicate a constitutive marking of the inhuman within the human that renders indeterminate the borderline between the two terms" (Pheng Cheah, *Inhuman Conditions: On Cosmopolitanism and Human Rights* [Cambridge: Harvard UP, 2006], 3, 230).

2. See, for example, Robert Fine, "Crimes against Humanity: Hannah Arendt and the Nuremburg Debates," *European Journal of Social Theory* 3.3 (2000): 293–311.

3. From the judgment of the Nuremberg Tribunal, qtd. in Geoffrey Robinson, *Crimes against Humanity: The Struggle for Global Justice* (London: Penguin, 1999), 207–8.

4. "Jurisdiction arises, in other words, wherever an offender is found, and it arises because he is alleged to have offended in a particularly outrageous way"

(ibid., 237). The doctrine of universal jurisdiction was, Robinson recalls, relevant in the Eichmann trial (ibid., 238).

5. Pauline Kleingeld and Eric Brown, "Cosmopolitanism," in *The Stanford Encyclopedia of Philosophy*, ed. Edward N. Zalta et al. (Stanford: Center for the Study of Language and Information, Stanford University, 2009).

6. Jacques Derrida, "On Forgiveness," in *On Cosmopolitanism and Forgiveness*, trans. Mark Dooley and Michael Hughes (London: Routledge, 2001), 30.

7. That crimes against humanity are interpreted today as "the most serious crimes" is not only what is reflected incessantly throughout the global Western media; it is also the terminology of the International Criminal Court, whose jurisdiction "shall be limited to the most serious crimes of concern to the international community as a whole" (see Article 5 of the Rome Statue of the International Criminal Court [1998], online, www.un.org/law/icc/statute).

8. Robinson, *Crimes against Humanity: The Struggle for Global Justice*, 220.

9. Ibid.

10. Jacques Derrida, "To Forgive: The Unforgivable and the Imprescriptible," ed. John D. Caputo, Mark Dooley, and Michael J Scanlon (Bloomington: Indiana UP, 2001), 35.

11. The Rome Statute of the International Criminal Court (1998). Unlike the definitions formally provided in the Nuremberg (1945) and Toyko (1946) Charters, or otherwise, by the Security Council in the Statutes of the Yugoslavia (1993) or Rwanda (1994) tribunals, the Rome Statute is the first formal definition of "crimes against humanity" that has been developed through multilateral negotiations among 160 states. The definition given in this statute makes clear that a "crime against humanity" (unlike a war crime) does not have to take place during a period of armed conflict (see Daryl Robinson, "Defining 'Crimes against Humanity' at the Rome Conference," *American Journal of International Law* 93.1 [January 1999]: 43–57).

12. Significantly, every formulation of the legal concept of "crimes against humanity" since Nuremberg has concluded its list of enumerated inhumane acts with the general phrase "other inhumane acts" (see Robinson, "Defining "Crimes against Humanity" at the Rome Conference," 55).

13. Extermination is defined as "intentional infliction of conditions of life, *inter alia* the deprivation of access to food and medicine, calculated to bring about the destruction of part of a population" (ibid.).The language is taken from the Genocide Convention (ibid., 52).

14. *Oxford English Dictionary*, 3rd ed., online, www.oed.com.

15. In this respect, it is useful to recall that *in addition* to the Jewish and especially Christian interpretation of the brotherhood of man (with which I am principally concerned here), Derrida identifies "the Abrahamic memory

of the religions of the Book" as indissociable from the concept of crimes against humanity and the logic that there is nothing worse. By "Abrahamic memory," he refers no doubt to the test of sacrificial responsibility to which the patriarch Abraham is called by God on Mount Moriah. With the help of Kierkegaard's *Fear and Trembling,* Derrida rereads the Abrahamic memory in one of his most important and powerful texts, *Donner la mort.* In this narrative of the origin of responsibility, which is foundational for the three monotheistic religions, it is worth recalling that in addition to the sacrifice of Isaac at the foreground of the drama (a sacrifice which takes place as a decision without taking place as such), there are in the background two additional sacrifices: (1) the sacrifice of Sarah, mother and wife, the sole woman in the drama, who does not speak, and who is left at the beginning, without ever being told of what happened; and (2) the blood sacrifice of an "animal," the lamb, which substitutes for the sacrifice of the son, Isaac (see Derrida, *The Gift of Death,* 2nd ed., trans. David Wills [Chicago: U of Chicago P, 2008]). To what extent the term "man" in English or "*l'homme*" in French refers to humanity in general or rather in an unacknowledged fashion exclusively to masculine gender is probably an undecidable question. What is undeniable, however, is that one gender (rather than another or others) has been—and still is—employed to name the universal. This procedure has been interpreted by many as the symptom of a patriarchal or *phallogocentric* privilege, for which I believe one is responsible when one reads, which is to say, when one repeats in a certain way. I will come back to this question also in chapter 4 in the reading of Jankélévitch's thought of forgiveness, which subscribes to the same privilege or conceit.

16. *OED*: a1639 W. WHATELY Prototypes II. xxvi. (1640) 76.

17. Ibid.

18. Commenting on the immunity of the Japanese Emperor Hirohito from prosecution at the Tokyo trials for crimes against humanity committed during World War II, Geoffrey Robinson writes: "The received wisdom in the US supreme command was that Japanese crimes against humanity were more readily forgivable than German, because the latter race were so much more civilized and hence deserved more punishment because they 'knew better.' This thinking, articulated by MacArthur in evidence to a US Senate inquiry, was ignorant as well as paternalistic . . . The absence of Hirohito, the supreme commander, undermined the trial both as a precedent and as a method of guilt acknowledgement" (Robinson, *Crimes against Humanity: The Struggle for Global Justice,* 223–25).

19. "On Forgiveness: A Roundtable Discussion with Jacques Derrida," in *Questioning God,* 67.

20. Jacques Derrida, "Faith and Knowledge: The Two Sources of Religion within the Limits of Reason Alone," in *Acts of Religion*, ed. Gil Anidjar [London: Routledge, 2002], 33.

21. See Martin Heidegger, *Elucidations of Hölderlin's Poetry,* trans. Keith Hoeller (Stony Brook: State U of New York P, 2000); and *Contributions to Philosophy (from Enowning),* trans. Parvis Emad and Kenneth Maly (Bloomington: Indiana UP, 1999).

22. See Robert H. Miller, "The Convention on the Non-Applicability of Statutory Limitations to War Crimes and Crimes against Humanity," *American Journal of International Law* 65.3 (July 1971): 476–501.

23. "The immunitary reaction protects the 'indemnity' of the body proper in producing anti-bodies against foreign antigens. As for the process of auto-immunization . . . it consists for a living organism . . . of protecting itself against its own self-protection by destroying its own immune system. As the phenomenon of these antibodies is extended to a broader zone of pathology and as one resorts increasingly to the positive virtues of immuno-depressants destined to limit the mechanisms of rejection and to facilitate the tolerance of certain organ transplants, we feel ourselves authorized to speak of a sort of general logic of auto-immunization. It seems indispensable for us today for thinking the relations between faith and knowledge, religion and science, as well as the duplicity of sources in general" (Derrida, "Faith and Knowledge," 80). Two pages earlier, Derrida explicitly relates the notion of auto-immunization to "all the projects which appeal to universal fraternization, to the reconciliation of men, sons of the same God" (ibid., 78).

24. Robert Antelme, *L'espèce humaine* (Paris: Gallimard, 1957).

25. Ibid., 11.

26. Ibid., 229–39; Robert Antelme, *The Human Race,* trans. Jeffrey Haight and Annie Mahler (Marlboro: Marlboro Press, 1992), 219–20.

27. Antelme, *L'espèce humaine,* 11.

28. Ibid.; Antelme, *The Human Race*, 5, translation modified.

29. It is in this direction that it is necessary to interpret, I believe, the paradoxical formulations proposed by Maurice Blanchot in his reading of *L'espèce humaine* in *L'entretien infini*: "Man is the indestructible who can be destroyed"; "That man can be destroyed is certainly not reassuring; but what is overwhelming [*acablant*] is that despite this and because of it, in this very movement, man remains indestructible, because we no longer have any chance to free ourselves from ourselves, nor from our responsibility" (Blanchot, *The Infinite Conversation* trans. Susan Hanson [Minneapolis: U of Minnesota P, 1993], 192, 200). In this sense, Blanchot, like Levinas, would remain committed to a fraternalist universalism (i.e., humanism).

30. Antelme, *L'espèce humaine*, 11.

31. "The essentially deported person, the one who no longer has either a face or speech, the work he is forced to do is designed only to exhaust his power to live and to deliver him over to the boundless insecurity of the elements. Nowhere any recourse: outside the cold, inside hunger; everywhere an indeterminate violence. *'The cold, SS,'* Antelme says profoundly. In precisely this way he blocks the enemy's endeavor" (Blanchot, *The Infinite Conversation*, 131; *L'entretien infini* [Paris: Gallimard 1969], 193).

32. Antelme, *L'espèce humaine*, 84–85/75, translation modified. It is significant that the speech act "*Langsam!*" must be reconfirmed with the holding out of the hand, so there may be no confusion as to the meaning of the first gesture. On the hand as a synecdoche for humanity, see J. Derrida, "Geschlecht 2: Heidegger's Hand," in *Deconstruction and Philosophy: The Texts of Jacques Derrida*, ed. J. Sallis (Chicago: U of Chicago P, 1999), 161–96.

33. Marguerite Duras, *La douleur* (Paris: P.O.L., 1985), 63; Marguerite Duras, *The War,* trans. Barbara Bray (New York: Pantheon, 1986), 53.

34. Thus, on the one hand, one can say that the "concrete" responsibility is diffused. But, on the other hand, it is also increased beyond measure (which was in all probability Antelme's ultimate intention): whoever may identify themselves henceforth as a human is responsible for what the Nazis and their collaborators have done. The Nazis and their collaborators may be regarded here as exemplary for the perpetrators of any "crime against humanity." *And yet, to what extent is such exemplarity justified?*

35. "La mise en question de la qualité d'homme provoque une revendication *presque* biologique d'appartenance à l'Espèce humaine" (Antelme, *L'espèce humaine* 11, emphasis mine.

36. On the question of the political and philosophical stakes of testing and falsifiablility, see A. Ronell, *The Test Drive* (Chicago: U of Illinois P, 2005); see, in particular, chapter 1, "Proving Grounds," 3–61.

37. Jacques Derrida, "Les fins de l'homme," in *Marges de la Philosophie* (Paris: Éditions de Minuit, 1972), 129–64; translated by Alan Bass as "The Ends of Man," in *Margins of Philosophy*, trans. Alan Bass (Chicago: U of Chicago P, 1986), 109–37.

38. "Thus is explained the fact that despite the critique of anthropologism, of which we have just given a few indices, man is the only *example*, the only case of a rational being that can ever be cited at the very moment when by all rights one distinguishes the universal concept of a rational being from the concept of the human being. It is through the offices of this *fact* that anthropology regains all the authority that been contested. It is at this point that the philosopher says 'we'" (ibid., 145–46/122).

39. Heidegger, *Sein und Zeit*, 5/25. Compare: "Dieses Seiende, das wir selbst je sind und das unter anderem die Seinsmöglichkeit des Fragens hat, fassen wir terminologisch als *Dasein*"; "This entity which each of us is himself and which includes inquiring as one of the possibilities of its Being, we shall denote by the term *Dasein*" (ibid., 27).

40. Ibid., 149–50, translation modified.

41. "Metaphysics thinks of man on the basis of *animalitas* and does not think in the direction of his *humanitas* . . . the highest determinations of the essence of man in humanism still do not realize the proper dignity of man [*die eigentliche Würde des Menschen*]." To this extent the thinking in *Being and Time* is against humanism . . . Humanism is opposed because it does not set the *humanitas* of man high enough" (ibid., 155–56).

42. "This something which is just present-at-hand-and no-more is 'more' than a *lifeless* material Thing. In it we encounter something *unalive,* which has lost its life. (Das Nur-noch-Vorhandene ist 'mehr' als ein lebloses materielles Ding. Mit ihm begegnet ein des Lebens verlustig gegangenes Unlebendiges.) The deceased [*Der 'Verstorbene'*] as distinct from the dead person [*dem Gestorbenen*] has been torn away from those who have 'remained behind' ('*Hinterbliebenen*'), and is an object of 'concern' in the ways of funeral rites, interment, and the cult of graves. And that is so because the deceased, in his kind of Being, is 'still more' than just an item of equipment, environmentally ready-to-hand, about which one can be concerned. In tarrying alongside him in their mourning and commemoration, those who have remained behind *are with him* in a mode of respectful solicitude. Thus the relationship-of-Being which one has towards the dead is not to be taken as a *concernful* Being alongside something ready-to-hand [*Zuhandenen*)]" (Heidegger, *Being and Time*, 282; *Sein und Zeit* [Tübingen: Max Niemeyer, 1993], 238).

43. Consider the comment of Imre Kertész in response to the final scene of Steven Spielberg's film *Schindler's List,* which portrays a triumphant crowd of people: "I regard as kitsch any representation of the Holocaust that fails to imply the wide-ranging ethical consequences of Auschwitz, and from which the PERSON in capital letters (and with it the idea of the human as such) emerges from the camps healthy and unharmed. If this were really possible, we wouldn't still be talking about the Holocaust" (Kertész, "Who Owns Auschwitz?," 267).

4. A Hyper-Ethics of Irreconcilable Contradictions: Vladimir Jankélévitch

1. Vladimir Jankélévitch, *Music and the Ineffable,* trans. Carolyn Abbate (Princeton: Princeton UP, 2003); Vladimir Jankélévitch, *Ravel,* trans. Margaret

Crossland (London: Greenword, 1976); Vladimir Jankélévitch, *Penser la mort? (Thinking Death)*, preface and supervision by Françoise Schwab (Paris: Liana Levi, 1994).

Critical Inquiry 22 (Spring 1996), ed. Arnold I. Davidson, includes an introduction and translations into English of several of Jankélévitch's essays, including the important 1966 polemical essay "Shall We Pardon Them?," which was written in response to the public debate in France over the abolition of statues of limitations for crimes against humanity.

2. Emmanuel Levinas, "Philosophy and the Idea of Infinity," in *Collected Philosophical Papers*, trans. Alphonso Lingus (Pittsburgh: Duquesne UP, 1998), 47, 63; see also "Vladimir Jankélévitch" in Emmanuel Levinas, *Hors Sujet* (Paris: Fata Morgana, 1987).

3. Vladimir Jankélévitch, *Henri Bergson* (Paris: Alcan, 1959).

4. Vladimir Jankélévitch, *L'odyssie de la conscience dans la dernière philosophie de Schelling* (Paris: Presse Universitaire de France, 1933).

5. Françoise Schwab, "Jankélévitch: Le parcours d'une vie," *Magazine Littéraire* 333 (June 1995): 17.

6. "Alors peut-être, alors surtout le pardon deviendrait un jour possible, qui n'a pas de sens aujourd'hui" (Vladimir Jankélévitch, "Dans l'honneur et la dignité," [1948] in *L'imprescriptible*, 102–3).

7. "Le pardon est mort dans les camps de mort" (Jankélévitch, "Pardonner?" [1971], in *L'imprescriptible* [Paris: Éditions du Seuil, 1986], 50).

8. Jankélévitch, "Dans l'honneur et la dignité," (1948), in *L'imprescriptible*, 103.

9. Jankélévitch, "Pardonner?," translated by Ann Hobart as "Shall We Pardon Them?," *Critical Inquiry* 22.3 (Spring 1996): 49–52/566–68.

10. Although in the book *Le pardon* Jankélévitch does not refer to the ethics of forgiveness as "hyperbolical," he does do so in an interview he gave several years later in 1977, which is quoted by Jacques Derrida: "*Le Pardon* . . . is a philosophy book in which I study forgiveness in itself, from the point of view of Christian and Jewish ethics. I draw out an ethics that could be qualified as hyperbolical" (Vladimir Jankélévitch qtd. in Derrida, "To Forgive: The Unforgivable and the Imprescriptible," 27). The expression "ethics beyond ethics" is Derrida's).

11. Jankélévitch, *Le pardon*, 991–1141. I have lightly modified most of translated citations.

12. Ibid., 1146/161.

13. "Le pardon, lui, n'est pas un monologue, mais un dialogue; le pardon, étant un rapport à deux, comporte un aléa supplémentaire: cet élément aventureux tient à la présence de l'autre" (ibid., 1137/151).

14. "Then God said, 'Let us make man in our image, according to our likeness; and let them have dominion over the fish of the sea, and over the birds of the air, and over the cattle, and over all the wild animals of the earth, and over every creeping thing that creeps upon the earth.' So God created man in his image" (Genesis 1:26–28).

15. "*L'amour des hommes est entre toutes les valeurs la plus sacré*" (Jankélévitch, *Le pardon*, 1147/162).

16. "On *doit*, à certains égards, pardonner l'impardonnable sans l'avoir compris" (ibid., 1144).

17. Ibid., 1144/159, 1146/160.

18. In her remarkable study *Male Subjectivity at the Margins* (New York: Routledge, 1992), Kaja Silverman employs a notion of *heteropathic identification* in order to research the ways in which various marginal forms of male sexuality may be related to political refusal and emancipation. Following the work of Max Scheler, she distinguishes between *incorporative identification* (articulated by Freud) which works to constitute the self at the expense of the other, who is in effect "swallowed", and heteropathic identification, which locates the self at the site of the other. "Within heteropathic identification, the "I" is so overwhelmed and hypnotically bound and fettered by the other "I" that its formal status as a subject is usurped by the other person's personality, with all *its* characteristic aspects. I live, not in myself, but entirely in the other person" (264). She notes that *heteropathic identification* is most often characterized by Scheler as a form of ecstasy, and turns not only upon the exteriorization of identity, but also upon a pleasurably painful acknowledgement of the "otherness" of all identity. Among the varieties of masochism enumerated by Freud it relates therefore to one kind only, i.e., what he calls feminine masochism (213).

19. Jankélévitch, *Le pardon*, 1134/148.

20. Contemporary philosophers such as Gilles Deleuze and Jean-Luc Nancy have also employed Lucretius's concept of the *clinamen* (see, for example, Jean-Luc Nancy, *La communauté dèsoeuvrée* [Paris: Bourgeois, 1996], 17; and Gilles Deleuze, *Différence et répetittion* [Paris: PUF, 1969], 184).

21. Cf. Friedrich Wilhelm Joseph Schelling, *Philosophische Untersuchungen über das Wesen der menschlichen Freiheit und die damit zusammenhängenden Gegenstände* (Frankfurt: Meiner, 2001).

22. Jankélévitch, *Le pardon*, 1142/157.

23. Ibid., 1142–43/158.

24. See Charles Baudelaire, "Au lecteur," in *Fleurs du mal.*

25. Jankélévitch, "Pardonner?," 50; Vladimir Jankélévitch and Ann Hobart, "Shall We Pardon Them?," 552. Jankélévitch's opposition to the application of

statutes of limitations to crimes against humanity was supported by the unanimous vote of the French government.

26. Ibid., 50–51/567.

27. While "Pardonner?" was first published in 1971, it was based on an essay "L'imprescriptible," which appeared in *La Revue Administrative* in January–February 1965 (see Kevin Hart, "Forgiveness," *Christianity and Literature* [Spring 2007]).

28. "Le pardon pur est un événement qui n'est peut-être jamais arrivé dans l'histoire de l'homme" (Jankélévitch, *Le pardon*, 1103) (Pure forgiveness is an event that has perhaps never happened in the history of Mankind).

29. Jankélévitch, "Pardonner?," 60; Jankélévitch and Hobart, "Shall We Pardon Them?," 558, translation modified.

30. "It is therefore quite significant, a structural element in the realm of human affairs, that men are unable to forgive what they cannot punish and that they cannot punish what has turned out to be unforgivable. This is the true hallmark of offences which, since Kant, we call 'radical evil'" (Arendt, *The Human Condition*, 241).

31. "De l'inexpiable ou de l'irréparable, Jankélévitch conclut à l'impardonnable. Et l'on ne pardonne pas, selon lui, à de l'impardonnable. Cet enchaînement ne me paraît pas aller de soi . . . 'Le pardon est mort dans les camps de la mort,' dit-il. Oui. À moins qu'il ne devienne possible qu'à partir du moment où il paraît impossible. Son histoire commencerait au contraire avec l'impardonnable" (Derrida, "Le siècle et le pardon," 112–13). "'Forgiveness died in the death camps,' he said. Yes. Unless it becomes possible from the moment it appears impossible. On the contrary, its history would begin with the unforgivable."

32. See chapter 3 of this volume, "The Self-Evidence of the Logic . . ." section.

33. On 8 December 1942, a small delegation of American Jewish leaders met with President Roosevelt about the Holocaust. The President was presented with a document outlining the Nazi intention to annihilate European Jews. As this report of the meeting indicates, the president was acquainted with details of the atrocities being committed by the Nazis. For more on the history of the American government's reaction to the Holocaust, see Samantha Power, *A Problem from Hell: American and the Age of Genocide* (New York: HarperCollins, 2003).

34. Consider the thesis of eminent holocaust historian Raul Hilberg, who argues that the destruction of the Jews was not so much a product of laws and commands as it was a matter of spirit, of shared comprehension, of consonance and synchronization. He writes of "countless decision makers in a far-flung bureaucratic machine" without "a basic plan." There had been "no one agency," "no single organization directed or coordinated the entire process."

The destruction of the Jews, he concludes, was "the work of a far-flung administrative machine," and "no special agency was created and no special budget was devised . . . Each organization was to play a specific role in the process, and each was to find the means to carry out its task" (Raul Hilberg, *The Destruction of the European Jews* [New Haven: Yale UP, 2003], 53–55, 62).

35. Jankélévitch, "Pardonner?," 61/567–68.

36. "Un crime qui fut perpétré au nom de la supériorité germanique engage la responsabilité nationale de tous les Allemands." "A crime perpetrated in the name of German superiority engages the national responsibility of all Germans." (ibid., 60/565).

37. Devour: "To swallow or eat up voraciously, as a beast of prey; to make a prey of, to prey upon" (*The Oxford English Dictionary* [Oxford: Oxford UP, 2009] online, www.oed.com.

38. See "The Quest for Romani Redress." in S. Wolfe, *The Politics of Reparations and Apologies* (New York: Springer, 2014), 122–29; and W/ Wippermann, "Compensation Withheld: The Denial of Reparations to the Sinti and Roma, *Gypsies during the Second World War: The Final Chapter*, ed. D. Kenrick (Hertfordshire: U of Hertfordshire P, 2006).

39. Between 200,000 and 250,000 mentally and physically handicapped persons were murdered from 1939 to 1945 under the T4 and other "euthanasia" programs. In addition, it is estimated that some 50,000 men served prison terms in concentration camps as convicted homosexuals between 1933 and 1945 (U.S. Holocaust Memorial Museum, online, www.ushmm.org/).

40. The following section is a testimony to my reading of Derrida's reading of this remarkable exchange of letters between Jankélévitch and Raveling in "To Forgive: The Unforgivable and the Imprescriptable," 38–46.

41. Wiard Raveling, "Lettre de Wiard Raveling," June 1980, in *Magazine Littéraire*, June 1995, 53.

42. Ibid.

43. Ibid., 57.

44. Ibid., 40.

45. The poets Dan Pagis and Czeslaw Milosz both imagine a reversibility of time, an undoing of what has been done (see Dan Pagis, "Draft of a Reparations Agreement," in *Art from the Ashes*, ed. Lawrence L. Langer [Oxford: Oxford UP, 1995], 592; and Czeslaw Milosz, "This World," in *New and Collected Poems, 1931–2001* [New York: HarperCollins, 2001], 634).

46. Countersigning Kafka's interdiction on hope, Derrida once spoke of "the possibility of a hopeless prayer" (Shapiro, Govrin, and Derrida, *Body of Prayer* [New York: The Irwin Chanin School of Architecture of the Cooper Union, 2001]). "You may pray without any reference to the future, just to

address the other, hopelessly, hopelessly: in reference only to the past. There is only repetition, no future. And, nevertheless, you pray" (3:16). One can say, thinking of Hélène Cixous, that forgiveness may be imagined, even found, but not hoped for (cf. Hélène Cixous, *Insister of Jacques Derrida*, trans. Peggy Kamuf [Stanford: Stanford UP, 2006], 92).

47. Derrida, "To Forgive the Unforgivable and the Imprescriptible," in 41.

48. See, in particular, the pages devoted to "transgression" (Maurice Blanchot, *Le pas au-delà* [Paris: Gallimard, 1973], 144f). See also Maurice Blanchot, *L'instant de ma mort* (Paris: Gallimard, 2002).

49. On the interpretation of the human as *subjectum* or *hypokaimenon*, see Martin Heidegger, "The Age of the World Picture," in *The Question Concerning Technology and Other Essays*, trans. William Lovitt (New York: Garland, 1997).

50. See Ronell, *Stupidity*.

51. See Jacques Derrida, *The Gift of Death*, 2nd ed., trans. David Wills (Chicago: U of Chicago P, 2008), 70–71.

52. Raphael Lemkin, "Genocide—A Modern Crime" (April 1945), online, www.preventgenocide.org.

53. Jacques Derrida, *Archive Fever: A Freudian Impression*, trans. Eric Prenowitz (Chicago: U of Chicago P, 1998), 100.

Conclusion: Forgiveness as a Jewish Joke

1. Jacques Derrida, *Archive Fever: A Freudian Impression*, trans. Eric Prenowitz (Chicago: U of Chicago P, 1998), 381.

2. Theodore Reik, *Jewish Wit* (New York: Gamut, 1962).

3. Jacques Derrida, ". . . . .," *Les cahiers du Grif*, no. 3 (Paris: Descartes and Cie, 1997), 131–65. Sarah Kofman committed suicide on October 15, 1994. At the time, I was writing a Diplôme d'Études Approfondies (D.E.A.) under her supervision in the Département de Philosophie at the Université de Paris I.

4. Sarah Kofman, *Pourquoi rit-on? Freud et le mot d'esprit* (Paris: Galilée, 1986) 198.

5. J. Derrida, ". . . . . ."; in Jacques Derrida, *The Work of Mourning*, trans. Pascale-Anne Brault and Michael Naas (Chicago: U of Chicago P, 2001), 172. For a reading of the philosophical and personal relation between Derrida and Kofman, see Penelope Deutscher, "Pardon: Sarah Kofman and Jacques Derrida (On Mourning, Debt and Seven Friendships)," *Journal of the British Society for Phenomenology* 31.1 (2000): 21–35.

6. See chapter 1 of this volume, "Before All Questioning" section.

7. Jacques Derrida, "Hostipitality," in *Acts of Religion*, ed. Gil Anidjar [London: Routledge, 2002], 396. In relation to humor and forgiveness, Sarah

Kofman writes of an "economy of pleasure allowed by the super-ego, the forgiveness of sorts that is granted by it and that brings humour closer to the manic phase, since thanks to its 'gifts', the diminished 'ego' finds itself if not euphoric at least inflated anew" (Kofman, *Pourquoi rit-on? Freud et le mot d'esprit*, 100–103).

8. Cf. Hélène Cixous's concept of "dreamexistence": "of which there is no more difference or lag between virtuality and actuality, between the desire of the phantasm and reality, between dream and reality, is the event that makes things happen in a dream. As if in a dream" (Jacques Derrida, *H. C. for Life, that is to say . . .* trans. Laurent Milesi and Stefan Herbrechter [Stanford: Stanford UP, 2006], 157; see also chapter 2 of this volume, "An Ethics or Politics of the Dream" section).

9. Derrida, *The Work of Mourning*, 188. See also Jacques Derrida, "Psyche: Inventions of the Other," in *Reading De Man Reading*, ed. Wlad Godzich and Lindsay Waters (Minneapolis: U of Minnesota P, 1989).

10. Derrida, "Hostipitality," 385.

11. Derrida, *The Work of Mourning*, 172.

12. Jacques Derrida, "Passages—from Traumatism to Promise," in *Points: Interviews 1974–1994*, ed. Elizabeth Weber, trans. Peggy Kamuf (Stanford: Stanford UP, 1995), 381–82.

13. Derrida, *The Work of Mourning*, 182.

14. Ibid., 169

15. Ibid., 172.

16. Ibid., 183.

17. Jacques Derrida, Seminar "Questions de Responsabilité III: Témoignage" (1993–94), Ecole des Hautes Etudes en Sciences Sociales, Paris.

18. "This treatment of memory called forgiveness" (Jacques Derrida, introduction to *Selected Writings: Sarah Kofman*, ed. Thomas Albrecht et al. [Stanford: Stanford UP, 2007], 27).

19. Ibid., 27–28.

20. Jacques Derrida, "To Forgive: The Unforgivable and the Imprescriptable, in *Questioning God*, ed. John D. Caputo, Mark Dooley, and Michael J Scanlon (Bloomington: Indiana UP, 2001), 44.

21. J. Derrida and E. Roudinesco, "Of the Anti-Semitism to Come," in *For What Tomorrow*, trans. Jeff Fort (Stanford: Stanford UP, 2004), 111.

22. C. McDonald "Sarah Kofman: Effecting Self-Translation," *TTR: Traduction, Terminologie, Rédaction* 11.2 (1998): 192. See also S. Kofman, *Rue Ordonner Rue Labat*, trans. Ann Smock (Lincoln: U of Nebraska P, 1996).

23. S. Kofman. "Damned Food," *SubStance* 49 (1986): 8–9.

24. Derrida *The Work of Mourning*, 184.

25. Ibid.

26. *Colporter* is the French translation of the German *zutragen* in Freud, who writes: "A new joke operates almost as an event of general interest; it is passed on (peddled, in Kofman's text) from mouth to mouth like a message of the most recent victory [neueste Sieges nachricht von dem einen dem anderen zugetragen]." S. Kofman *Pourquoi rit-on? Freud et le mot d'esprit* (Paris: Galilée 1986), 106–7, translation mine. *Mot d'esprit* is the French rendering of the German *Witz*, which is habitually (albeit inexactly) translated into English as "joke," as in the title of Freud's book: *Jokes and Their Relation to the Unconscious.*

27. Ibid., 198.

28. Jacques Derrida, *Memoires for Paul de Man*, trans. Avital Ronell and Eduardo Cadava (New York: Columbia UP, 1986), 11. See also Paul de Man, "The Rhetoric of Temporality," in *Blindness and Insight: Essays in the Rhetoric of Contemporary Criticism* (Minneapolis: U of Minnesota P, 1983), 187–228. See also Jacques Derrida, "Typewriter Ribbon: Limited Ink (2)," in *Without Alibi*, trans. Peggy Kamuf (Stanford: Stanford UP, 2002).

29. In an argument similar to the one he makes elsewhere concerning the gift beyond exchange, forgiveness does not present itself as such to what is commonly called an experience or consciousness (Derrida, "To Forgive: The Unforgivable and the Imprescriptible," 36).

30. See the chapter entitled "Deconstruction Is America?," in Catherine Malabou and Jacques Derrida, *Counterpath: Traveling with Jacques Derrida*, trans. David Wills (Stanford: Stanford UP, 2004), 219–29.

31. Ibid.

32. Paul de Man, "Les Juifs dans la littérature actuelle," *Le Soir*, 4 March 1941. This has been republished in Paul de Man, *Wartime Journalism 1939–1943*, ed. Werner Hamacher, Neil Hertz, and Thomas Keenen (Lincoln: U of Nebraska P, 1988).

33. Jacques Derrida, "Like the Sound of the Sea Deep within a Shell: Paul de Man's War," in "The Sociology of Literature," special issue of *Critical Inquiry* 14.3 (Spring 1988): 623. In the first publication of this article in English, Peggy Kamuf translated *impardonable* as "unpardonable" rather than "unforgiveable." Unpardonable is undoubtedly a correct translation, but one cannot help but ask if this more Latin translation did not also attenuate, if ever so slightly, Derrida's appraisal of de Man's offense to English speaking readers and making it easier to go past without notice. Even in italics, the word "unpardonable" in English is less striking than the word "unforgivable." That many commentators at the time (both within and outside of academia) did not see or wish to see that Derrida had condemned what de Man had done is well documented

(see, for example, Jacques Derrida, "Biodegradables Seven Diary Fragments," *Critical Inquiry* 15.4 [Summer 1989]: 812–73; and Benoit Peeters, *Derrida: A Biography*, trans. Andrew Brown [Cambridge: Polity, 2013], 389–413).

34. Derrida, "An Interview with Professor Derrida," Shoah Resource Center, 17.

35. Ibid.

36. Derrida "Like the Sound of the Sea Deep within a Shell: Paul de Man's War," 621.

37. Peeters, *Derrida: A Biography*, 397.

38. Derrida, "To Forgive: The Unforgivable and the Imprescriptible," in *Questioning God*, 42.

39. Derrida "Typewriter Ribbon: Limited Ink (2)," 71–161; Derrida, "Le parjure, perhaps," in *Without Alibi*, 161–202.

40. "Do not forgive. Forgiveness accuses before it forgives. By accusing, by stating the injury, it makes the wrong irredeemable. It carries the blow all the way to culpability. Thus, all becomes irreparable; giving and forgiving cease to be possible . . . Forgive me for forgiving you" (Maurice Blanchot, *L'écriture du désastre* [Paris: Gallimard, 1980], 89; see also chapter 1 of this volume).

41. Derrida *Memoires for Paul de Man*, 98.

42. Jacques Derrida, "On Forgiveness: A Roundtable Discussion with Jacques Derrida," in *Questioning God*, 56.

43. Jacques Derrida, "Signature Event Context," in *Margins of Philosophy*, trans. Alan Bass (Chicago: U of Chicago P, 1986), 307–30.

44. Ibid., 316.

45. Jacques Derrida, "There Is No One Narcissism," in *Points: Interviews 1974–1994*, ed. Elizabeth Weber, trans. Peggy Kamuf (Stanford: Stanford UP, 1995), 209.

46. "We must understand this word *subjectum*, however, as the translation of the Greek *hypokeimenon*. The word names that-which-lies-before (*das Vorliegende*), which, as ground, gathers everything onto itself. This metaphysical meaning of the concept of subject has first of all no special relationship to man (*Mensch*) and none at all to the I. However, when man becomes the primary and only real *subjectum*, that means: Man becomes that being upon which all that is, is grounded as regards the manner of its Being and its truth" (Martin Heidegger, "The Age of the World Picture," in *The Question Concerning Technology and Other Essays*, trans. William Lovitt [New York: Garland, 1997], 129). The philosophical determination of the human as subject is, for Heidegger, characteristic of the modern age, which begins with Descartes's *ego cogito*.

47. "Deconstruction and the Philosophers (the very idea)," in Geoffrey Bennington, *Legislations: The Politics of Deconstruction* (London: Verso, 1994), 25.

48. For more on this aporia, see Dana Hollander, "Is Deconstruction a Jewish Science? Reflections on Jewish Philosophy in Light of Derrida's Judéïtés," *Philosophy Today* 50.1 (Spring 2006): 128–38.

49. Malabou and Derrida, *Counterpath*, 90.

50. Jacques Derrida, "Hostipitality," 397. In French, the Day of Atonement is called Le Jour du Grand Pardon.

51. Cf. Simon Wiesenthal *Every Day Remembrance Day: A Chronicle of Jewish Martyrdom* (New York: H. Holt, 1987).

52. Jacques Derrida, *Learning to Live Finally: The Last Interview*, trans. Pascale-Anne Brault and Michael Naas (Brooklyn: Melville House), 24.

53. Simon Wiesenthal, "How to Deal with Opponents," in *Justice not Vengeance*, trans. Ewald Osers (London: Weidenfeld and Nicolson, 1989), 347.

54. For more on the proximity of Hegel and Derrida, see Stuart Barnett, ed., *Hegel after Derrida* (London: Routledge, 1998).

55. Ibid. "There can be absolute hostility only *for* a brother." Derrida has analyzed the logic of fraternal enmity in *Politics of Friendship* (trans. George Collins [London: Verso, 1997], see, in particular, 148). Within a traditional orthodox Jewish synagogue on Yom Kippur, it would be impossible for a man and a woman to address one another, since the sexes are separated. By addressing and remembering the Jewish joke for Sarah Kofman, Derrida also attempts to mark what the Abrahamic, patriarchal mirror of fraternal love and enmity leaves invisible, i.e., that a daughter and/or sister may arrive as a frenemy in a similar or different way.

56. Derrida, "Hostipitality," 396–97. To read Derrida's "And yet" (*Et pourtant*) above, one should also read Maurice Blanchot's very beautiful analysis of "Prophetic Speech" in *The Book to Come*: "When everything is impossible, when the future given over to fire burns, when there is no more rest except in the land of midnight, then prophetic speech which tells of the impossible future, also says the 'yet' ['*pourtant*'] which breaks the impossible and restores time." In a footnote, Blanchot adds: "When Kafka puts all his hope in the word '*trotzdem*' ('yet' [*et pourtant*]) and 'despite everything' [*en dépit de tout*]), it is the prophetic hope which speaks in him" (Blanchot, *The Book to Come*, 81, translation modified; *Le livre à venir* [Paris: Gallimard, 1959], 112).

57. "One must perhaps be able to think the perhaps, which is to say that one must be able to *say* it and to *make* of it, in saying it, an event"; "the thought of the 'perhaps' perhaps engages the only possible thought of the event—of friendship to come and friendship for the future . . . there is no more just category for the future than that of the 'perhaps.'" "The *arrivant* will arrive perhaps . . . but the *arrivant* will also be the perhaps itself, the unheard-of, totally new experience of the perhaps" (Derrida, *Politics of Friendship*, 29–30). Elisabeth Weber

has undertaken a reading of Derrida's perhaps in "Suspended from the Other's Heartbeat," *South Atlantic Quarterly* 106.2 (Spring 2007): 325–44.

58. Derrida, *Politics of Friendship*, 29.

59. "The promise promises in the fundamental mode of 'perhaps,' and even the 'dangerous perhaps' which will open, as *Beyond Good and Evil* prophesies, the speech of the philosophers to come" (ibid., 28–29).

60. Derrida, "There Is No *One* Narcissis," in *Points: Interviews 1974–1994*, 205.

61. "There is," Derrida believes, "a relative specificity . . . a 'relative purity' of performatives . . . one must [therefore] . . . construct a differential typology of forms of iteration" (Derrida, "Signature Event Contex," in *Margins of Philosophy*, 326. For another reading of the role of Jewish jokes for Derrida, see Elizabeth Rottenberg, "The Laughter of Jacques Derrida," *Oxford Literary Review* 36.2 (December 2014): 296–99.

62. Jacques Derrida, "Faith and Knowledge: The Two Sources of Religion within the Limits of Reason Alone," in *Acts of Religion*, 90.

63. For a recent critique of Jewish exceptionalism, see Judith Butler, *Parting Ways: Jewishness and the Critique of Zionism* (New York: Columbia UP, 2012).

64. See Philippe Lacoue-Labarthe, "Transcendence Ends in Politics," *Typographies: Mimesis, Philosophy, Politics* (Cambridge: Harvard UP, 1989), 267–300.

65. Derrida, "Faith and Knowledge: The Two Sources of 'Religion' at the Limits of Reason Alone," 90–91, translation modified.

66. Sigmund Freud, "The Advance in Intellectuality/Spirituality" (*Fortschritt in der Geistigkeit*), in *Moses and Monotheism*, 362. On her father's request during the International Psychoanalytic Congress in 1939, Anna Freud read out this section of the book. Freud was too ill to appear. This gesture is analyzed in Yosef Hayim Yerushalmi's *Freud's Moses: Judaism Terminable and Interminable* (New Haven: Yale UP, 1991), 51ff., 128. In Paris in 1833, Heinrich Heine made the same point as Freud did over a century later: "The Jews, who appreciate the value of precious things, knew right well what they did when, at the burning of the second temple, they left to their fate the gold and silver implements of sacrifice, the candlesticks and lamps, even the breastplate of the High Priest adorned with great jewels, but saved the Bible. This was the real treasure of the Temple, and, thanks be to God!" (Heinrich Heine, *Religion and Philosophy in Germany: A Fragment*, trans. John Snodgrass [Albany: State U of New York P, 1986], 15). On the question of psychoanalysis (and implicitly deconstruction) as a Jewish science, see Jacques Derrida *Archive Fever: A Freudian Impression*, trans. Eric Prenowitz, *Diacritics* 25.2 (Summer 1995): 9–63.

67. At a recent conference I attended, an Aboriginal Elder, Aunty Fran Bodkin, who is a D'harawal Elder (Bidjigal clan), attested that she thought

the safest place today to guard the knowledge of her people is the university ("Honouring Our Songlines: Connection, Collaboration and Co-Creation," 24–25 October 2016, Western Sydney University).

68. Jacques Derrida, "The Eyes of Language: The Abyss and the Volcano," in *Acts of Religion*, 226.

69. Jacques Derrida, *On Cosmopolitanism and Forgiveness*, trans. Mark Dooley and Michael Hughes (London: Routledge, 2001), 28, translation modified. See also chapter 2 of this volume.

70. Ibid. See also Derrida, "Hostipitality," 356–421.

71. Derrida, *The Gift of Death.*

72. Jacques Derrida, "Abraham, the Other," in *Judeities*, trans. Bettina Bergo and Michael B. Smith (New York: Fordham UP, 2007), 1–36.

73. Jacques Derrida, "Circumfession," in *Jacques Derrida*, trans. Geoffrey Bennington (Chicago: U of Chicago P, 1993), 182.

74. Jacques Derrida and Elizabeth Roudinesco, *For What Tomorrow*, trans. Jeff Fort (Stanford: Stanford UP, 2004), 165.

75. Jacques Derrida, "How to Avoid Speaking: Denials," in *Derrida and Negative Theology*, ed. Harold Coward and Toby Foshay (Albany: State U of New York P, 1992), 127–28.

76. Derrida, *On Cosmopolitalism and Forgiveness*, 54.

77. Jacques Derrida, *Adieu to Emmanuel Levinas,* trans. Pascale-Anne Brault and Michael Naas (Stanford: Stanford UP, 1999), 81–82.

78. Derrida, "How to Avoid Speaking: Denials," 135. Compare also: "Yesterday he [Genet] let me know that he was in Beirut, among the Palestinians at war, encircled outcasts. I know that what interests me always takes place over there [*là-bas*], but how to show that?" (Derrida, *Glas*, 36).

79. Some indeed will have already attempted it, notably Gil Anidjar, "Derrida, the Jew, the Arab," in *The Jew, The Arab: A History of the Enemy* (Stanford: Stanford UP, 2003), 40–61. See also Gil Anidjar, "Once More, Once More: Derrida, the Arab, the Jew," introduction to Derrida, *Acts of Religion*, 1–40.

80. Jill Robbins, "Circumcising Confession: Derrida, Autobiography, Judaism," *Diacritics* 25.4 (Winter 1995): 29.

81. Derrida, "How to Avoid Speaking: Denials," 126–27.

82. Ibid., 128.

83. Martin Heidegger, "The Nature of Language," in *On the Way to Language*, trans. Peter D. Hertz (New York: Harper and Row, 1982), 71–73. See also Jacques Derrida, *Of Spirit: Heidegger and the Question*, trans. Geoffrey Bennington and Rachel Bowlby (Chicago: U of Chicago P), 129–36.

84. Jacques Derrida, "Différance," in *Margins of Philosophy*, 22.

85. Martin Heidegger, *Gesamtausgabe*, 96:243 (Überlegungen XIV) (1941), qtd. in *Reading Heidegger's Black Notebooks 1931–1941*, ed. Ingo Farin and Jeff Malpas (Cambridge: MIT Press, 2016), 257.

86. For Heidegger's rejection of biologism, see Heidegger, *Contributions to Philosophy (from Enowning)*, trans. Parvis Emad and Kenneth Maly (Bloomington: Indiana UP, 1999), 122, 152–55; and Mahon O'Brien, *Heidegger History and the Holocaust* (London: Bloomsbury Academic, 2015).

87. Jean-Luc Nancy "Heidegger et Nous," 21 June 2014 by J-C Martin, online, http://strassdelaphilosophie.blogspot.com.au/2014/06/heidegger-et-nous-jean-luc-nancy.html.

88. Peter Trawny, "Eine neue Dimension," *Die Zeit*, 27 December 2013, online, www.zeit.de/2014/01/heidegger-schwarze-hefte-herausgeber-peter-trawny.

89. Nancy, "Heidegger et Nous."

90. Derrida, "To Forgive the Unforgivable and the Imprescriptible," in *Questioning God*, 41.

91. "Our resentments-emotional source of every genuine morality, which was always a morality for the losers [*Unterlegenen*]-have little or no chance at all to make the evil work of the overwhelmers [*Überwältigern*] bitter for them" (Jean Améry, "Ressentiments," in *Beyond Guilt and Atonement*, 81/58; see also chapter 1 of this volume, "Before All Questioning" section).

92. Derrida, "An Interview with Professor Jacques Derrida," Shoah Resource Center, 11.

93. Cf. Blanchot, *Le livre à venir*; and also the Derridean concept of "la démocratie á venir," in Jacques Derrida, *Rogues: Two Essays on Reason*, trans. Pascale-Anne Brault and Michael Naas (Stanford: Stanford UP, 2001).

94. Derrida, "Hostipitality," 381. Cf. Maurice Blanchot: "Prophetic speech announces an impossible future, or makes the future it announces . . . When speech becomes prophetic, it is not the future that is given, it is the present that is taken away, and with it any possibility of a firm, stable, lasting presence" ("Prophetic Speech," in *The Book to Come*, 79).

95. "Everything has either a price [*Preis*] or a dignity [*Würde*]. What has a price can be replaced by something else as its equivalent; what on the other hand is raised above all price and therefore admits of no equivalent has a dignity" (Immanuel Kant, *Groundwork of the Metaphysics of Morals: A German-English Edition*, ed. and trans. Mary Gregor and Jens Timmermann [Cambridge: Cambridge UP, 2011], 97).

96. René Char qtd. in Blanchot, *The Infinite Conversation*, 53.

97. "Un type qui fait attention à ce qu'il dit" me dit-il un jour de Heidegger, comme de lui-même. Attention à ce qu'il dit. (Hélène Cixous, "Le Bouc lié," in *Salut à Jacques Derrida* [Paris: PUF, 2005], 26).

98. Ibid.

99. Cixous, *Insister of Jacques Derrida*, 78–79.

100. See, for example, Samuel Weber, *The Legend of Freud*, expanded ed. (Stanford: Stanford UP, 2000), and "The Diverticator: Remarks on Freud's *Witz*," *Glyph* 1 (1977): 1–27.

101. Derrida, *Of Spirit: Heidegger and the Question*, 129–36.

102. Martin Heidegger, "The Nature of Language," 76.

103. "De telles blagues, et surtout le rire qu'ils déclenchent, me semblent être associées à ce que, dans une longue note de son livre, *De l'esprit*, il appelle le 'gage.' Dans cette lecture de Heidegger, Jacques Derrida est remonté au-delà ou en deça du questionnement, qui était, pour Heidegger, 'la piété de la pensée,' pour discerner comme sa condition de possibilité un engagement 'dans la langue—et donc toujours dans *une* langue.' Cet engagement revoie à un 'gage' qui 'précède le langage' sans 'lui être étranger' (*De l'esprit*, 148). Dans cette même note, il propose une relecture de Heidegger à partir de ce 'gage' et de son 'appel' (*Zusage*)" (Sam Weber, "Le seul 'moi' du monde . . . ," *Salut à Jacques Derrida Rue Descartes* 48.2 [2005]: 40, translation mine. The rapport in French between "*gage*" and "*langage*" is not reproducible in English).

104. See, for example, Jacques Derrida, "Nombre de oui," in *Psyché: Inventions de l'autre* (Paris: Galilée, 1987), 639–50. Weber ends his eulogy by recalling the "yes": "Ce mot parfois sans mot que nous nommons le 'oui'" (Weber, "Le seul 'moi' du monde . . . ," 41). For more on forgiveness as grant or *Zusage*, see chapter 1 of this volume, "The Survival of the Question" section.

105. Wiesenthal, *The Sunflower*, 12.

Afterword: "What an Art of Living!"

1. See Jacques Derrida, *Glas*, trans. John P. Leavy and Richard Rand (Lincoln: U of Nebraska P, 1990), 242–44; and Jacques Derrida *The Post-Card: From Socrates to Freud and Beyond*, trans. Alan Bass (Chicago: U of Chicago P, 1987), 40, 71.

2. Jacques Derrida, "An Interview with Professor Derrida," Shoah Resource Center, 21–25.

3. Jacques Derrida, "Of an Apocalyptic Tone Recently Adopted in Philosophy," *Oxford Literary Review* 6.2 (1984): 4.

4. Emmanuel Levinas, "Wholly Otherwise," in *Re-Reading Levinas*, ed. Robert Bernasconi and Simon Critchley (Bloomington: Indiana UP, 1991), 4.

5. Sarah Kofman, *Pourquoi rit-on? Freud et le mot d'esprit?*, 104, also qtd. in Jacques Derrida, "Sarah Kofman: September 14, 1934–October 15 1994," in *The*

Work of Mourning, trans. Pascale-Anne Brault and Michael Naas (Chicago: U of Chicago P, 2001), 185.

6. Jacques Derrida, 'From a Restricted Economy to a General Economy: An Hegelianism Without Reserve' in *Writing and Difference*, trans. (Alan Bass. Chicago: U of Chicago P, 1978), 319.

Works Cited

Abraham, Nicolas, and Maria Torok. *The Shell and the Kernel: Renewals of Psychoanalysis*. Vol. 1. Edited by Richard T. Rand. Chicago: U of Chicago P, 1994.

Amery, Jean. *At the Mind's Limits: Contemplations by a Survivor on Auschwitz and its Realities*. Translated by Sidney Rosenfeld and Stella P. Rosenfeld. Bloomington: Indiana UP, 1980.

———. *On Suicide: A Discourse on Voluntary Death*. Translated by John D. Barlow. Bloomington: Indiana UP, 1999.

———. *Werke Band 2*. Stuttgart: Klett-Cotta, 2002.

Améry, J. *Hand an sich legen: Diskurs über den Freitod*. Stuttgart: Klett-Cotta, 1983.

Anidjar, Gil. *The Jew, the Arab: A History of the Enemy*. Stanford: Stanford UP, 2003.

Antelme, Robert. *L'espèce humaine*. Paris: Gallimard, 1957.

———. *The Human Race*. Translated by Jeffrey Haight and Annie Mahler. Marlboro: Marlboro Press, 1992.

Arendt, Hannah. *The Human Condition*. Chicago: U of Chicago P, 1998.

———. *Vita Activa oder Vom tätigen Leben*. Munich: Piper, 1999.

Austin, J. L. *How to Do Things with Words*. Oxford: Clarendon, 1969.

Bachmann, Ingeborg. *Das Buch Franza/Requiem für Fanny Goldmann*. Munich: Piper, 1995.

———. "Drei Wege zum See." In *Ingeborg Bachmann, Gesamtausgabe*, edited by Christine Koschel, Inge von Weidenbaum, and Clemens Münster, vol. 2. Munich: Piper, 1993.

———. *The Book of Franza and Requiem for Fanny Goldmann*. Translated by Peter Filkins. Evanston: Northwestern UP, 2010.

Baer, Ulrich. "The Hubris of Humility: Günter Grass, Peter Schneider and German Guilt after 1989." *Germanic Review* 80 (Winter 2005): 50–73.

Barkan, Elazar. *The Guilt of Nations: Restitution and Negotiating Historical Injustices.* New York: Norton, 2000.

Barkan, Elazar, and Alexander Karn. "Group Apology as an Ethical Imperative." In *Taking Wrongs Seriously: Apologies and Reconciliation.* Stanford: Stanford UP, 2006.

Bar-On, Dan. *Fear and Hope: Three Generations of the Holocaust.* Cambridge: Harvard UP, 1995.

———. *The Indescribable and the Undiscussable: Reconstructing Human Discourse after Trauma.* Budapest: Central European UP, 1999.

———. *Legacy of Silence: Encounters with Children of the Third Reich.* Cambridge: Harvard UP, 1989.

Baudelaire, Charles. *Les fleurs du mal.* Paris: Gallimard, 2002.

Bennington, Geoffrey. *Legislations: The Politics of Deconstruction.* London: Verso, 1994.

Blanchot, Maurice. *The Book to Come.* Translated by Charlotte Mandel. Stanford: Stanford UP, 2003.

———. *L'écriture du désastre.* Paris: Gallimard, 1980.

———. *L'entretien infini.* Paris: Gallimard, 1969.

———. *The Infinite Conversation.* Translated by Susan Hanson. Minneapolis: U of Minnesota P, 1993.

———. *L'instant de ma mort.* Paris: Gallimard, 2002.

———. *Le livre à venir.* Paris: Gallimard, 1959.

———. *Le pas au-delà.* Paris: Gallimard, 1973.

Brudholm, Thomas. "The Justice of Truth and Reconciliation." *Hypatia: A Journal of Feminist Philosophy* 18 (Spring, 2003): 189–96.

———. *Resentment's Virtue: Jean Améry and the Refusal to Forgive.* Philadelphia: Temple UP, 2008.

Butler, Judith. *Parting Ways: Jewishness and the Critique of Zionism.* New York: Columbia UP, 2012.

Caputo, John D., Mark Dooley, and Michael J Scanlon, eds. *Questioning God.* Bloomington: Indiana UP, 2001.

Celan, Paul, and Niko Grafenauer. *Todtnauberg.* n.p., n.d.

Charny, I. W. *Encyclopedia of Genocide.* Santa Barbara, CA: ABV-Clio, 1999.

Cixous, Hélène. "Le Bouc lié." *Salut à Jacques Derrida*, Special issue, *Rue Descartes* 48 (2005). y

———. *Insister: A Jacques Derrida*. Paris: Galilée, 2006.

———. *Insister of Jacques Derrida*. Translated by Peggy Kamuf. Stanford: Stanford UP, 2006.

Cohn-Sherbok, Dan. *Judaism: History, Belief, and Practice*. London: Routledge, 2003.

De Man, Paul. *Wartime Journalism 1939–1943*. Edited by Werner Hamacher, Neil Hertz, and Thomas Keenen. Lincoln: U of Nebraska P, 1988.

De Vries, Hent. *Philosophy and the Turn to Religion*. Baltimore: Johns Hopkins UP, 1999.

———. *Religion and Violence: Philosophical Perspectives from Kant to Derrida*. Baltimore: Johns Hopkins UP, 2001.

De Vries, Hent, and Samuel Weber, eds. *Religion and Media*. Stanford: Stanford UP, 2001.

Derrida, Jacques. ". . . . ." *Les cahiers du grif*. Hors- Sérien 3 (1997).

———. "Abraham, the Other." In *Judeities*, translated by Bettina Bergo and Michael B. Smith. 1–36. New York: Fordham UP, 2007.

———. *Acts of Religion*. Edited by Gil Anidjar. London: Routledge, 2002.

———. *Adieu to Emmanuel Levinas*. Translated by Pascale-Anne Brault and Michael Naas. Stanford: Stanford UP, 1999.

———. *L'animal que donc je suis*. Paris: Galilée, 2006.

———. *The Animal That Therefore I Am*. Translated by David Wills. New York: Fordham UP, 2008.

———. *Aporias*. Translated by Thomas Dutoit. Stanford: Stanford UP, 1993.

———. *Apories: Mourir—s'attendre aux limites de la vérité*. Paris: Galilée, 1996.

———. *Archive Fever: A Freudian Impression*. Translated by Eric Prenowitz. Chicago: U of Chicago P, 1998.

———. *The Beast and the Sovereign, Volume I. (The Seminars of Jacques Derrida)*. Edited by Michel Lisse et al. Translated by Geoffrey Bennington. Chicago: U of Chicago P, 2009.

———. *Béliers: Le dialogue ininterrompu: entre deux infinis, le poème*. Translated by Thomas Dutoit. Paris: Galilée, 2003.

———. "Biodegradables Seven Diary Fragments." *Critical Inquiry* 15.4 (Summer 1989).

———. "Choreographies." *Diacritics* 12.2 (Summer 1982): 66–76.

———. "'Comment Donner Raison?' How to Concede, with Reasons?" Translated by John P. Leavey Jr. *Diacritics* 19.3 (1989): 4–9.

———. *De la grammatologie.* Paris: Éditions de Minuit, 1967.

———. "Demeure: Fiction and Testimony." In *The Instant of My Death.* Translated by Elizabeth Rottenberg. Stanford: Stanford UP, 2000.

———. *Derrida and Negative Theology.* Edited by Harold Coward and Toby Foshay. Albany: State University at New York Press, 1992.

———. *Donner la mort.* Paris: Galilée, 1999.

———. *Donner le temps 1: La Fausse Monnaie.* Paris: Galilée, 1991.

———. *The Ear of the Other: Otobiography, Transference, Translation: Texts and Discussions with Jacques Derrida.* Edited by Christine V. McDonald. Translated by Peggy Kamuf. New York: Schocken, 1985.

———. "'Eating Well' or the Calculation of the Subject: An Interview with Jacques Derrida." In *Who Comes After the Subject?,* edited by E. Cadava, P. Connor, and Jean-Luc Nancy. New York: Routledge, 1991.

———. *L'écriture et la différence.* Paris: Seuil, 1967.

———. "Epoché and Faith: An Interview with Jacques Derrida." In *Derrida and Religion: Other Testaments,* edited by Yvonne Sherwood and Kevin Hart. New York and London: Routledge, 2005.

———. "Faith and Knowledge: The Two Sources of 'Religion' at the Limits of Reason Alone." In *Religion,* edited by Gianni Vattimo and Derrida, translated by David Webb et al. Stanford: Stanford UP, 1998.

———. *Fichus, Discours de Francfort.* Paris: Galilée, 2002.

———. *Foi et savoir: Suivi de le siècle et le pardon.* Paris: Éditions du Seuil, 2007.

———. *For What Tomorrow.* Translated by Jeff Fort. Stanford: Stanford UP, 2004.

———. "Force of Law: The Mystical Foundations of Authority." *Cardozo Law Review* 11.919 (1990).

———. "Geschlecht 2: Heidegger's Hand." In *Deconstruction and Philosophy: The Texts of Jacques Derrida,* edited by J. Sallis, 161–96. Chicago: U of Chicago P, 1999.

———. *The Gift of Death.* Translated by David Wills. Chicago: U of Chicago P, 1995.

———. *Given Time.* Translated by Peggy Kamuf. Chicago: U of Chicago P, 1992.

———. *Glas.* Translated by John P. Leavy and Richard Rand. Lincoln: U of Nebraska P, 1990.

———. *HC for Life, That Is to Say—.* Translated by Laurent Milesi and Stephen Herbrechter. Stanford: Stanford UP, 2006.

———. "Hostipitality: Session of January 8, 1997." In *Acts of Religion*, edited by Gil Anidjar. London: Routledge, 2001.

———. "An Interview with Professor Jacques Derrida." Shoah Resource Center, the International School for Holocaust Studies. January 8, 1998. Online. June 2014. www.yadvashem.org.

———. *Jacques Derrida.* Translated by Geoffrey Bennington. Chicago: U of Chicago P, 1999.

———. *Learning to Live Finally: The Last Interview.* Translated by Pascale-Anne Brault and Michael Naas. Brooklyn: Melville House, 2007.

———."Like the Sound of the Sea Deep within a Shell: Paul de Man's War." In "The Sociology of Literature," special issue, *Critical Inquiry* 14.3 (Spring 1988).

———. *Marges de la philosophie.* Paris: Éditions de Minuit, 1972.

———. *Margins of Philosophy.* Translated by Alan Bass. Chicago: U of Chicago P, 1986.

———. "Marx and Sons." In *Ghostly Demarcations: A Symposium on Jacques Derrida's Specters of Marx*, edited by Michael Sprinker. London: Verso, 1999.

———. *Memoires for Paul de Man.* Translations edited by Avital Ronell and Eduardo Cadava. New York: Columbia UP, 1986.

———. "Mochlos: or, the Conflict of the Faculties." In *Logomachia: The Conflict of the Faculties*, edited by Richard Rand. Lincoln: U of Nebraska P, 1992.

———. "Niemand ist unschuldig." Interview by Ulrich Raulff. *Süddeutsche Zeitung*, September 24, 2001.

———. "Nombre de oui." In *Psyché: Inventions de l'autre*, 639–50. Paris: Galilée, 1987.

———."Of an Apocalyptic Tone Recently Adopted in Philosophy." *Oxford Literary Review* 6.2 (1984): 3–37.

———. *Of Grammatology.* Translated by Gayatri Chakravorty Spivak. Baltimore: Johns Hopkins UP, 1997.

———. *Of Spirit: Heidegger and the Question.* Translated by Geoffrey Bennington and Rachel Bowlby. Chicago: U of Chicago P, 1989.

———. *On Cosmopolitanism and Forgiveness.* Translated by Mark Dooley and Michael Hughes. London: Routledge, 2001.

———. "On Forgiveness: A Roundtable Discussion with Jacques Derrida." In *Questioning God*, edited by John D. Caputo, Mark Dooley, and Michael J Scanlon. Bloomington: Indiana UP, 2001.

———. "On Forgiveness." European Graduate School, 2004. Available online at www.egs.edu.

———. *Paper Machine.* Translated by Rachel Bowlby. Stanford: Stanford UP, 2005.

———. "Philosophie et mondialisation." Rencontre de Jacques Derrida et Etienne Balibar." *Philosophie, Philosophie* (Revue des Etudiants de Philosophie Paris) 8.7 (2007).

———. *Points: Interviews 1974–1994.* Edited by Elizabeth Weber. Translated by Peggy Kamuf. Stanford: Stanford UP, 1995.

———. *Points de suspension: Entretiens.* Paris: Galilée, 1992.

———. "The Politics of Friendship." *Journal of Philosophy* (1988): 632–44.

———. *Politics of Friendship.* Translated by George Collins. London: Verso, 1997.

———. *The Post-Card from Socrates to Freud and Beyond.* Translated by Alan Bass. Chicago: U of Chicago P, 1987.

———. "Psyche: Inventions of the Other." In *Reading de Man Reading*, edited by Wlad Godzich and Lindsay Waters; translated by Catherine Porter. Minneapolis: U of Minnesota P, 1989.

———. *Rogues: Two Essays on Reason.* Translated by Pascale-Anne Brault and Michael Naas. Stanford: Stanford UP, 2001.

———. "Le siècle et le pardon." Interview by Michel Wieviorka. *Le monde des débats*, December 1999.

———. *Sovereignties in Question: The Poetics of Paul Celan.* Translated by Thomas Dutoit. New York: Fordham UP, 2005.

———. *Spectres de Marx: L'etat de la dette, Le travail du deuil et la nouvelle internationale.* Paris: Galilée, 1997.

———. "To Forgive: The Unforgivable and the Imprescriptible." In *Questioning God.* Edited by John D. Caputo et al. Bloomington: Indiana UP, 2001.

———. *Without Alibi.* Translated by Peggy Kamuf. Stanford: Stanford UP, 2002.

———. *The Work of Mourning.* Translated by Pascale-Anne Brault and Michael Naas. Chicago: U of Chicago P, 2001.

———. *Writing and Difference.* Translated by Alan Bass. Chicago: U of Chicago P, 1978.

Derrida, J, and C. Malabou. *Counterpath: Traveling with Jacques Derrida.* Translated by David Wills. Stanford: Stanford UP, 2004.

Dostoyevsky, Fyodor. *The Brothers Karamazov.* Translated by Constance Garnett. New York: Lowell, 1969.

Duras, Marguerite. *La douleur.* Paris: P.O.L., 1985.

———. *The War.* Translated by Barbara Bray. New York: Pantheon, 1986.

Farin, Ingo, and Jeff Malpas, eds. *Reading Heidegger's Black Notebooks 1931–1941.* Cambridge: MIT Press, 2016.

Fathy, Safaa. *D'ailleurs, Derrida.* Produced by La Sept/Arte. Gloria Films Production, 1999.

Felman, Shoshana, and Dori Laub. *Testimony: Crises of Witnessing in Literature, Psychoanalysis, and History.* New York: Routledge, 1992.

Fine, R. "Crimes against Humanity: Hannah Arendt and the Nuremberg Debates." *European Journal of Social Theory* 3.3 (2000): 293.

Freud, Sigmund. *Der Mann Moses und die Monotheistische Religion.* Frankfurt: Fischer, 1999.

———. *Moses and Monotheism.* Translated by Katherine Jones. London: Hogarth, 1939.

———. *The Standard Edition of the Complete Psychological Works of Sigmund Freud: The Future of an Illusion, Civilization and Its Discontents and Other Works.* Edited by James Strachey. London: Hogarth, 1953–74.

———. *Trauer und Melancholie.* Rahway, NJ: Merck, 1972.

Gasché, Rodolphe. "L'expérience aporétique aux origines de la pensée: Platon, Heidegger, Derrida." *Derrida lecteur* 38.1–2 (2002).

Gellhaus, Axel. *Paul Celan bei Martin Heidegger in Todtnauberg.* Marbach am Necker: Literaturhaus Museum, 2002.

Gerl-Falkovitz, Hanna-Barbara. *Verzeihung des Unverzeihlichen? Ausflüge in Landschaften der Schuld, der Reue und der Vergebung.* Dresden: Bibliothek der Unruhe und des Bewahrens, 2006.

Gouhier, Alain. "Le temps de l'impardonable et le temps du pardon selon Jankélévitch." In *Le Point Théologique, Forgiveness.* Proceedings of the Colloquium organized by the Centre Histoire des Idées, Université de Picardie. Edited by Michel Perrin. Paris: Beauchesnes, 1987.

Grunebaum, Heidi. "Talking to Ourselves" among the Innocent Dead": On

Reconciliation, Forgiveness, and Mourning." *Publications of the Modern Language Association of America* 117.2 (2002): 306–10.

Guyer, Sara. "The Pardon of the Disaster." *SubStance* 35.1 (2006): 85–105.

Guyer, Sara Emilie. *Romanticism after Auschwitz* Stanford, Calif.: Stanford UP, 2007.

Hamacher, Werner. "Afformative, Strike." Translated by Dana Hollander. *Cardozo Law Review* 13.4 (December 1991): 1133.

Hancock, Ian. "Beyond Poverty, beyond Europe." *SAIS Review* 23.2 (2005).

Hegel, G. W. F. *Early Theological Writing.* Translated by T. M. Knox. Philadelphia: U of Pennsylvania P, 2011.

———. *Elements of the Philosophy of Right.* Edited by Allen W. Wood. Translated by H. B. Nisbet. Cambridge: Cambridge UP, 1991.

———. *Frühe Schriften.* Frankfurt: Suhrkamp, 1986.

———. *Phänomenologie des Geistes.* Hamburg: F. Meiner, 1988.

———. *The Phenomenology of Spirit.* Translated by A. V. Miller. Oxford: Clarendon, 1977.

———. *Werke, Band 7: Grundlinien der Philosophie des Rechts.* Edited by Eva Moldenhauer and Karl Markus Michel. Frankfurt: Suhrkamp, 1970.

Heidegger, Martin. "The Age of the World Picture." In *The Question Concerning Technology and Other Essays,* translated by William Lovitt. New York: Harper Torchbooks, 1977.

———. *Being and Time.* Translated by John Macquarrie. Edited by Edward Robinson. Oxford: Basil Blackwell, 1978.

———. *Contributions to Philosophy (from Enowning).* Translated by Parvis Emad and Kenneth Maly. Bloomington: Indiana UP, 1999.

———. *Early Greek Thinking.* San Francisco: Harper, 1975.

———. *Elucidations of Hölderlin's Poetry.* Translated by Keith Hoeller. Stony Brook: State U of New York P, 2000.

———. "Letter on Humanism, Trans. F. A. Capuzzi." In *Basic Writings—Martin Heidegger.* London: Routledge, 1993.

———. "The Nature of Language." In *On the Way to Language.* New York: Harper and Row, 1971.

———. *Sein und Zeit.* Tübingen: Max Niemeyer, 1993.

Heidelberger-Leonard, I. *Über Jean Améry.* Heidelberg: C. Winter, 1990.

Heine, Heinrich. *Religion and Philosophy in Germany: A Fragment.* Translated by John Snodgrass. Albany: State U of New York P, 1986.

Hercules, Bob, and Cheri Pugh. *Forgiving Dr. Mengele.* Brooklyn: First Run/ Icarus Films, 2005.

Hilberg, Raul. *The Destruction of the European Jews.* New Haven: Yale UP, 2003.

Hollander, Dana. "Is Deconstruction a Jewish Science? Reflections on Jewish Philosophy in Light of Derrida's Judéïtés." *Philosophy Today* 50.1 (Spring 2006). 128–38.

Höller, Hans. *Ingeborg Bachmann.* Hamburg: Rowatt, 1995.

Hyppolite, Jean. *Genèse et structure de la Phénoménologie de l'esprit de Hegel.* Vol. 2. Paris: Aubier, 1946.

Jankélévitch, Vladimir. *Forgiveness.* Translated by Andrew Kelly. Chicago: U of Chicago P, 2005.

———. *Henri Bergson.* Paris: Alcan, 1959.

———. *La mort.* Paris: Flammarion, 1966.

———. *Le pardon.* Paris: Aubier-Montaigne, 1967.

———. Lettre de Wiard Raveling, juin 1980. *Magazine Littéraire,* June 1995.

———. *L'imprescriptible: Pardonner?: Dans L'honneur et la Dignité.* Paris: Éditions du Seuil, 1986.

———. *L'odyssée de la conscience dans la dernière philosophie de Schelling.* Paris: Presse Universitaire de France, 1933.

———. *Music and the Ineffable.* Translated by Carolyn Abbate. Princeton: Princeton UP, 2003.

———. *Penser la mort? (Thinking Death).* Preface and supervision by Françoise Schwab. Paris: Liana Levi, 1994.

———. *Philosophie morale.* Paris: Flammarion, 1998.

———. *Ravel.* Translated by Margaret Crossland. London: Greenword, 1976.

———. "Should We Pardon Them?" *Critical Inquiry* 22.3 (Spring 1996): 552–72.

Kafka, Franz. *Erzählungen, Taschenbuchausgabe in 8 Bänden.* Edited by Max Brod. Frankfurt: Fischer, 1989.

Kant, Immanuel. "Die Streit der Fakultäten." In *Immanuel Kant's Sämmtliche Werke,* edited by Karl Rosenkranz und Friedrich Wilhelm Schubert. Vol 10. Leipzig: Leopold Voss, 1938.

———. *Groundwork of the Metaphysics of Morals.* Translated by Mary Gregor. Cambridge: Cambridge University Press, 2012.

———. *Religion within the Limits of Reason Alone* (1793). Translated by

Theodore M. Greene and Hoyt H. Hudson with John R. Silber. New York: Harper Torchbooks, 1960.

Kertész, Imre. "Who Owns Auschwitz?" Translated by John Kay. *Yale Journal of Criticism* 14.1 (2001): 267–72.

King James Bible. "Authorized Version." Cambridge edition.

Kleingeld, Pauline, and Eric Brown. "Cosmopolitanism." In *The Stanford Encyclopedia of Philosophy*, edited by Edward N. Zalta et al. Center for the Study of Language and Information. Stanford: Stanford UP, 2009.

Klüger, Ruth. "Forgiving and Remembering." *Publications of the Modern Language Association of America* 117.2 (March 2002): 311–13.

Kofman, Sarah. "Damned Food." *SubStance* 49 (1986): 8–9.

———. *Pourquoi rit-on? Freud et le mot d'esprit.* Paris: Galilée, 1996.

———. *Rue Ordonner Rue Labat.* Translated by Ann Smock. Lincoln: U of Nebraska P, 1996.

———. *Selected Writings: Sarah Kofman.* Edited by Thomas Albrecht et al. Stanford: Stanford UP, 2007.

Köhler, Dietmar, and Otto Pöggeler. *G. W. F. Hegel, Phänomenologie des Geistes.* 2nd. ed. Akademie Verlag, 2006.

Kok, Ruth R. *Statutory Limitations in International Criminal Law.* Cambridge: Cambridge UP 2007

Kristeva, J. "Forgiveness: An Interview." *PMLA* 117.2 (March 2002): 278–85.

Lacoue-Labarthe, Philippe. *Typography: Mimesis, Philosophy, Politics.* Edited by Christopher Fynsk. Cambridge: Harvard UP, 1989.

Lang, B. *The Future of the Holocaust: Between History and Memory.* Ithaca, NY: Cornell UP, 1999.

Langer, Lawrence L. *Art from the Ashes: A Holocaust Anthology.* Reprint, illustrated ed. New York: Oxford UP, 1995.

———. *Preempting the Holocaust.* New Haven: Yale UP, 2000.

Lawlor, Leonard. *Derrida and Husserl: The Basic Problem of Phenomenology.* Bloomington: Indiana UP, 2002.

Lemkin, Raphael. "Genocide—A Modern Crime." April 1945. Online. www.preventgenocide.org

Levi, Primo. *The Reawakening.* 1965. New York: Touchstone, 1995.

———.*The Voice of Memory: Interviews 1961–1987.* Edited by Marco Belpoliti and Robert Gordon. Translated from the Italian by Robert Gordon. New York: New Press, 2001.

Levinas, Emmanuel. *Collected Philosophical Papers.* Translated by Alphonso Lingis. Pittsburg: Duquesne UP, 1998.

———. *Hors sujet.* Paris: Fata Morgana, 1987.

———. *Quatre lectures Talmudiques.* Paris: Éditions de Minuit, 1997.

———. *Re-Reading Levinas.* Edited by Robert Bernasconi and Simon Critchley. Bloomington: Indiana UP, 1991.

Lyon, James K. *Paul Celan and Martin Heidegger: An Unresolved Conversation.* Baltimore: Johns Hopkins UP, 2006.

Lyotard, Jean-Francois. *The Differend: Phrases in Dispute.* Translated by Georges Van Den Abbeele. Minneapolis: U of Minnesota P, 1989.

Marrati, Paula. *Genesis and Trace: Derrida Reading Husserl and Heidegger.* Translated by Simon Sparks. Stanford: Stanford UP, 2005.

Miller, Robert H. "The Convention on the Non-Applicability of Statutory Limitations to War Crimes and Crimes against Humanity." *American Journal of International Law* 65.3 (July 1971): 476–501.

Mozes Kor, Eva, and Mary Wright. *Echoes from Auschwitz.* Terre Haute: CANDLES, 1995.

Nancy, Lean-Luc. *Dis-Enclosure: The Deconstruction of Christianity.* Translated by Bettina Bergo, Gabriel Malenfant, and Michael B. Smith. New York: Fordham UP, 2008

———. *La création du monde ou la mondialisation.* Paris: Galilée, 2002.

———. *La déclosion: Déconstruction du Christianisme 1.* Paris: Galilee, 2005.

———. "Heidegger et Nous." Published June 21, 2014, by J-C Martin. Online. http://strassdelaphilosophie.blogspot.com.au/2014/06/heidegger-et-nous-jean-luc-nancy.html

———. "On Derrida A Conversation of Sergio Benvenuto with Jean-Luc Nancy." Translated by Marcel Lieberman. *Journal of European Psychoanalysis* 19.2 (2004).

Nietzsche, Friedrich Wilhelm. *The Genealogy of Morals.* Translated by Walter Kaufmann and R. J. Hollingdale New York: Vintage, 1989.

———. *Human All Too Human: A Book for Free Spirits.* Translated by R. J. Hollingdale. Cambridge: Cambridge UP, 1996.

———. *Kritische Studienausgabe.* Vol. 2. Edited by Giorgio Colli and Mazzino Montinari. Berlin: Deutscher Taschenbuch Verlag de Gruyter, 1988.

———. *Kritische Studienausgabe.* Vol. 5. Edited by Giorgio Colli and Mazzino Montinari. Berlin: Deutscher Taschenbuch Verlag de Gruyter, 1988.

———. *Thus Spoke Zarathustra.* Translated by Adrian Del Caro. Cambridge: Cambridge UP, 2006.

Oliver, K. *The Colonization of Psychic Space: A Psychoanalytic Social Theory of Oppression.* Minneapolis: U of Minnesota P, 2004.

Ortiz, D. "Spokes in the Wheel: An Account of Torture" in *Tikkun.* Vol. 22, No. 3. May/June 2007. 36-39.

Oxford English Dictionary. 3rd. ed. Online. www.oed.com

Passerin d'Entrèves, Maurizio, 1953. *The Political Philosophy of Hannah Arendt* London and New York: Routledge, 1994.

Payne, M. "Kofman, Sarah. 2007". *Selected Writings,* edited by Thomas Albrecht. Stanford: Stanford UP." *College Literature* 35.3 (Summer 2008).

Peeters, Benoit. *Derrida: A Biography.* Translated by Andrew Brown. Cambridge: Polity, 2013.

Pick, Hella. *Simon Wiesenthal: A Life in Search of Justice.* Boston: Northeastern UP, 1996.

Power, Samantha. *A Problem from Hell: America and the Age of Genocide.* New York: HarperCollins, 2003.

Reik, Theodore. *Jewish Wit.* New York: Gamut, 1962.

Robbins, Jill. "Circumcising Confession: Derrida, Autobiography, Judaism." *Diacritics* 25.4 (Winter 1995): 20–38.

Robinson, Daryl. "Defining" Crimes Against Humanity" at the Rome Conference." *American Journal of International Law* 93.1 (1999): 43–57.

Robinson, Geoffrey. *Crimes Against Humanity: The Struggle for Global Justice.* London: Penguin, 1999.

Ronell, Avital. *Finitude's Score: Essays for the End of the Millennium.* Lincoln: U of Nebraska P, 1998.

———. *Loser Sons: Politics and Authority.* Chicago: U of Illinois P, 2012.

———. *Stupidity.* Champaign: U of Illinois P, 2003.

———. *The Test Drive.* Chicago: U of Illinois P, 2005.

Rosen, David. "The Concept of Forgiveness in Judaism." January 2003. www.rabbidavidrosen.net/the-concept-of-forgiveness-in-judaism/.

Rottenberg, Elizabeth, "The Laughter of Jacques Derrida." *Oxford Literary Review* 36.2 (December 2014): 296–99.

Sanders, Mark. *Ambiguities of Witnessing: Law and Literature in the Time of a Truth Commission.* Stanford: Stanford UP, 2007.

Schelling, Friedrich Wilhelm Joseph. *Philosophische Untersuchungen über das*

Wesen der menschlichen Freiheit und die damit zusammenhängenden Gegenstände. Frankfurt: Meiner, 2001.

Schwab, Françoise. "Jankélévitch: Le parcours d'une vie." *Magazine Littéraire,* June 1995.

Searle, John R. *Speech Acts.* Cambridge: Cambridge UP, 1969.

Shakespeare, William. *Hamlet, Prince of Denmark.* Edited by Philip Edwards. Cambridge: Cambridge UP, 2003.

Shriver, Donald. *An Ethic for Enemies Forgiveness in Politics.* Oxford: Oxford UP, 1995.

Silverman, Kaja. *Male Subjectivity at the Margins.* New York: Routledge, 1992.

Sporrer, Maria, and Herbert Steiner. *Simon Wiesenthal: Ein unbequemer Zeitgenosse.* Vienna: Orac, 1992.

Trank, Richard, and Marvin Hier. *I Have Never Forgotten You: The Life and Legacy of Simon Wiesenthal.* Documentary video. Simon Wiesenthal Center, 2007.

Trawny, Peter. "Eine neue Dimension." *Die Zeit,* December 27, 2013. www.zeit.de/2014/01/heidegger-schwarze-hefte-herausgeber-peter-trawny.

Tutu, Desmond. *No Future without Forgiveness.* New York: Image, 2004.

Ure, Michael. "The Politics of Mercy, Forgiveness and Love: A Nietzschean Appraisal." *South African Journal of Philosophy* 26.1 (2007).

Victoria, Brian Diazen. *Zen at War.* London: Rowman and Littlefield, 2006.

———. *Zen War Stories.* London: RoutledgeCurzon, 2003.

Weber, Elizabeth. "Suspended from the Other's Heartbeat." *South Atlantic Quarterly* 106.2 (Spring 2007): 325–44.

Weber, Samuel. *The Legend of Freud.* Stanford: Stanford UP, 2000.

———. "Once and for All." *Grey Room* 20 (2005): 105–16.

———. "Le seul 'moi ' du monde . . . "Salut à Jacques Derrida." Special issue of *Rue Descartes* 48.2 (2005). (Revue du Collège International de Philosophie).

Weigel, Sigrid. *Ingeborg Bachmann: Hinterlassenschaften unter Wahrung des Briefgeheimnisses.* Vienna: Zsolnay, 1999.

———. "Secularization and Sacralization, Normalization and Rupture: Kristeva and Arendt on Forgiveness." Translated by Mark Kyburz. *Publications of the Modern Language Association of America* 117.2 (2002): 320–23.

Wiesenthal, Simon. *Antisemitism: The Generic Hatred: Essays in Memory of Simon Wiesenthal.* United Nations Educational Scientific and Cultural Organization; Verbe et Lumière-Vigilance, 2007.

———. *Die Sonnenblume: Eine Erzählung von Schuld und Vergebung.* Frankfurt: Ullstein, 1998.

———. *Every Day Remembrance Day: A Chronicle of Jewish Martyrdom.* New York: Holt, 1987.

———. *Les fleurs de soleil.* Translated by Denise Meunier. Paris: Stock, 1969.

———. "How to Deal with Opponents." In *Justice not Vengeance,* translated by Ewald Osers. London: Weidenfeld and Nicolson, 1989.

———. *Max und Helen.* Frankfurt: Ullstein, 1981

———. *Recht, nicht Rache.* Frankfurt: Ullstein, 1988.

———. "The Sunflower." In *Anti-Semitism: The Generic Hatred: Essays in Honor of Simon Wiesenthal.* Edited by Michael Fineberg et al. London: Vallentine Mitchell, 2007.

———. *The Sunflower: On the Possibilities and Limits of Forgiveness.* New York: Schocken, 1998.

———. "Überleben der Shoah" im Wiener Rathaus. November 1997. Online. www.simon-wiesenthal-archiv.at.

———. *Verjährung?: 200 Persönlichkeiten des öffentlichen Lebens sagen nein: Eine Dokumentation.* Frankfurt: Europäische Verlagsanstalt, 1965.

Yovel, Yirmiyahu. *Other Within: The Marranos: Split Identity and Emerging Modernity.* Princeton: Princeton UP, 2008.

———. *Spinoza and Other Heretics.* Vol. 1, *The Marrano of Reason.* Princeton: Princeton UP, 1989.

Zolkos, Magdalena, ed. *On Jean Améry: Philosophy of Catastrophe.* Lanham, MD : Lexington, 2011.

Index

just ideas

Roger Berkowitz, *The Gift of Science: Leibniz and the Modern Legal Tradition*

Jean-Luc Nancy, translated by Pascale-Anne Brault and Michael Naas, *The Truth of Democracy*

Drucilla Cornell and Kenneth Michael Panfilio, *Symbolic Forms for a New Humanity: Cultural and Racial Reconfigurations of Critical Theory*

Karl Shoemaker, *Sanctuary and Crime in the Middle Ages, 400–1500*

Michael J. Monahan, T*he Creolizing Subject: Race, Reason, and the Politics of Purity*

Drucilla Cornell and Nyoko Muvangua (eds.), *uBuntu and the Law: African Ideals and Postapartheid Jurisprudence*

Drucilla Cornell, Stu Woolman, Sam Fuller, Jason Brickhill, Michael Bishop, and Diana Dunbar (eds.), *The Dignity Jurisprudence of the Constitutional Court of South Africa: Cases and Materials, Volumes I & II*

Nicholas Tampio, *Kantian Courage: Advancing the Enlightenment in Contemporary Political Theory*

Carroll Clarkson, *Drawing the Line: Toward an Aesthetics of Transitional Justice*

Jane Anna Gordon, *Creolizing Political Theory: Reading Rousseau through Fanon*

Jimmy Casas Klausen, *Fugitive Rousseau: Slavery, Primitivism, and Political Freedom*

Drucilla Cornell, *Law and Revolution in South Africa: uBuntu, Dignity, and the Struggle for Constitutional Transformation*

Abraham Acosta, *Thresholds of Illiteracy: Theory, Latin America, and the Crisis of Resistance*

Andrew Dilts, *Punishment and Inclusion: Race, Membership, and the Limits of American Liberalism*

Lewis R. Gordon, *What Fanon Said: A Philosophical Introduction to His Life and Thought.* Foreword by Sonia Dayan-Herzbrun, Afterword by Drucilla Cornell

Gaymon Bennett, *Technicians of Human Dignity: On the Politics of Intrinsic Worth*

Drucilla Cornell and Nick Friedman, *The Mandate of Dignity: Ronald Dworkin, Revolutionary Constitutionalism, and the Claims of Justice*

Richard A. Lynch, *Foucault's Critical Ethics*

Peter Banki, *The Forgiveness to Come: The Holocaust and the Hyper-Ethical*